# Life Course Research and Social Policies

Volume 5

**Series editors**
Laura Bernardi
Dario Spini
Michel Oris

Life course research has been developing quickly these last decades for good reasons. Life course approaches focus on essential questions about individuals' trajectories, longitudinal analyses, cross-fertilization across disciplines like life-span psychology, developmental social psychology, sociology of the life course, social demography, socio-economics, social history. Life course is also at the crossroads of several fields of specialization like family and social relationships, migration, education, professional training and employment, and health. This Series invites academic scholars to present theoretical, methodological, and empirical advances in the analysis of the life course, and to elaborate on possible implications for society and social policies applications.

More information about this series at http://www.springer.com/series/10158

Isabel Baumann

# The Plight of Older Workers

Labor Market Experience after Plant Closure
in the Swiss Manufacturing Sector

Isabel Baumann
Center for Health Sciences
Zurich University of Applied Sciences
Winterthur, Switzerland

National Centre of Competence in Research
 "Overcoming Vulnerability - Life Course
 Perspectives" - NCCR LIVES
Lausanne, Switzerland

ISSN 2211-7776      ISSN 2211-7784  (electronic)
Life Course Research and Social Policies
ISBN 978-3-319-39752-8      ISBN 978-3-319-39754-2  (eBook)
DOI 10.1007/978-3-319-39754-2

Library of Congress Control Number: 2016945030

© The Editor(s) (if applicable) and the Author(s) 2016. This book is published open access.
**Open Access** This book is distributed under the terms of the Creative Commons Attribution 4.0 International License (http://creativecommons.org/licenses/by/4.0/), which permits use, duplication, adaptation, distribution and reproduction in any medium or format, as long as you give appropriate credit to the original author(s) and the source, a link is provided to the Creative Commons license, and any changes made are indicated.
The images or other third party material in this book are included in the work's Creative Commons license, unless indicated otherwise in the credit line; if such material is not included in the work's Creative Commons license and the respective action is not permitted by statutory regulation, users will need to obtain permission from the license holder to duplicate, adapt or reproduce the material.
The use of general descriptive names, registered names, trademarks, service marks, etc. in this publication does not imply, even in the absence of a specific statement, that such names are exempt from the relevant protective laws and regulations and therefore free for general use.
The publisher, the authors and the editors are safe to assume that the advice and information in this book are believed to be true and accurate at the date of publication. Neither the publisher nor the authors or the editors give a warranty, express or implied, with respect to the material contained herein or for any errors or omissions that may have been made.

Printed on acid-free paper

This Springer imprint is published by Springer Nature
The registered company is Springer International Publishing AG Switzerland

# Acknowledgments

This study emanates from a research project conducted together with Professor Daniel Oesch at the University of Lausanne. He initiated this project and was crucially involved at all stages of the process. The PhD thesis that resulted from the project was supervised by him with impressive academic knowledge and scientific rigor. It was a great pleasure and an enormous privilege to work with him and I would like to thank him for his encouragement and inspiration.

The realization of this study would not have been possible without the survey participation of workers who lost their job because their plant closed down. I would like to sincerely thank them for offering us their precious time to respond to the questionnaire and for their willingness to share their experiences. In order to collect the data we received indispensable help from representatives of the works councils, plants, cantonal employment offices and trade unions. I would like to particularly thank Pierre Niederhauser who facilitated meetings with workers who experienced plant closure, provided me with profound insights to the process of a plant closure and enormously supported our study. Moreover, my gratitude goes to Urs Schor for taking the time to share his knowledge and experience, and for his continuous encouragement. I am highly thankful to Jessica Garcia, Lorenza Visetti and Katrina Riva for their research assistance and for the pleasant collaboration. My thanks go to Roman Graf, Grégoire Metral and Stefan Floethkoetter who provided the project with IT support, to Robert DiCapua for the title page of the questionnaire and to Emmanuelle Marendaz Colle for communication assistance. I appreciated the methodological expertise of Maurizio Bigotta, Eliane Ferrez, Francesco Laganà, Oliver Lipps, Alexandre Pollien, Caroline Roberts, Alexandra Stam and Boris Wernli who helped with the survey procedure, data analysis and data management.

My gratitude goes to Lucio Baccaro, Marina Dieckhoff, Duncan Gallie, and Dominique Joye, who accepted to be the members of my PhD committee and provided me with very valuable insights that have importantly contributed to this study. I am very grateful to Gaëlle Aeby, Karen Brändle, Carolina Carvalho Arruda, Julie Falcon, Claire Johnston, Maïlys Korber, Sebastian Lotz, Christian Maggiori, Emily Murphy, Laura Ravazzini, Jacob Reidhead, Rosa Sanchez Tome, Emanuela Struffolino, and Nicolas Turtschi for their helpful comments from their reading of my work. In particular, I would like to express my gratitude to Anna von Ow who took the time to carefully read and comment on the entire manuscript. Parts of this study were presented at WIP workshops at the Institute of Social Sciences between 2010 and 2015, at workshops of the NCCR LIVES at the University of Lausanne in 2012, at the Congress of the European Consortium for Sociological Research in Stockholm in 2012, at the Economic Sociology Workshop and the Inequality Workshop at Stanford University in 2013, at the ISA World Congress in Yokohama in 2014, and at the Economics, Health and Happiness Conference in Lugano in 2016. I am very grateful for all the inputs to this study that I received on these occasions.

Procedural and financial support from the State Secretariat for Economic Affairs (SECO) is acknowledged. My thanks go to Werner Aeberhardt, Andrea Bonanomi, Bruno Burri, Jonathan Gast, Thomas Ragni, and Bernhard Weber for their inputs and assistance. This study has been conducted within and the publication of the manuscript has been encouraged by the National Centre of Competence in Research (NCCR) "LIVES – Overcoming Vulnerability: Life Course Perspectives," funded by the Swiss National Science Foundation. I would like to thank Bernadette Deelen-Mans and Evelien Bakker at Springer for their assistance and an anonymous reviewer for her/his valuable comments on the manuscript. Richard Nice is gratefully acknowledged for his careful proofreading.

My final thanks go to Victor Garcia to whom I am deeply grateful for his support, inspiring conversations, and shared academic experiences such as a research stay abroad.

# Contents

**1 The Debate About the Consequences of Job Displacement** .................. 1
   1.1  Career Prospects After Job Loss ......................................................... 1
        1.1.1   A Growing Body of Plant Closure Literature ........................ 1
        1.1.2   Reemployment ....................................................................... 3
        1.1.3   Job Search ............................................................................. 8
        1.1.4   Retirement, Exit from the Labor Force
                and Repeated Job Loss .......................................................... 10
   1.2  Type and Quality of the Post-displacement Job ................................ 12
        1.2.1   Reemployment Sectors and Occupations.............................. 12
        1.2.2   Determinants of Post-displacement Wages .......................... 14
        1.2.3   Changes in Job Quality ......................................................... 16
   1.3  Sociability and Well-Being ............................................................... 18
        1.3.1   Coping Strategies on the Household Level .......................... 18
        1.3.2   Sociability ............................................................................. 19
        1.3.3   Subjective Well-Being........................................................... 21
   1.4  Our Model of Occupational Transition After Plant Closure
        and Hypotheses ................................................................................. 24
   References............................................................................................... 27

**2 A Tailor-Made Plant Closure Survey** ................................................. 35
   2.1  Plant Closure Data as a Way to Avoid Selection Bias....................... 35
   2.2  Sampling ........................................................................................... 36
   2.3  Survey Bias ....................................................................................... 40
   2.4  Data Collection.................................................................................. 42
   2.5  Identifying the Presence of Bias in Our Data.................................... 47
   2.6  Constructing a Non-experimental Control Group............................. 52
   2.7  Limits ................................................................................................ 54
   2.8  The Institutional Context of the Swiss Labor Market....................... 55
   2.9  Aggregate Unemployment ................................................................ 57
   References............................................................................................... 58

## 3 Reemployment or Unemployment ... 63
- 3.1 Labor Market Status Two Years After Displacement ... 64
- 3.2 Labor Market Status by Socio-demographic Characteristics ... 68
- 3.3 Determinants of Reemployment ... 71
- 3.4 Conclusion ... 78
- References ... 79

## 4 Early Retirement and Exit from the Labor Force ... 81
- 4.1 Transition into Early Retirement ... 81
- 4.2 Determinants of Early Retirement ... 83
- 4.3 Exit from the Labor Force ... 88
- 4.4 Conclusion ... 89
- References ... 90

## 5 Job Search Strategies and Unemployment Duration ... 91
- 5.1 Job Search Strategies ... 91
  - 5.1.1 The Application Process ... 92
- 5.2 Other Strategies of Job Search: Commuting, Training, Temporary Jobs ... 95
- 5.3 Unemployment Duration ... 97
- 5.4 Conclusion ... 104
- References ... 105

## 6 Sectors and Occupations of the New Jobs ... 109
- 6.1 Sectors ... 110
- 6.2 Sectors in Which Workers Were Reemployed ... 110
- 6.3 Determinants of Sectoral Change ... 112
- 6.4 Determinants of Switching into Different Subsector in the Services ... 115
- 6.5 Occupations of Reemployment ... 118
- 6.6 Determinants of Occupational Change ... 122
- 6.7 Conclusion ... 124
- References ... 125

## 7 Wages ... 127
- 7.1 Wage Distribution Before and After Displacement ... 128
- 7.2 Average Wage Change ... 129
- 7.3 Distribution of Wage Change ... 133
- 7.4 Determinants of Wage Change ... 135
- 7.5 Conclusion ... 140
- References ... 141

| | | | |
|---|---|---|---|
| **8** | **Job Quality** | | 143 |
| | 8.1 Contract Type | | 144 |
| | 8.2 Subjective Job Security | | 146 |
| | 8.3 Skill Match | | 147 |
| | 8.4 Job Authority | | 149 |
| | 8.5 Job Satisfaction | | 151 |
| | 8.6 Conclusion | | 155 |
| | References | | 156 |
| **9** | **Linked Lives and Well-Being** | | 157 |
| | 9.1 Coping Strategies | | 158 |
| | 9.2 Sociability | | 161 |
| | 9.3 Subjective Well-Being | | 165 |
| | 9.4 Unemployed Workers' Changes in Life Satisfaction | | 168 |
| | 9.5 Reemployed Workers' Change in Life Satisfaction | | 170 |
| | 9.6 Changes in Workers' Health | | 173 |
| | 9.7 Conclusion | | 174 |
| | References | | 176 |

**Conclusion** ......... 179
   Robust Job Prospects in Manufacturing ......... 180
   Polarization in Labor Market Experiences ......... 180
   Old Age as the Main Disadvantage ......... 182
   Tackling the Plight of Older Workers ......... 184

**References** ......... 187

**Annex** ......... 189
   Tables ......... 189
   Figures ......... 191

**Index** ......... 193

# Introduction

This study examines the impact of job loss on individuals' careers and lives. This topic has been widely studied by social scientists, but our study innovates on three accounts. First, by examining the effect of plant closure on an array of outcomes ranging from workers' wages and their social lives to their subjective well-being, we offer an interdisciplinary perspective on plant closure. We focus not only on economic factors as has been done by a large part of the plant closure literature but integrate an analysis of the social and psychological consequences of job displacement. Second, by conducting our own survey, we are able to analyze a population on which very little data is publicly available in Switzerland or in Europe. We conducted our own survey among 1200 workers from five companies. Using plant closure data and a tailor-made study design, we address typical methodological limits of observational data such as selection or nonresponse bias. In addition, we had the opportunity to personally meet some of the affected workers and thereby receive qualitative insight into their experience. Third, our study is situated in the context of the financial crisis of 2008. The companies that we examine closed down soon after, in 2009 or 2010. Our study thus contributes to a strand of the scholarly literature that emerged in the aftermath of the crisis, aiming at analyzing its consequences for the societies affected. Moreover, focusing on the manufacturing sector, we provide evidence on labor adjustment processes in the secondary sector and thus contribute to the debate about deindustrialization.

From a perspective integrating sociological, economic, and psychological theory, it is interesting to understand how job loss affects different dimensions of workers' quality of life. Since in Western societies individuals' social status depends heavily on participation in the labor market, being made redundant usually induces a feeling of failure and threatens workers' identity (Gallie and Paugam 2000, Sennett 1998). Durkheim (1933 [1893]) argued that in modern societies employment has an integrative function and that individuals' social status is significantly determined by their particular occupational function. Consequently, plant closure constitutes a major social issue with possibly far-reaching consequences, not only for the laid-off individuals and their families but also for entire regions.

A seminal study conducted in Austria during the Great Depression of the 1930s by Jahoda et al. (1971 [1933]) documented the disrupting effects of massive job displacement on a village community. The researchers found that joblessness not only put families in a difficult financial situation but also paralyzed the workers in their efforts to keep up a regular daily structure and pursue leisure activities as they had before losing their job. At the community level, this adversity led to a corrosion of common activities and shared responsibilities. Similarly, the financial crisis of the early twenty-first century has produced severe economic damage. The Great Recession has led to massive job destruction, not only in the financial sector but also in manufacturing, services, and the public sector (Baccaro 2010: 342). This situation both gives rise to a need and provides an opportunity to collect and analyze data about how workers deal with the critical situation of job loss.

## Understanding the Impact of Plant Closure on Workers' Careers and Lives

Our first research question addresses the workers' reemployment prospects. It has been argued that workers made redundant because of plant closure return more easily to employment than those who are laid off individually (Gibbons and Katz 1991). This has been explained by individual layoff acting as a negative signal to future employers, indicating a lower ability of the worker. In the case of plant closure in contrast, such a signal does not exist since employers know that workers lost their job simply because their plant closed down. Nevertheless, although workers affected by plant closure are obviously employable – as they were working before displacement – their career prospects are curtailed in comparison with workers who were never displaced (Kuhn 2002).

A second set of research questions examines the characteristics of the jobs in which workers are reemployed. Employment in the tertiary sector has been steadily increasing in the recent decades, while employment in the secondary sector stagnated. This process raises the question whether displaced manufacturing workers have to change sector in order to avoid long-term unemployment. The skills of manufacturing workers may be little transferable to the service sector, thereby forcing workers to accept low-end jobs which do not correspond to their skill profile (Iversen and Cusack 2000: 326). As a consequence, they would not receive the same financial returns in their new job and have to put up with wage losses. In addition, having experienced a spell of unemployment seems to increase the risk of being reemployed in less stable jobs (Payne and Payne 1993: 528). Accordingly, displaced workers may be at risk of being reemployed in more precarious jobs as compared with both their pre-displacement job and with workers who were continuously employed.

Third, based on the assumption of negative spillover effects from employment relationship on other realms of workers' lives, our study aims to inquire how job loss affects workers' sociability. Gallie (2003: 61–2) highlights that the two most influential traditions of labor market research since the 1960s, the neo-Marxist and the liberal theories, share the view that the nature of work tasks and work organization is at the center of individuals' well-being and broader social cohesion. In a similar vein, Kalleberg (2009: 1–2) argues that if workers experience occupational downgrading, their work experience and economic security are likely to be negatively affected, which in turn has far-reaching consequences for their family life and social participation. In addition, it is of crucial interest to examine how plant closure affects workers' life satisfaction. Mass displacement usually comes as a shock for the workers concerned and leaves them with anxiety about their future careers (Gallo et al. 2006). Subjective well-being is closely linked to the quality of the workers' new job but also to their social relationships, which may have suffered as a consequence of the uncertainty following displacement.

Fourth, our study emphasizes that workers have different levels of vulnerability to critical events such as plant closure. One of the principal aims of our study is to identify the individual characteristics which acted as resources or constraints in the occupational transition after job loss. We thus strive to provide insights into the mechanisms behind smooth and difficult transitions. Plant closure may be a triggering factor of completely divergent career outcomes, thereby contributing to labor market segmentation or even social exclusion (Kalleberg and Sorensen 1979: 354). Referring to a concept from the life course paradigm, we endeavor to understand whether the critical event of plant closure rather constitutes a "turning point" or a "transition" in workers' lives. In this context, the term transition stands for gradual change connected with acquiring or relinquishing new roles. The notion of turning point refers to the stages at which a life trajectory shifts in direction or is discontinuous in form (Settersten 2003: 25). In the context of our study, the concept of transition describes the passage into an occupational position that is similar to the one occupied before displacement. The notion of turning point, by contrast, is used to describe the situation of individuals who completely leave the labor market after displacement or who experience a radical change with respect to their job-related social status.

## Using Plant Closure Data and a Tailor-Made Survey Design

We analyze our research questions by drawing on a survey of the complete workforce of five manufacturing plants which closed down in 2009 or 2010 for reasons such as bankruptcy or delocalization of production. We exclusively considered plants that closed down completely, in order to avoid the sampling of workers who were made redundant individually. In fact, individual layoff is probably not random, which makes the causal analysis of the impact of job loss on the ensuing work career tricky: the same factors causing the workers to lose their jobs, such as poor health or lack of motivation, may also reduce their reemployment prospects (Brand 2015).

The workers were surveyed about 2 years after their job loss, which allows us to examine the mid-term effects of job displacement. However, our data is cross-sectional, and only the retrospective information about workers' pre-displacement job provides us with a quasi-longitudinal structure. Even though longitudinal studies are always to be preferred, cross-sectional studies using retrospective recall constitute a second-best solution (Hardt and Rutter 2004). The advantage of having two assessments of workers' situation – one before and one after displacement – is that we can measure within-individual changes such as changes in wages, job quality, or well-being.

Our data was complemented with register data from the public unemployment insurance and from firm registers. This combination not only extends the number of observations and enhances the reliability of the data but also allows us to control for nonresponse bias. Nonresponse bias is a typical problem in observational data that arises from the fact that some types of individuals are more likely to participate in a survey than others. Whenever possible, we use a difference-in-difference design to measure the causal effect of plant closure on workers' lives. Using data from the Swiss Household Panel and a technique known as propensity score matching, we construct a control group in order to compare the outcomes of displaced workers with those of non-displaced workers.

## Unequal Outcomes

Our analysis reveals that about two-thirds of the displaced workers managed to return to a job within 2 years of displacement, while about a sixth were still or again unemployed. Among the reemployed, more than two-thirds returned to a job in manufacturing and thus were not forced into a low-end service job in order to avoid unemployment. This seems to show that within the secondary sector labor churning is paralleled by the creation of new employment and that the pace of deindustrialization in Switzerland is rather slow. On average, reemployed workers experience a slight wage decrease, but variance is substantial. Asked about their subjective evaluation of wage losses, twice as many workers indicate having experienced strong wage losses as those reporting strong wage gains. Also in terms of other job quality indicators, some lose out heavily, while others experience an improvement as compared with their pre-displacement job.

Which factor best explains whether workers were more positively or negatively affected by plant closure? Our analysis strikingly shows that an age over 55 most strongly hampers workers' career prospects. Older workers face strong hurdles in returning to employment. If they manage to find a new job, they are often reemployed in jobs of lower quality and have to put with the largest wage losses of all age cohorts. Only if older workers were able to enter retirement – either regularly or through early retirement plans – did they experience a smooth transition. The retired constitute the subgroup of workers who evaluate the change in their life satisfaction between before and after displacement most positively. Since most of the retirees retired *early*, their high levels of well-being suggest that a majority of them decided voluntarily to take this path and were not pushed out of the labor force. Still, a minority seems to have been forced into this pathway as an alternative to long-term unemployment.

The finding that older workers are the most vulnerable subgroup in the labor market after job loss is interesting in the context of a large body of literature that argues that labor market institutions are mainly biased against young workers. A study covering 27 OECD countries shows that in most countries the rate of unemployment is substantially higher for young than prime-age workers (Breen 2005). Youth unemployment is particularly high where employment protection is high and where the educational system fails to clearly signal the candidate's suitability for a particular job (Gangl 2002: 48). Since Switzerland has weak employment protection and a highly standardized vocational education system certifying credentials and linking the educational system closely with the labor market, young people manage the transition from school to work much better than in most other countries (Buchmann and Stefan 1998, Breen and Buchmann 2002: 294, Breen 2005: 130). Yet an educational system that strongly accentuates vocational training may negatively affect labor force integration in workers' late careers.

In sum, we find that plant closure has unequal consequence on the examined workers' careers and lives. While the majority of the workers overcame this occupational rupture with only minor mid-term effects, for a small proportion of the workers, plant closure had a strongly harmful effect. For these individuals, hard-earned achievements and expectations in terms of career prospects and financial security have been destroyed by an exogenous event.

## Contributions to the Scholarly Literature

Our descriptive findings provide knowledge about the dimension of the impact plant closure has on workers' lives. Our analysis of workers' reemployment prospects shows that over two-thirds manage to return to a job within 2 years but that a significant share of workers remained unemployed. While the average unemployment rate in Switzerland was about 4.5% at the time of our survey, the workers in our study had an unemployment risk of 17% on average. This finding clearly shows that experiencing non-self-inflicted job loss leads to disadvantages for the affected individuals in terms of unemployment risk as compared with non-displaced workers.

Moreover, our study shows that job loss goes along with wage losses and decreased job quality even for workers who return to a job. The literature on wage losses after plant closure has shown strongly diverging outcomes, in particular between the United States and Europe. While displaced workers in the United States tend to experience losses up to 25% as compared with non-displaced workers, European displaced workers are on average less negatively affected. Most European studies report wage losses between 0 and 5%. Our finding of wage losses of 4% on average (or 6% compared with the control group) is thus of about the same order of magnitude. To our knowledge, our study is the first from Switzerland to provide an analysis of the *average* percentage of wage loss. The average percentage is the number that has been reported in most international studies on job displacement and thus allows us to compare the result from Switzerland with results from other countries. With respect to job quality, our finding contributes to the consensus in the previous literature that job loss leads to disadvantages in comparison with workers who never lost their job.

Our regression analyses contribute to the scholarly literature by providing evidence on the different degrees of vulnerability of different worker subgroups. The previous literature suggests that education is the most important determinant of displaced workers' career prospects. Our study in contrast reveals that age most crucially affects their labor market outcomes. In the context of an aging workforce, this finding may point to an increasing number of workers negatively affected in the case of plant closure. Moreover, our results shed light on the potential mechanisms underlying the older workers' vulnerability. The finding that age *per se* better predicts workers' career outcomes than – as we would expect from labor market theory – seniority in a company or education seems to indicate that signaling theory better describes the mechanisms in place than human capital theory.

Finally, our study contributes to the discussion among life course scholars of how unemployment affects other domains of life. We look into the spillover effects of job loss on workers' social life. Our research shows that job loss is not an isolated phenomenon and that it does not affect workers only in terms of their career. In contrast, it highlights that relationships with workers' spouses, families, and friends are affected – surprisingly most often in a positive way, improving these relationships. Moreover, our analysis confirms earlier findings that job loss causes strong decreases in life satisfaction. It thus confirms the hypothesis put forward by numerous scholars that job loss leaves deep and long-lasting traces in displaced workers' lives.

## Contributions to the Policy Debate

Our findings provide insights that may help policy makers to take informed decisions with respect to plant closure. A possible conclusion of our study is that related policies may provide displaced workers with a support structure that offers intensive assistance to the most vulnerable. Job opportunities for workers within 10 years before the official retirement age – the category of workers that our study found to be at the highest risk of unemployment – may be facilitated through unemployment agencies. Plans targeted at this age group such as subsidies for adjustment for new jobs[1] or subsidies for self-employed workers may be promoted intensively.

---

[1] Einarbeitungszuschüsse/Allocations d'initiation au travail.

Moreover, as older workers may not be up to date about current application procedures, they would probably benefit from special support with job applications. If workers nevertheless and despite intensive job search efforts do not manage to return to the labor force, redundancy plans providing them with indemnities constitute an important financial support. Elsewise, displaced workers who are unable to find a job may be forced to rely on welfare benefits. Such a situation may be interpreted as an outsourcing of support by the downsizing companies to the society as a whole.

Our results seem to show that returning to employment quickly after displacement enhances workers' chances of being reemployed in a high-quality job. A second characteristic of effective policies should thus be to allow workers to anticipate their job loss and search for new employment before they are without a job. A possible way of addressing this issue is to motivate closing companies to announce their closure several months before they are going to displace the workers. This procedure may be of little interest for companies who rely on their workers to finish the production of the ordered goods. However, workers may be incentivized through wage supplements to stay until the end of their contract and start their new job subsequently.

Finally, we consider that in addition to policies that cushion the hardship induced by plant closure, measures to enhance workers' resilience and capability to adjust to job changes should be promoted. Higher investments in employees' continuous training with a focus on new learning opportunities until the end of the career are probably the best way to address this challenge. As firms may have little interest in covering the costs that these measures entail (since they may even increase the likelihood that employees quit their company for a new one), a public fund for continuous training, supplied by contributions from employees and employers, may be implemented. As employees would contribute to this fund, they would equally have an interest in making use of training opportunities, maintaining a career-long professional self-development.

## Structure

We set out by presenting the theoretical approach used in this study and discussing the scholarly literature on job loss and its consequences for the workers affected. The discussion is based on both research about the experience of unemployment in general and studies on plant closures more specifically. The most solid studies offer a comparison between the outcomes of workers who experience job displacement and workers who were continuously employed. This research setting offers a post hoc reconstruction of an experiment and is assumed to provide results that allow a causal interpretation of the effect of job loss on occupational trajectories as it addresses the problem of self-selection into job loss. Our first chapter is completed by the presentation of our theoretical model and the hypotheses.

The second chapter presents our tailor-made survey. We discuss biases that typically arise when observational data is collected. We describe the survey design we used to address these potential problems as well as the data collection procedure. We examine whether the measures we take to enhance data quality are successful in this endeavor. We present the construction of a control group of non-displaced workers and discuss the institutional context of the Swiss labor market.

The following chapters present the empirical results of our study. Chapter 3 examines whether workers have found a job or are still unemployed 2 years after displacement. We begin with a descriptive analysis based on the data from our own survey, add the administrative data source, and then compare the outcome with the labor market prospects of non-displaced workers. We proceed with identifying the sociodemographic and contextual factors that potentially explain the workers' reemployment prospects and finish with a discussion of our results in the context of the previous literature.

In Chap. 4, we address older workers' transition into early retirement and discuss possible drivers behind this pathway. We put emphasis on early retirement plans provided by most firms in our sample and discuss how they affect older workers' occupational transitions after plant closure.

The fifth chapter explores workers' job search strategies and the duration of unemployment for both the reemployed and the still unemployed. We examine how sociodemographic characteristics, contextual factors, and individual strategies affect the workers' success in job search. We also briefly discuss the situation of workers who quit the labor force for training, childcare, or disability.

Chapter 6 analyzes the sectors and occupations in which workers are reemployed. We begin with a descriptive analysis of the reemployment sectors before we analyze which factors favored workers' reemployment in their pre-displacement sector. We then address the question of which factors are most strongly associated with reemployment in different service sub-sectors. Finally, we analyze in which occupations workers are reemployed and try to identify which factors had an effect on change of occupation.

The seventh chapter focuses on workers' wages. We begin by comparing the overall wage distribution before and after displacement. Although this analysis provides us with important information about whether the median wage changed as a consequence of plant closure, it does not offer clear indication about the scope of wage change at the individual level. We therefore go on to assess the within-individual wage change between the pre- and post-displacement job. This outcome is then compared with the evolution of the wages of non-displaced workers in order to simulate the counterfactual outcome. Finally, we discuss possible drivers of the observed individual-level wage changes.

Chapter 8 examines workers' job quality in the new job. Finding a job does not in itself guarantee that displaced workers experience a successful occupational transition after plant closure. Indeed, workers may have accepted jobs of lower quality in order to avoid long-term unemployment. We discuss the contract types, job security, skill match, and job authority of the new jobs before we scrutinize whether the occupational transition after plant closure leads to changes in job satisfaction.

Chapter 9 looks into the question of how plant closure affects the social relationship between the displaced workers and their significant others. We begin with the discussion of the coping strategies workers developed on the household level. We then analyze how the quality of their sociability has changed. Finally, we describe the impact of plant closure on workers' well-being and discuss how changes in workers' social and occupational lives have affected their life satisfaction.

The conclusion comes back to our central research questions. We review the main findings of our study, discuss them in the context of the broader literature on the topic, and sketch out their policy implications. We briefly address the question whether our findings can be generalized and show how our results contribute to a comprehensive understanding of occupational transitions after plant closure.

An important concern of this book is to make it intelligible to a broad readership. We have therefore chosen to present as many results as possible in the form of diagrams. An innovative technique, developed by Jann (2014), allowed us to represent not only the results of descriptive analyses but also the results of regression analyses in diagram form. Using diagrams instead of tables should render the reading of our findings more intuitive and accessible to readers from outside the field. To further improve intelligibility, whenever it seemed helpful, we have provided a reading example of how to interpret the results. For most regression analyses, we computed four to six models stepwise including the variables. For reasons of simplicity, this book usually only displays the full models. Readers who wish to access the complete results can find them in the PhD thesis, defended at the University of Lausanne, that is the basis of this book (Baumann 2015).

# References

Baccaro, L. (2010). Does the global financial crisis mark a turning point for labour? *Socio-Economic Review, 8*, 341–376.

Baumann, I. (2015). *Labor market experience and well-being after firm closure. Survey evidence on displaced manufacturing workers in Switzerland*. Dissertation, Supervisor: Oesch, D. Université de Lausanne.

Brand, J. E. (2015). The far-reaching impact of job loss and unemployment. *Annual Review of Sociology, 41*, 359–375.

Breen, R. (2005). Explaining cross-national variation in youth unemployment. Market and institutional factors. *European Sociological Review, 21*(2), 125–134.

Breen, R., & Buchmann, M. (2002). Institutional variation in the position of young people: A comparative perspective. *Annals of the American Society of Social and Political Sciences, 580*, 288–305.

Buchmann, M., & Stefan, S. (1998). The transition from school to work in Switzerland: Do characteristics of the educational system and class barriers matter? In Y. Shavit & W. Müller (Eds.), *From school to work: A comparative study of educational qualifications and occupational destinations* (pp. 407–442). Oxford: Oxford University Press.

Durkheim, E. (1933 [1893]). *Division of labor in society*. New York: MacMillan.

Gallie, D. (2003). The quality of working life: Is Scandinavia different? *European Sociological Review, 19*(1), 61–79.

Gallie, D., & Paugam, S. (2000). The experience of unemployment in Europe: The debate. In D. Gallie & S. Paugam (Eds.), *Welfare regimes and the experience of unemployment in Europe* (pp. 1–22). Oxford: Oxford University Press.

Gallo, W. T., Bradley, E. H., Dubin, J. A., Jones, R. N., Falba, T. A., Teng, H.-M., & Kasl, S. V. (2006). The persistence of depressive symptoms in older workers who experience involuntary job loss: Results from the health and retirement survey. *Journal of Gerontology: Social Sciences, 61*(4), S221–S228.

Gangl, M. (2002). *The only way is up? Employment protection and job mobility among recent entrants to European labour markets* (Working paper of the Mannheimer Zentrum für Europäische Sozialforschung no 48). Mannheim: MZES.

Gibbons, R., & Katz, L. F. (1991). Layoffs and lemons. *Journal of Labor Economics, 9*(4), 351–380.

Hardt, J., & Rutter, M. (2004). Validity of adult retrospective reports of adverse childhood experiences: Review of the evidence. *Journal of Child Psychology and Psychiatry, and Allied Disciplines, 45*(2), 260–273.

Iversen, T., & Cusack, T. R. (2000). The causes of welfare state expansion: Deindustrialization or globalization? *World Politics, 52*(3), 313–349.

Jahoda, M., Lazarsfeld, P., & Zeisel, H. (1971 [1933]). *Marienthal: The sociography of an unemployed community*. Chicago: Aldine.

Kalleberg, A. L. (2009). Precarious work, insecure workers: Employment relations in transition. *American Sociological Review, 74*(1), 1–22.

Kalleberg, A. L., & Sorensen, A. B. (1979). The sociology of labor markets. *Annual Review of Sociology, 5*(1979), 351–379.

Payne, J., & Payne, C. (1993). Unemployment and peripheral work. *Work, Employment & Society, 7*(4), 513–534.

Sennett, R. (1998). *The corrosion of character: The personal consequences of work in the new capitalism*. New York: W.W. Norton.

Settersten, R. A. (Ed.). (2003). *Invitation to the life course. Toward new understandings of later life*. Amityville: Baywood Publishing Company.

# Chapter 1
# The Debate About the Consequences of Job Displacement

Since the 1970s scholars have shown an increasing interest in the study of the social and economic consequences of plant closure. One strand of research addresses the topic from an economic perspective, investigating the impact of plant closure on workers' occupational trajectory and financial situation. The main interests of these studies are reemployment rates, unemployment durations and wage differences between the pre- and post-displacement job. Another strand of research strives at understanding the nonpecuniary costs of unemployment, addressing the consequences of job displacement in terms of workers' well-being and social life. We try to bridge these different research interests and will propose a model to investigate the impact of plant closure on workers' lives in a more encompassing way.

In this chapter we discuss the literature on the consequences of job displacement on displaced workers' occupational situation, their sociability and well-being. The first section focuses on reemployment, unemployment and labor force exit. A second section discusses the type and quality of the post-displacement jobs. Third, we address how workers' sociability and subjective well-being are affected by job loss. We conclude by suggesting a theoretical model of occupational transitions after plant closure and present our hypotheses.

## 1.1 Career Prospects After Job Loss

### 1.1.1 A Growing Body of Plant Closure Literature

The growing academic interest in job displacement may stem from the increasing number of workers affected by plant closures, relocations, restructurings and downsizings. In the United States, the displacement rate has risen significantly since the early 1970s (Hamermesh 1989: 52–3; Brand 2006: 275–6). The increase in the number of plant closure studies thus possibly reflects the growing public attention to this phenomenon. However, there may be another reason for this expansion.

The study of the consequences of job displacement requires appropriate data. In the United States, the launch of the Displaced Worker Survey (DWS) in 1984, conducted biannually as a complement to the Current Population Survey (CPS), made it possible to study the relevant population in more detail. The availability of this data source triggered many publications on job displacement. Where register data is accessible, as in Sweden (see Eliason and Storrie 2003) or in the state of Pennsylvania (see Jacobsen et al. 1993), this type of data provides an even more valuable source of information, being more reliable and exhaustive than survey data. Finally, for the study of the long-term consequences of plant closure longitudinal data is indispensable. However, the availability of this type of data is relatively novel since the two longest running panel surveys based on representative national samples such as the Panel Study of Income Dynamics in the US (PSID) or the Socio-Economic Panel Study in Germany (GSOEP) were established in 1968 and 1984 respectively. The increasing accessibility of appropriate data thus may be an alternative explanation for the growing interest in studying the impact of job displacement on workers' ensuing life trajectories.

To date, most plant closure studies have been based on US data. "Earning Losses of Displaced Workers" by Jacobson et al. (1993) is one of the most influential early studies. The innovation of this study was the use of a longitudinal *administrative* dataset from Pennsylvania. Earlier studies usually used survey data from the Displaced Workers Survey (Podgursky and Swaim 1987; Kletzer 1989; Addison and Portugal 1989; Gibbons and Katz 1991; Carrington 1993; Fallick 1993), or the Michigan Panel Study of Income Dynamics (Ruhm 1991). Another novelty in job displacement studies of the early 1990s was the inclusion of a control group of non-displaced workers (Ruhm 1991; Jacobson et al. 1993). Offering a counterfactual for workers who continued to be employed, this approach made it possible to more precisely measure the causal effect of displacement on wages.

In the late 1990s and early 2000s European job displacement studies emerged. Based on administrative data, Margolis (1999) discusses wage losses of French displaced workers as compared to non-displaced workers. Couch (2001) and Burda and Mertens (2001) use longitudinal data from the German Socio-Economic Panel. Kriechel and Pfann (e.g. 2002, 2005, 2011) use data from a large firm closure in the Netherlands and discuss different problems such as the role of specific and general human capital in the reemployment prospects of displaced workers. Plant closure in Northern Europe was investigated by Eliason and Storrie (2006) who rely on a unique Swedish administrative dataset, linking employer with employee data. Appelqvist (2007) uses a similar dataset from Finland, analyzing the effect of the business cycle on job displacement outcomes. Jolkonnen et al. (2012) conduct their own survey on manufacturing workers in Finland and analyze the workers' reemployment prospects about a year after displacement. For Switzerland a study has been conducted based on a survey among three large industrial plants that closed down between 2001 and 2006, a phase of economic boom (e.g. Wyss 2009; Wyss 2010; Weder and Wyss 2010).

To our knowledge, only one piece of research has chosen a comparative approach: the book *Losing Work, Moving On*, edited by Peter J. Kuhn (2002), which offers not only an in-depth description of the labor market of ten countries under study, but also detailed data on a standardized set of indicators and measures. This approach significantly improves the comparability of the results within a broad series of industrialized countries in Europe, Northern America, Australia and Japan. Finally, there are four literature reviews, all of them focusing on US studies (Hamermesh 1989; Fallick 1996; Couch and Placzek 2010; Brand 2015). Couch and Placzek's article additionally replicates the methodology applied by Jacobson et al. (1993), using a different dataset.

## 1.1.2 Reemployment

There is a broad consensus that job seekers experience decreasing reemployment chances over the course of unemployment. The adverse effect of long periods of unemployment is called "negative duration dependence" (Gebel 2009: 663). On the one hand, this phenomenon may come about because of self-selection into longer unemployment durations: better employable workers flow out of unemployment early, and over time only the less employable workers stay in the group of the unemployed. In this view, individual employability remains constant over time.

On the other hand, "true duration dependence" may be at stake, a situation where the duration of unemployment itself reduces workers' employability (Machin and Manning 1999: 12). If this mechanism is at work, all individuals who are unlucky enough to stay unemployed for a while will experience a decreasing probability of finding a job. How could "true duration dependence" be explained? A first approach is the signaling theory, which goes back to Spence (1973) and suggests that employers interpret the unemployment duration as an indicator for unobservable characteristics such as productivity or motivation (Blanchard and Diamond 1994). In this view a long spell of unemployment stigmatizes workers as being unproductive or having low motivation. Second, proponents of the human capital theory argue that if workers do not use their occupational skills for a long period they lose their routine and thus are less productive when returning to work (Pissarides 1992: 1371). A third explanation is that long spells of unemployment have negative effects on job seekers' self-confidence and motivation (Newman 1999). This in turn reduces the intensity of their job search, which reduces their chances of finding a new job (Young 2012b: 19; Flückiger 2002: 15–6).

It is, however, difficult to determine which mechanisms are at work since an analysis requires information about (usually) unobserved factors such as motivation, productivity, self-confidence and skills. Machin and Manning (1999: 17) claim based on an international comparison of OECD data that there is little evidence for true duration dependence but that instead unobserved heterogeneity explains the outcome of negative duration dependence. In contrast, two studies based on longitudinal data from the UK, the US and Germany find no support for pure heterogeneity for any of these countries (Jackman and Layard 1991: 97; Gangl 2004: 178). Other studies using experimental data equally reject the unobserved heterogeneity argument: Oberholzer-Gee (2008), Kroft et al. (2013) and Eriksson and Rooth (2014) show, based on data from Switzerland, the US and Sweden respectively, that if fictive job applications with identical profiles but varying unemployment spells are sent to companies, employers consider a long unemployment duration as a signal of workers' low productivity. Erikson and Rooth (2014: 1029) find that for low and mid-skilled jobs unemployment spells of over 9 months lead to a stigma effect while Kroft et al. (2013: 1128) find the strongest stigma occurring during the first 8 months. Although not consistent with respect to the effect of varying durations, these findings provide evidence that true duration dependence is at work. Additionally, the studies suggest that – at least in part – the signaling theory explains the phenomenon.

We now turn to the socio-demographic factors that drive workers' reemployment prospects. Previous findings suggest that education plays an important role, higher educational levels being assumed to generate better reemployment chances (Fallick 1993: 317). One explanation is that employers may be interested in the educational attainments of individuals not only as certifying specific competences, but further as an indicator for attributes that employers consider desirable but that cannot be known with any certainty before a candidate is actually taken on (Jackson et al. 2005: 11). In other words, education serves as a signal to the employer for characteristics that are not apparent in a job seeker's application such as productivity, motivation, self-discipline or the ability to learn quickly (Sauer et al. 2010: 1110; Rider and Roberts 2011: 30).

Another explanation of why higher levels of education are likely to enhance workers' reemployment prospects is that in OECD countries demand for highly educated workers has risen over the last decades (OECD 2008: 166). A study that analyzes the occupational structure of the US manufacturing sector observes that the proportion of high-skilled labor grew substantially between the late 1950s and the late 1980s as compared to low-skilled labor (Berman et al. 1994: 372–3, 369). This shift went along with a relative increase in high-skilled workers' wages in the same period. This phenomenon – named skill-biased technological change – has been attributed to technological advance as a growing number of routine tasks, traditionally carried out by low-skilled workers, are replaced by machines (Liu and Grusky 2013: 1335). At the same time, the finding that industries with particularly high levels of investment in automation also experience a strong demand for skilled labor suggests that the skills of highly educated workers are complementary to these new technologies (Berman et al. 1994: 372, 387).

The finding, based on US and UK data, of growth in both low-end and high-end occupations challenged this view (Autor and Dorn 2009: 27, Goos and Manning 2007: 122). This phenomenon of job polarization may be explained by the inability of machines to replace low-skilled but still nonroutine tasks involving hand-eye coordination such as caring, serving or cleaning (Autor and Dorn 2009: 31). Routine tasks, however, which are typically carried out by mid-skilled workers such as clerks or machine operators, can more easily be automated.

For Switzerland, evidence suggests that the occupational change in the last two decades is best described as a combination of both phenomena: jobs in the middle of the occupational hierarchy decreased most strongly, pointing to a process of polarization (Oesch and Rodriguez Menes 2011: 514). At the same time, low-skilled jobs decreased too – though to a weaker extent than mid-skilled jobs – while jobs with high skill requirements experienced strong growth, a pattern that implies occupational upgrading (Oesch and Rodriguez Menes 2011: 517; Oesch 2013: 76). This result makes the prediction of low-educated workers' reemployment prospects difficult but suggests that the highly educated are likely to have the most promising reemployment prospects after job loss.

Research on displaced workers' reemployment prospects suggests that age plays a paramount role, older displaced workers consistently experiencing more difficulties in finding a new job than younger workers. A study based on the US Health and Retirement Survey, focusing on workers aged over 50, finds that prospects of returning to work decline from about the age of 56 and are very low after the age of 60 (Chan and Stevens 2001: 496). As compared to workers aged 50, workers aged 56 have a 5 percentage points lower reemployment rate and at the age of 62 it is about 30 percentage points lower. A study based on US Displaced Worker Survey data from 1984 to 1996 finds that as compared to the 25–34 year olds, the 45–54 year old cohort have about a 5 percentage points lower and the 55–64 year old cohort about a 19 percentage points lower reemployment rate (Farber 1997: 93, see also Farber 2005: 19).

For Europe the results point in the same direction. A Finnish study shows that older workers from the age of 40 have much lower reemployment prospects than younger workers: the reemployment prospects of workers over the age of 50 are only a third of those under the age of 35 (Jolkkonen et al. 2012: 88–9). Likewise, in Switzerland older displaced workers have a hard time in finding new jobs. In their study on workers of three large industrial plants in Switzerland that closed, Wyss (2009: 40–1) shows that age is the factor with the most adverse effect on the workers' reemployment prospects.

In addition, older workers face generally longer unemployment durations than younger workers. Flückiger (2002: 20) documents this phenomenon for Switzerland based on data from the Swiss Labour Force Survey (SLFS). Similarly, in their study on reemployment patterns of older workers who experienced job loss, Chan and Stevens (2001: 491–2) report that workers over the age of 60 are more likely to experience longer spells of unemployment than workers in their 50s: 2 years after displacement, about 60 % of workers aged 50–55 and about 45 % of those aged 55–60 are reemployed, but only 20 % of those aged 60–64. The large body of empirical evidence for older workers' bleak labor market prospects in different countries thus points to the fact that we are confronted with a widespread phenomenon. However, the mechanism underlying this phenomenon is still a puzzle.

A first potential explanation refers to internal labor markets and suggests that firms want to promote careers *within* their organization (Daniel and Heywood 2007: 37). Generally speaking, employers prefer to hire young workers who will stay in the firm throughout their career. For the companies this has the advantage that the returns to the workers' on-the-job training are higher. To incite employees to stay in their organization firms apply steep wage profiles where firm tenure is strongly rewarded (so-called "deferred compensation").

A second explanation for older workers' reduced labor market prospects is the cohort effect of education. As a result of educational expansion, younger workers are on average better-educated than the older and therefore have better chances on the labor market. The older workers who completed their education a long time ago may also be less flexible since it is more difficult to adjust to new job requirements and technologies (Cha and Morgan 2010: 1137). This places them in a disadvantaged position in comparison with younger workers.

Third, older workers may have difficulties in finding a job because of high firm tenure. High tenure implies high specialization for one firm and high-tenured workers may not have many skills transferable to other companies (Couch and Placzek 2010: 574). The negative effect of tenure on reemployment prospects has, however, been contested: it has been argued that high firm tenure may be a positive signal to the future employer in terms of a good job match (Greenaway et al. 2000: 66; Arulampalam 2001: F590). Other authors have argued that the association between tenure and reemployment prospects is U-shaped. Evidence for this third option is provided by a Finnish study which found that an intermediate tenure offers workers the best reemployment perspective after plant closure (Jolkkonen et al. 2012: 89). Hence, the impact of tenure for workers' reemployment chances seems to be ambiguous.

Fourth, there is a widespread belief that older workers are less productive than younger workers because of reduced mental and physical capacities and because of being more frequently affected by injuries or sickness. In addition, older workers are assumed to experience declining abilities to learn, as a study from the US emphasizes (Wrenn and Maurer 2004: 234). Older workers are therefore likely to be disadvantaged in labor markets where rapidly developing technologies require constant adaptation to new tasks. However, studies that thoroughly examine this question highlight that the link between age and performance is not clear-cut: while some studies find a negative relation between age and performance, others find a positive relation or none at all (Hansson et al. 1997: 206; Ng and Feldman 2008: 392). A possible explanation for these inconclusive results is that while workers' mental and physical capacities indeed decrease with age, older workers are able to compensate for this loss with their experience and knowledge and consequently maintain a similar performance to in previous years (Park 1994: 195). Regarding the risk of accidents, two studies from the US have revealed that older workers experience injuries that are more serious. However, the study also shows that older workers are injured less frequently and – in terms of reduced working hours – less consequentially than younger workers (Silverstein 2008: 273; Pransky et al. 2005: 108). The assumption that older workers exhibit a lower performance at work than younger workers thus does not seem to be justified.

Another factor likely to influence labor market success in Switzerland is workers' nationality, national origin or ethnic background. The Swiss study by Weder and Wyss (2010: 43) observes that foreigners had a four times higher risk of remaining unemployed than the Swiss after controlling for socio-demographic factors such as age and education. In addition, a field experiment conducted in Switzerland in which employers received two applications that were similar regarding all job-related factors with the exception of the applicant's name (Fibbi et al. 2003). The results reveal that applicants with a typical Kosovar name were about 60 percentage points less likely and applicants with a typical Turkish name about 30 percentage points less likely to be invited to a job interview than applicants with a typical Swiss name. For applications where a Portuguese name was used there was no significant difference in the frequency of invitations. A study with a similar design from Sweden finds that job applicants with local names are about 50 percentage points more often invited to interviews (Carlsson and Rooth 2007).

These differences may be explained by discrimination, employers having a general aversion to individuals with particular backgrounds (Sheldon 2007: 40). Another explanation is that employers use workers' nationality or surname as a signal for unobserved skills and knowledge. This hypothesis is plausible since in hiring procedures there is an information asymmetry about workers' abilities. All other characteristics being constant, employers prefer applicants with a national origin that correlates (or is believed to correlate) with higher performance (Bonoli and Hinrichs 2012: 340). Since the quality of the same type of education differs between countries, job seekers with a foreign national origin may indeed perform better or worse than natives even if they have the same formal qualifications (Sheldon 2007: 41). Moreover, natives are likely to have a better command of the local language and may – but of course may not – be better informed about the local context (e.g. political situation, customers of a company) than immigrants. Evidence for this assumption is provided by a study conducted in Switzerland that finds that the wage returns on education and work experience are lower if they were acquired abroad (De Coulon et al. 2003).

Research shows that workers' unemployment durations and reemployment prospects are not only mediated by individual characteristics but also by contextual factors. The prevailing unemployment rate at the moment of displacement is clearly relevant: the higher the unemployment rate, the lower the demand for labor. This leads to higher competition among job seekers and results in longer spells of unemployment. This effect seems to be consistent across different countries. For the US it has been shown that mid-age displaced manufacturing workers had a 20 percentage points higher reemployment chance in the boom period between 1993 and 1996 as compared to the recession of 1981–1983 (Kletzer 2001: 49). A Finnish study observes that reemployment is much more difficult for workers displaced during the recession in the early 1990s than those who lost their job in the more prosperous late 1990s: in the 3 years after plant closure, workers displaced in 1992 were employed, on average, only about 8 months a year while those displaced in 1997 were employed about 11 months a year (Appelqvist 2007: 18). Likewise, Swedish workers experienced a stronger negative effect of displacement if they lost their job during the recession of the early 1990s than under better cyclical conditions in the late 1980s and late 1990s (Eliason and Storrie 2003: 13).

## 1.1.3 Job Search

An extensive literature has explored how individuals search for jobs. One strand of the literature examines the strategies job seekers adopt, suggesting that they possess the capacity to exert control over their career by anticipating future scenarios and adjusting actions accordingly (Sweet and Moen 2011: 3). Obviously, job seekers may face constraints on the demand side of labor, be it because of employers' preferences and hiring procedures or because of adverse macroeconomic conditions. Using a particular job search strategy thus does not automatically lead to more and better job opportunities, but is assumed to have a positive impact on reemployment as compared to not using the strategy.

One strategy that is expected to have an effect is the intensity of the job search, measured as the number of applications someone writes within a defined time. The higher workers' search intensity, the more employers learn that they are looking for a job, which in turn likely increases the number of job opportunities (Burgess and Low 1998: 242). A second strategy is to apply unsolicited. Unsolicited applications are a signal to potential employers that the job seeker is highly interested in the job and in general strongly motivated. A qualitative study on the low-skilled sectors in six European countries suggests that employers appreciate unsolicited applications most of all recruitment channels (Bonoli and Hinrichs 2012: 352).

Third, job seekers may inform their friends and acquaintances that they are looking for a job. The activation of the social network is a strategy that seems to help finding better jobs and to reduce the duration of the job search (Franzen and Hangartner 2006: 364). Two arguments are brought forward to explain the mechanisms behind this strategy: First, the information asymmetry involved in hiring processes leads employers to look for information about future employees – such as motivation or social skills – that is not apparent in a formal application. A third party who knows the candidate personally may provide this lacking information to the employer (Marsden and Gorman 2001: 470). Second, contacts have been described as channels of information through which news about a vacancy reaches the job seeker or employers learn about possible candidates.

According to Granovetter (1995), the most valuable information about jobs and candidates flows though networks of acquaintances, so-called "weak ties". In contrast to "strong ties" – such as family and friends – "weak ties" function as bridges to socially more distant groups of closely related individuals and thus allow information to circulate in a wide network. However, Granovetter's research focuses only on employed workers. A Swedish study based on longitudinal data focusing on unemployed workers reports that only strong ties had a positive effect on displaced workers' reemployment prospects (Korpi 2001: 166–7). At the same time the study shows that the size of the network is in fact more relevant than the types of the contacts: every additional contact increases the workers' reemployment probability more than any other job search strategy.

In a Swiss study on the use of informal contacts among unemployed workers, Oesch and von Ow (2015: 14–6) distinguish between work-related and communal social contacts; the latter refers to non-work related contacts such as family, friends, neighbors or acquaintances from a sports club or a volunteering activity. The authors show that both types of contacts are important for the job search of unemployed workers, but while work-related contacts are mainly used by highly educated male job seekers, communal ties seem to be important for job seekers with weaker employability such as working-class Southern European immigrants with low levels of education and workers over 55.

When job seekers remain unemployed for a longer time, work-related contacts tend to gradually fade away. Evidence for this phenomenon is provided by a Danish study which observed that 1 year after losing their job, two-thirds of the workers no longer had contact with their former colleagues (Larsen 2008: 11). Long-term unemployed workers who may already be disadvantaged due to particular characteristics or labor market conditions are additionally marginalized by this mechanism.

The claim that the use of social contacts *per se* improves workers' reemployment prospects has been challenged by Mouw (2003: 890–891). He maintains that the previous analyses of this topic face an endogeneity problem and instead of showing a causal effect of individuals' social contacts, the existing literature merely shows that those individuals who have a large and helpful network also have good labor market prospects. Because of homophily, higher-ranked individuals tend to have higher-ranked friends and therefore have better chances of finding their job through their contacts. In other words, the same individual characteristics that lead to – in terms of job search – a useful social network also lead to better reemployment chances. To underline his argument, he provides evidence from fixed-effect analysis of longitudinal data showing that controlling for other characteristics, workers who do use contacts do not have better job prospects than those who do not use contacts. His analysis furthermore reveals that jobs found through the social network do not differ in terms of wages, occupational prestige or unemployment duration for jobs found through other channels.

A fourth strategy that workers may adopt in order to find a job is to enlarge the geographical scope of job search (Kaufmann et al. 2004). However, accepting a job that involves long commuting distances seems to constitute a burden to the workers. A study based on women in Texas shows that commuting is one of the daily activities that individuals dislike most (Kahneman et al. 2004: 431–2). Economists have assumed that workers' acceptance of commuting increases if they are compensated in terms of wages or other benefits. However, a study based on German longitudinal data suggests that even if commuters are compensated, they are less satisfied than those who do not commute (Stutzer and Frey 2008: 349). This result seems paradoxical and raises the question why individuals accept long distance commuting – sometimes even without compensation. To explain this puzzle, the authors test whether job seekers with less opportunities and more financial pressure accept commuting more readily, which neither seems to be the case.

## 1.1.4 Retirement, Exit from the Labor Force and Repeated Job Loss

There is a debate in the literature whether older workers who retire early or quit the labor force are "pushed" or "pulled" out of the labor market. Proponents of the "push-out" argument have claimed that older displaced workers are forced into early retirement because they do not find a new job and thus have no better alternative than retiring (Desmet et al. 2005). This argument has been empirically supported by studies from the US and Europe that show that older workers who have difficulties in finding a job after plant closure are likely to choose this pathway (Chan and Stevens 2001; Ichino et al. 2007). In line with these results, a study that compares the transition into early retirement in OECD countries finds a positive link between the overall unemployment rate and the proportion of workers who retire early (Dorn and Sousa-Poza 2010: 434).

Second, "pull mechanisms" such as generous early retirement plans may incite older workers to leave the labor force before the official retirement age. A comparative study across 19 industrialized countries reports that the proportion of workers retiring rises with an increasing pension benefit replacement rate (Dorn and Sousa-Poza 2010: 343).[1] However, since Swiss institutions – in contrast to other continental European countries (for the case of Austria see Lalive 2008: 805) – do not promote early retirement, workers in Switzerland are generally less likely to enter early retirement.

Other factors that may incite workers to retire early are institutionalized retirement savings. Men are probably more likely to retire early than women because they accumulate larger savings, less often experiencing career interruptions due to child-rearing and being less often part-time employed (Bonoli 2003: 407–410). Moreover, workers who earned high wages during their active life are more likely to retire early than those with low wages. Early-retired workers may even be forced to use their savings in order to make ends meet – a situation that is easier to cope with for workers who had higher wages when still working, since higher wages translate into higher occupational pensions. Finally, having an economically inactive partner may promote workers' transition into early retirement. Evidence from Switzerland and Germany suggests that men with a non-active partner and with higher wages are more likely to transit into early retirement (Dorn and Sousa-Poza 2005: 269; Knuth and Kalina 2002: 412). The reason for this phenomenon may be that partners often have a preference for being in the same occupational situation. Thus having a retired (or for other reasons non-working) partner may incite workers to retire early.

As an alternative to reemployment, unemployment or retirement, job displacement may lead workers of all ages to persistently exit the labor force, for instance for training, child care, disability or leisure (Knuth and Kalina 2002). On the one hand, workers with significant difficulties in finding a job may exit the labor market

---

[1] The replacement rate is the proportion of the former wage that is provided by the old-age pension.

as an alternative to long-term unemployment. This "push-out" hypothesis suggests that workers were forced to leave because of a lack of opportunities in the labor market. On the other hand, the "pull-out" hypothesis assumes that specific incentives – such as early retirement, disability insurance or taxation rules – constitute a gateway for workers out of the labor force.

Exit from the labor force after job displacement seems to be determined by an interaction mechanism between sex and civil status: based on data from the US Health and Retirement Survey it has been shown that among unemployed workers married women have a 15 percentage points lower probability of going back to work than unmarried women, while for men marital status makes no difference (Chan and Stevens 2001: 496). This seems to point to a pull mechanism being at work, where displaced married women who probably have a husband with a stable income choose not to take on a new job.

Displaced workers face an increased risk of multiple job losses. A study using US data from the Panel Study of Income Dynamics for the period 1968–1988 observes that multiple job loss was frequent in the US in the 1970s and 1980s: about 40 % of the workers who had lost their job once were displaced or laid off a second or a third time (Stevens 1997: 172). Most of the multiple displacements happened within 5 years of the first displacement. Another US study based on a labor market simulation confirms these results, showing that recently (re-)employed workers face a higher propensity to lose their job than longer tenured workers (Pries 2004: 214). This suggests that a first job loss makes workers vulnerable to experiencing subsequent involuntary job separations or that some workers are generally more vulnerable to job loss than others.

Two explanations account for these findings. First, as Farber emphasizes in a literature review (1998) and in his own analysis of US longitudinal data (1994), a large proportion of all new job matches are destroyed within a short time. Displaced workers thus have a higher risk of repeated job loss than average workers, simply because they have recently entered a new employment. New employment relationships are unstable as they often turn out to be bad matches and thus are more likely to be terminated prematurely. Second, the above-cited studies by Stevens (1997) and Pries (2004) rely on data containing workers displaced both because of plant closure and because of layoff, without distinguishing between the two reasons for job loss. This may be misleading since it is less surprising that workers dismissed for just cause lose their job repeatedly. Indeed, these workers may have individual characteristics that are generally unpopular among employers.

## 1.2 Type and Quality of the Post-displacement Job

### 1.2.1 Reemployment Sectors and Occupations

Structural change in the economy leads to labor reallocation across industries. In recent decades a shift of employment from the goods-production industry to the services has taken place throughout the OECD. In the UK for instance, large labor reallocations take place from declining to expanding industries and they are often intermitted by a spell of unemployment (Greenaway et al. 2000: 58, 60). It is possible that plant closures in the manufacturing sector constitute a mechanism that mediates this adjustment process. In this logic, manufacturing workers who lose their job would then be absorbed mainly by expanding sectors such as services. Alternatively, an adjustment process may come about through cohort renewal if young workers enter sectors and occupations that are different from those that older workers were active in.

The view that displaced workers have to change sector in order to find a new job has been challenged by the finding that even larger labor reallocation processes take place *within* the same industries (OECD 2009: 121). While the net change of employment *across* industries in OECD countries between 1997 and 2004 was 4%, it was on average 18% *within* industries. This suggests that within OECD countries job destruction in a sector is paralleled by job creation in the same sector. For displaced manufacturing workers this would imply that they may find a new job in their pre-displacement sectors.

Human capital theory suggests that workers prefer to stay in their pre-displacement sector because it is there where they receive the highest returns on their skills (Fallick 1993; Neal 1995: 657; Haynes et al. 2002: 251). Yet, if the prospects in the pre-displacement sector are bleak, workers are pushed into other sectors (Fallick 1993: 314). A study based on longitudinal micro-data shows for the US and Germany that sectoral mobility increases with the duration of the spell of unemployment (Gangl 2003: 206). Similar results are found for the US and the UK, showing that the spells of unemployment are shortest for workers who find their jobs in their pre-displacement sector (Greenaway et al. 2000: 68).

The transition from one sector to another may be difficult. However, for some groups of workers sectoral change is easier than for others. Much depends on the transferability of the workers' skills to their reemployment sectors. If the workers' skills are very specific to their former sector of employment – as it is the case for workers with high sectoral tenure – they are likely to experience difficulties, for instance in form of wage losses (Neal 1995: 664; Cha and Morgan 2010: 1144). Moreover, the workers' education seems to influence their propensity to switch sector. Credentials, diplomas or certifications are considered objective attestations of skills. They help employers in other sectors to evaluate the portability of the workers' skills to another sector and are a signal for the workers' ability to learn the skills required in the new sector (Estevez-Abe 2005: 188). This explanation is supported by a study based on data from the US Current Population Survey that finds that

## 1.2 Type and Quality of the Post-displacement Job

higher levels of education only improve workers' reemployment prospects in another industry, but not in their former industry (Fallick 1993: 317).

In addition, women seem to experience better employment prospects in the expanding private service sectors and the public sector than men. A study comparing OECD countries shows that the occupational structure in the public service sector is strongly biased towards women (Estevez-Abe 2005: 197). This horizontal segregation seems to hold not only for the public sector: evidence from Germany suggests that in recent decades most of the jobs created in services – whether in the private or the public sector – were filled by women (Spitz-Oener 2006: 266; Black and Spitz-Oener 2010: 190). An explanation for women's overrepresentation in service jobs is the increasing demand for skills such as dealing with people, training and teaching or counseling and advising in Western economies, which have been shown to be used at work more often by women than by men (Nickell 2001: 621). Moreover, women's tendency to be employed in the public sector may be due to the fact that a large proportion of women prefer jobs that are compatible with care work, such as part-time employment and jobs with flexible working hours (Hakim 2006: 289). Jobs of this type are more abundant in the public sector.

Besides changing sector, workers may change occupation in order to find a new job. Different factors seem to promote workers' occupational change after plant closure. First, long spells of unemployment lead job seekers to consider accepting jobs in other occupations. This has been demonstrated in a study on West Germany: every additional month of unemployment increases the likelihood of changing occupation by 6 % (Velling and Bender 1994: 224). Second, in the US younger workers change occupation more often than older ones (Parrado et al. 2007: 446). The effect of age may be explained by tenure. Older workers have acquired a large amount of occupation-specific skills over their career and thus receive lower financial returns if they switch to other occupations. However, a study based on British and German data only partially confirms the tenure hypothesis: while the authors find supportive evidence for the UK, workers with longer experience being less likely to switch occupation, the is opposite is the case in Germany (Longhi and Brynin 2010: 660).

With respect to the question of which occupations workers who switch adopt, considering the evolution of the demand for labor may provide a possible answer. In Switzerland and the Scandinavian countries, an increase in employment at the top end of the occupational hierarchy has been documented for the recent decades. More precisely, jobs in management and the professions were expanding, whereas routine jobs held by production workers and clerks were decreasing (Oesch and Rodriguez Menes 2011: 514; Fernández-Macías 2012: 15). Accordingly, it is likely that the displaced workers are more often employed in managerial or professional occupations after displacement than they were before displacement. Moreover, as a consequence of service sector growth we may expect many manufacturing workers, above all women, to transit to service occupations (Oesch and Rodriguez Menes 2011: 512).

## 1.2.2 Determinants of Post-displacement Wages

A large body of research has shown that displaced workers, once reemployed, suffer from wage losses (Couch and Placzek 2010). Underlying to this phenomenon, two different mechanisms may be at work. According to the human capital theory, introduced by Becker (1962: 9), wage losses are caused by the loss of job-relevant knowledge and resources. In the context of plant closure, this approach interprets workers' change in wages as an expression of the different level of valuation of their skills by pre- and post-displacement employers.

A decrease in valuation may be the result of several mechanisms. First, such a situation may come about if the displaced workers' skill profiles and the requirements of their new jobs are not compatible. In this case of skill mismatch, workers' post-displacement wages are likely to be lower than in their pre-displacement job (Allen and Van der Velden 2001: 444–5, Payne and Payne 1993). A British study shows that, for workers with the same level of education, those who are overqualified in their jobs earn 18 % less than individuals who work in jobs for which they are appropriately qualified. At the same time, underqualified workers earn 18 % more than workers with appropriate qualification for their job – holding the level of education constant (Green and McIntosh 2007: 436). Thus, workers who end up in a job requiring skills below their own level will earn less than those working exactly at their skill level, regardless of their actual level of skills (Allen and Van der Velden 2001: 450).

Second, long spells of unemployment may lead to the depreciation of workers' skills (Pissarides 1992: 1386). This in turn results in wage losses upon reemployment. Based on data from the US Displaced Worker Survey and correcting for selection effects, it has been shown that a 10 % longer unemployment duration is associated with a 1 % wage decrease upon reemployment (Addison and Portugal 1989: 295).

Third, several studies have demonstrated a negative relationship between workers' education and wage losses. A study from the US finds that every additional year of education attenuates displaced workers' wage losses by a third (Chan and Stevens 2001: 568). A Dutch study reports that workers with more than intermediate vocational training experience lower wage losses than workers with lower levels of education (Kriechel and Pfann 2005: 231–2). Similarly, a Finnish study provides evidence for a linear relationship between education and wage losses – with the lowest losses for workers with a tertiary degree (Appelqvist 2007: 38). These findings suggest that pre- and post-displacement employers value higher levels of education more similarly than they do lower levels of education. While less educated workers may receive considerable returns in their pre-displacement firm because of the firm-specific knowledge they acquired, a new employer does not equally value their skills. Changing their job thus leads to substantial wage losses.

Fourth, research based on the US Displaced Worker Survey suggests that *sectoral* tenure leads to wage losses upon unemployment. A study based on the US Displaced Worker Survey has reported that tenure negatively affects wages twice as much if workers change sector as compared to staying (Neal 1995: 657). Moreover, high *firm* tenure leads to large wage losses upon reemployment (Carrington 1993; Greenaway et al. 2000: 66; Kletzer 2001: 59; Cha and Morgan 2010: 1145; Couch and Placzek 2010). These findings have been explained with the argument that workers with high tenure received returns on firm-specific knowledge in their pre-displacement job but not from a new employer. In contrast, workers with short tenure received no compensation for firm-specific skills before displacement and thus do not experience substantial wage losses when reemployed. Finally, a study based on UK panel data finds that *occupational* tenure has the most negative effects on wage changes: while the wage returns for *occupational* tenure of 10 years are 13 %, they are only 3 % for *sector* tenure (Haynes et al. 2002: 249). Changing occupation thus is likely to induce higher wage losses than changing sector while staying in the pre-displacement occupation. For instance, a mechanic who worked in manufacturing before job loss hired as a mechanic in a company in the services is likely to experience almost no wage changes. In contrast, a mechanic who worked in manufacturing and remains in the sector but is reemployed as a stocks clerk is likely to experience wage losses. This suggests that skills are better transferable between sectors than between occupations (Lee and Wolpin 2006: 28).

A second theory to explain displaced workers' wage losses focuses on deferred compensation. Deferred compensation is a practice where younger workers are underpaid and older workers overpaid with respect to their productivity. Accordingly, over their career, workers' wages rise more strongly than their productivity. Deferred compensation is a strategy used by companies to motivate young employees to stay in the company and reward those who stay for their loyalty (Lazear 1990: 275). If workers instead change their job, for instance because of plant closure, this loyalty bonus is lost. Evidence for this theory is provided by a British study that shows that those firms which defer compensation – for example in the form of pensions – hire fewer older workers (Daniel and Heywood 2007: 43). In firms that offer pensions, only 3 % of all the hirings are older workers as compared with 14 % in average firms. Similarly, firms with steeper wage profiles hire fewer older workers than firms with flatter wage profiles. In addition, the findings about the negative effect of high firm tenure may corroborate the deferred compensation theory.

Finally, wage levels differ substantially between sectors or firms. As a consequence, if workers change sector or firm they may experience a wage change. Since in Switzerland collective wage bargaining is mostly organized on a sectoral level, workers may experience wage losses (gains) simply by changing into a sector with generally lower (higher) wages (Mach and Oesch 2003: 166). Based on data from the US, Jacobson et al. (1993: 703) maintain that the loss of firm rents such as union premiums increase the workers' wage losses.

For those workers who experience wage losses, these often turn out to be long-lasting. An analysis of the Panel Study of Income Dynamics shows that 4 years after involuntary job loss, workers in the US still earn about 14 % less than non-displaced workers (Ruhm 1991: 322). Another study using the same dataset but for another time period finds that 4 years after displacement workers earn 10 % less than the non-displaced (Stevens 1997: 174). A study based on administrative data from

Pennsylvania found even wage losses of 20 % compared to non-displaced workers 6 years after job loss. Moreover, wage losses in the US seem to be most severe for workers with the lowest incomes before displacement (Feather 1997: 37).

### 1.2.3 Changes in Job Quality

Displaced workers are vulnerable to reemployment in precarious jobs. A study based on UK Labor Force Survey data reveals that workers who have recently been unemployed end up much more frequently in non-standard employment than workers who were continuously employed (Payne and Payne 1993: 526–8). Similarly, evidence from the analysis of the European Community Household Panel (ECHP) shows that workers who go through a spell of unemployment are negatively affected in their job quality, even 2 years after returning to the active labor force (Dieckhoff 2011).

One reasons for this outcome may be a general change of employment relations (Hipp et al. 2015: 355). Some authors have suggested that labor markets in Western societies are segmented and consist of secure "core" jobs on the one hand and insecure "peripheral" jobs on the other (Berger and Piore 1980). From this perspective, displaced workers may end up in peripheral jobs if they lack alternative opportunities, for instance because of high aggregate unemployment (Kalleberg 2009: 2). Workers are then likely to accept low-end jobs in order to avoid long-term unemployment or exclusion from the labor market (Payne and Payne 1993: 530–1). However, Kalleberg (2009: 5–6) claims that precarious work – such as temporary jobs – is becoming more generalized and even concerns managers and professionals. It may thus be due to the current evolution of the labor market that the new jobs of displaced workers are less secure and of lower quality than their former ones. In the long run, non-displaced workers would then also be exposed to a similar risk of precarious work.

What do we understand by precarious jobs and which aspects does the concept of job quality encompass? Precarious work has been defined as employment that is uncertain and unpredictable from the workers' point of view and that does not permit workers to obtain or maintain occupational skills (Kalleberg 2009: 2). Job quality reflects the variety in the tasks, the level of personal initiative in carrying out the job, the opportunities for learning and self-development, the ability to participate in decision-making, and job security (Gallie 2003: 62,65). Indicators for job quality are for example contract type, job security, skill match or job authority.

Contract type is an indicator for job quality since it reflects workers' job security and career prospects (Green 2008: 151). Permanent contracts are usually more advantageous than fixed-term or temporary contracts and imply better job security (Green 2008: 151). Data from the OECD countries shows that temporarily employed workers receive on average lower wages, less fringe benefits and are less satisfied with their jobs than the permanently employed (OECD 2002: 141, 145, 150). Workers who have experienced a phase of unemployment – such as displaced workers – seem to end up more often in temporary jobs than workers changing from employment to a new job. A study based on the UK Labour Force Survey shows that unemployed workers are five to ten times more likely to be reemployed in temporary jobs than the employed (Payne and Payne 1993: 528). Nevertheless, temporary employment is probably more advantageous than long-term unemployment and may in some cases serve as a stepping stone into permanent employment (Gerfin et al. 2005: 824; De Graaf-Zijl et al. 2011: 126).

Job security is central to the concept of job quality. Job insecurity represents the anticipation of an involuntary and stressful event (Sverke et al. 2002: 243). This anticipation is often as important a source of anxiety as the event of job loss itself (Sverke et al. 2002: 244). Job insecurity is widely understood as a subjective measure assessing an individual experience. However, a Finnish study has shown a close relation between the subjective perception of job insecurity and the unemployment level at a given time (Nätti et al. 2005). Job insecurity is thus not "just in your head" (De Witte 2005). Worker categories that are particularly affected by job insecurity in four European countries are blue-collars, manufacturing, low-skilled and older workers (Näswall and De Witte 2003: 199–202).

Job quality can furthermore be assessed in terms of skill mismatch. A mismatch between individuals' skills and the requirements of the job usually results in unsatisfactory employment relations. A small-scale study from the US finds that displaced workers suffer more often from skill mismatch than non-displaced workers (Leana and Feldman 1995: 1385). Particularly prevalent among displaced workers is overqualification. Being overqualified for a job usually comes along with lower job authority, lower earnings and may result in a lower social status (Green and McIntosh 2007: 436). Overqualification would be of minor importance if it were only a temporary phenomenon. But empirical evidence shows that among workers who are overqualified in their first job, two-thirds are still working in a job for which they are overqualified 6 years later (Green and McIntosh 2007: 428).

A final aspect of job quality that we discuss is job authority. Job authority reflects whether workers supervise the work of others. It expresses the hierarchical position of the workers and represents the autonomy they have in their job. A study based on longitudinal data from Wisconsin shows that as compared to non-displaced workers, displaced workers experience a reduction in job authority as a consequence of dismissal (Brand 2006: 290). In line with these results, a longitudinal study based on data from ECHP for Denmark, Austria, Spain and the UK finds that formerly unemployed workers were more likely to experience lower job authority in all countries except Austria (Dieckhoff 2011: 242).

## 1.3 Sociability and Well-Being

### 1.3.1 *Coping Strategies on the Household Level*

Life-course sociologists have emphasized that individuals' lives are interdependent (Elder 1994: 5). Accordingly, with respect to plant closure the question arises of how the significant others of the displaced worker respond to this critical event. For instance, workers' spouses or families may be involved in coping strategies adopted at the household level.

Earlier research has shown that job displacement often causes financial strains for the household members concerned. A Danish study on workers who become unemployed finds that nearly twice as many unemployed workers face difficulties in meeting their current expenses as compared to the employed (Andersen 2002: 186). Workers with low wages, few savings or experiencing long-term unemployment may adopt strategies to cope with income losses.

A first possible coping strategy that may be considered by couple households is to increase the employment activity of the non-displaced partner. However, most research does not find evidence for this strategy being used. A study based on data from the UK observes that the wives of unemployed workers become even more likely to leave the workforce when their husbands become unemployed (Davies et al. 1994). Similarly, based on Swedish longitudinal data on workers displaced in 1987, it has been shown that the wives of these workers experience a decrease in wages which suggests that they quit their jobs following their husband's job displacement (Eliason 2011: 609). A third study reveals compatible results for the UK but opposite outcomes for the Czech Republic and Slovakia (Gallie et al. 2001: 46–7). The findings from the two Eastern European countries are thus the only ones that support the assumption that spouses enter or increase employment when their partners lose their jobs. More generally, the studies cited above seem to provide evidence for a polarization of dual-earner versus no-earner families (Gallie et al. 2001: 46). Possible explanations are either a selection effect where individuals with a similar likelihood of losing their job become spouses, or that both partners experience the same constraints to being in employment because of adverse labor market conditions such as an economic crisis (Eliason 2011: 612).

Another possible response to the experience of financial strains is adjusting expenditures – a strategy that can also be adopted by single-person households. A longitudinal study based on the Panel Study of Income Dynamics addresses spending on food. The author observes a drop of 22 percentage points in food consumption for workers who do not receive unemployment benefits (Gruber 1997: 195). In contrast, at an unemployment benefit replacement rate of 84 % workers were able to keep their food consumption at their pre-job loss level.

We cannot infer from food consumption to overall household spending since food – with the exception of buying high-end products and dining out – is a basic need and its consumption thus relatively inelastic to income changes. In addition, food consumption only represents about 20 % of a household's overall consumption bundle and the related results thus cannot be extrapolated to workers' overall spending adjustment after job loss (Gruber 1997: 195). This assumption has been confirmed by a Canadian study showing that workers who experience an income loss reduce their spending on clothes much more than on food (Browning and Crossley 2009: 1190). It seems therefore likely that households reduce spending on goods that are not indispensable while they continue to spend as much on necessities as they did before job loss.

## 1.3.2 Sociability

Job loss has been shown to affect workers' social relationships. We may expect that workers who lose their job face the risk of being socially isolated, for example because individuals bow out as a consequence of stigmatization or a lack of money that renders maintaining a social life difficult. Social isolation tends to have negative impacts on individuals' well-being and may cut off workers' from information networks that are particularly important for job seekers (Gallie et al. 2003: 3, 12). However, studies on unemployed workers' sociability are inconclusive with respect to the risk of social isolation in the aftermath of job loss.

Based on data from the ECHP, Gallie et al. (2003: 16) find that sociability patterns do not change when workers become unemployed. But they find that patterns of sociability for workers becoming unemployed and workers being continuously employed differed already before the unemployed lose their job. Workers becoming unemployed have on average larger social networks than those who are continuously employed but they are less active in associations. Another European study based on data from the UK, the Czech Republic, Slovakia and Bulgaria observes similar results: the unemployed see friends and relatives more frequently than the employed (Gallie et al. 2001: 47). However, the unemployed receive less practical and psychological support than the employed (Gallie et al. 2001: 48). By contrast, a small-scale longitudinal study from the US finds contrasting results: employed workers have larger networks than the unemployed, but there is no difference in support received between unemployed and employed workers (Atkinson et al. 1986: 321). In sum, this leaves us with a puzzle about how individuals' sociability is affected when they experience job displacement.

With respect to contacts with colleagues, it has been shown that these contacts decline shortly after individuals' have quit their job. A study from Denmark comparing the social relations of unemployed and employed workers finds that contacts with former colleagues drastically decrease after job loss. One year after job loss, 62% of the unemployed no longer have contact with their former co-workers (Larsen 2008: 11). This development is problematic with regard to displaced workers' job search since the rupture from occupational networks may marginalize them in the labor market and reduce their chance of finding a new job.

With respect to relationships with spouses and the family, job loss seems to negatively affect these social ties. In a small-scale longitudinal study from the US studying the change in marital relationship after the husband became unemployed, Atkinson et al. (1986: 320) find that job loss decreases the quality of the marital relationship. However, they maintain that more cohesive family structures have a stress-buffering effect. The reasons for the adverse effect of job loss on marital relationships is however less clear. Tensions may stem from families' financial (Gallie et al. 2003: 3). A study based on longitudinal administrative data from Norway supports this argument, showing that families receiving social security benefits – and thus being at the lower income end – before one of the spouses becomes unemployed are more likely to experience marital dissolution than families without such benefits (Hansen 2005: 142).

Another argument that was brought forward is that workers may be blamed for the job loss by their spouse. A study from the US reveals that the incidence of divorce rises only for workers subject to individual layoffs but not for those experiencing plant closure (Charles and Stephens 2004: 516–9). They explain this finding by indicating that spouses of individually laid off workers may blame their partner while spouses of workers who experienced plant closure understand that it was not their fault. However, there may be an alternative explanation for their finding: reverse causality or unobserved heterogeneity, whereas workers who experience strong tensions in their marital relationship become depressed or distracted and therefore more likely to lose their job.

Finally, there seem to be different expectations of spouses towards their partner depending on their sex. Evidence from Norway based on longitudinal administrative data reveals that divorce is significantly more likely in couples where the *husband* experiences plant closure than where the husband is continuously employed, even if they control for selection effects and potential effects of income losses (Rege et al. 2007: 13, 18). Accordingly, marital dissolution results from the decline in husbands' indispensability because their spouses (or perhaps they themselves) consider them to be failing to fulfill the traditional breadwinner role. Support for this thesis is provided by a study from Sweden which finds large risks of divorce after displacement in couples where men lost their jobs but no significant effects if women were displaced (Eliason 2012: 1392). Accordingly, if unemployment stigmatizes men more strongly than women in Scandinavian countries where mothers are highly involved in the labor market and often work full-time, we may assume that the effect is even stronger in Switzerland where mothers are less strongly attached to the labor market.

Independently of workers' sex, displaced workers experience more pressure to find a new job if they have family obligations (Leana and Feldman 1995: 1383). The life-cycle stage of a family may thus determine how much hardship job loss causes (Moen 1980: 183). Families with lower household incomes are likely to be more distressed by job loss than those with higher incomes. Evidence for this has been provided by a panel study from the US that finds that children of single mothers are particularly vulnerable when their mothers lose their job (Brand and Simon Thomas 2014: 982). The authors find that young adults were negatively affected in their educational attainment and subjective well-being when their mothers were displaced while they were adolescent.

## 1.3.3 Subjective Well-Being

It is widely understood that losing a job leads to a substantial decrease in subjective well-being.[2] A meta-study reassessing the results of about a hundred studies mainly from the US shows that there is a broad consensus and substantial evidence for the reduction of mental health after job displacement (McKee-Ryan et al. 2005: 63). For instance, a study based on German panel data shows that workers who are displaced by plant closures suffer from reductions in life satisfaction (Winkelmann and Winkelmann 1998: 7). Likewise, a more recent study based on German and Swiss panel data finds that workers becoming unemployment experience a substantial decrease in well-being (Oesch and Lipps 2013: 963).

While there exists agreement on job loss leading to a drop in workers' well-being, there is a controversy going on about the mechanisms underlying this phenomenon. An influential explanation, called "latent deprivation model", goes back to Jahoda (1982). She argues that becoming unemployed is harmful for workers' well-being since work not only provides individuals' with an income but also fulfills some of their latent needs such as providing them with an identity, a social status, a daily structure and allowing them to engage in activities meant for collective purposes. This approach has been challenged by findings from Denmark that show that unemployed workers do not worry much about "having no purpose to get up in the morning" or that they lose their social status (Andersen 2002: 185). In contrast, their largest concern was economic insecurity. Psychologists in turn claim that economic insecurity induced by job loss generates stress and uncertainty (McKee-Ryan et al. 2005: 68). In line with these findings, displaced workers are more likely to experience anxiety, depression and loss of self-esteem (Brand 2015: 15).

Which individuals are particularly affected in their well-being by job displacement? Evidence from German and Swiss longitudinal data indicates that men experience stronger decreases in well-being than women when losing their job (Oesch and Lipps 2013: 963). Similar results are found for Germany (Clark et al. 2008: F238) and for Catalonia (Artazcoz et al. 2004: 83). A possible explanation is that the main responsibility to provide household income is still assigned to men and losing the ability to comply with this role makes them suffer more strongly (Ernst Stähli et al. 2009: 334).

It has been suggested that unemployed workers become used to their situation, as the duration of their unemployment spell increases – the so-called "habituation effect" hypothesis. Yet there is little evidence in support of that claim. The analysis of German and Swiss longitudinal data reveals no evidence for such an effect to be acting (Clark et al. 2008: F231; Oesch and Lipps 2013: 963). In contrast, these studies rather showed that unemployed workers' well-being slightly but continuously

---

[2] The notion of subjective well-being expresses the degree to which individuals judge the quality of their lives favorable (Veenhoven et al. 1993: 19). Theoretically the concept goes back to Bentham and aims at capturing individuals' pleasure and pain (Dolan et al. 2011: 6).

decreases over time, possibly as a consequence of their increasing frustration over rejected job applications (Strandh 2000: 469; Flückiger 2002: 15).

When unemployed workers are reemployed, their well-being seems to recover. A study on recent waves of the US Panel Study of Income Dynamics finds that unemployed people who return to employment experience a significant increase in well-being (Young 2012a: 16). However, they do not achieve their pre-displacement level of well-being. The author assumes that reemployed workers either experience a lingering sense of labor market insecurity or that they suffer from occupational downward mobility.

Hence, the characteristics of the new job may explain workers' well-being when reemployed. There may be a link between wage losses and well-being. Traditionally, economists have assumed that the financial return on work substantially affects workers' level of job satisfaction. A quasi-experimental study on lottery winners in Great Britain simulating wage increases observes strongly positive effects of winning on workers' well-being – even in the long-term (Gardner and Oswald 2007: 53). Yet a recent meta-analysis reports that the majority of studies find only a weak correlation between workers' well-being and their wage (Judge et al. 2010). As an example, two studies based on German longitudinal data find only extremely small effects of wage losses on well-being (Winkelmann and Winkelmann 1998: 12; Ferrer-i-Carbonell and Frijters 2004: 656). In fact, it has been shown that relative wage – the worker's wage as compared to the average wage in similar jobs – is a much better determinant of individuals' job satisfaction (Clark and Oswald 1996: 361).

From these findings we may infer that wage losses per se do not threaten workers' well-being as long as they permit them to keep up a similar standard of living. Only if the wage reduction is large enough to restrict the fulfillment of individuals' daily needs, do negative repercussions on their life satisfaction become apparent. This argument is supported by results from two US studies, one based on data from Tennessee and the other from Utah, which find that perceived economic well-being is a much better determinant of individuals' well-being than measured household income (Mills et al. 1992: 61; Fox and Chancey 1998: 74).

Displaced workers' well-being may also be affected by changes in job quality that are frequent after job loss (Dieckhoff 2011: 242; Brand 2006: 290). For instance, workers may be unable to find a job in which they are hired at an activity level that corresponds to their working hour preferences, or in other words, they may be "under-" or "overemployed" in their new position A meta-analysis reports that underemployment has harmful effects on individuals' well-being, perhaps because it involves a lower income or a lower social status than full-time employment (Winefield 2002: 142). At the same time, working overtime may have similarly negative consequences on workers' well-being as shown by a study based on the British Household Panel Survey (Rose 2003: 520).

Additional burdens that displaced workers may endure in order to become reemployed are longer commuting distances. Kahneman et al. (2004: 431–2) show for female workers in Texas that commuting is the most out-of-favor of all daily activities. A study based on German data controlling for selection effects suggests that

## 1.3 Sociability and Well-Being

even if commuters are financially compensated for the inconvenience of traveling, they are less satisfied with their lives than those who do not commute (Stutzer and Frey 2008: 349). This finding points to a strongly negative effect of commuting on individuals' subjective well-being.

An alternative to the argument that reemployed displaced workers do not regain their pre-displacement level of well-being because they are reemployed in low-quality jobs, is that job displacement negatively affects other domains of workers' lives, such as their social status or social relationships. For instance, reemployment in jobs of lower quality or in lower hierarchical positions goes along with loss of occupational prestige (Kalleberg 2009: 9), social status being a central determinant of individuals' well-being (Clark and D'Angelo 2013: 14). Another longitudinal British study examining the well-being of managers who – voluntarily or involuntarily – changed jobs has revealed that downward mobility led to substantial decreases in their life satisfaction (West et al. 1990: 127).

But most prominently, the literature has pointed out that social relationships matter for individuals' well-being. A British study comparing the effect of a large number of life domains on individuals' well-being finds the strongest correlations between life satisfaction and satisfaction with social life (Dolan et al. 2011: 7). Accordingly, it seems plausible that if social relationships suffer as a consequence of job loss, workers' life satisfaction is negatively affected.

The study by Dolan et al. (2011) highlights that among different types of social ties the relationship with their spouse matters most for their well-being. If workers' marital relationship suffers – for example as a consequence of a degradation of the financial household situation – they are likely to be negatively affected in their general life satisfaction, in particular if they are the main breadwinner (Hansen 2005: 142). A small-scale longitudinal study from the US shows that job loss leads to a decrease in the quality of the marital relationship, but that it recovers after reemployment (Atkinson et al. 1986: 320–7). Moreover, the study shows that cohesive family structures may be stress-buffering and displaced workers experiencing solidarity and receiving emotional assistance may see their family and spousal relationships improving.

Other studies claim that friendship is a better determinant of individuals' well-being than family and spousal relationships. A study based on data from Canada and the US shows that relationships with friends are associated more than twice as strongly with workers' well-being as the relationships with their family (Helliwell and Putnam 2004: 1439). A similar result has been found in a meta-analysis on this issue. The authors argue that the encounter with friends is associated with enjoyment and sharing of good times (Pinquart and Sörensen 2000: 194).

Finally, it has been argued that for some workers seeing their plant closing down may be a relief. This may be the case if the job security in the pre-displacement plant was very low and the workers experienced great uncertainty regarding their future career. A qualitative longitudinal study conducted in the State of New York reports positive effects of job displacement on workers' well-being (Sweet and Moen 2011: 24–5). More displaced workers reported health improvements than health declines following their job loss. Even for individuals where the financial situation worsened, other aspects of their lives – such as emotional well-being and physical health – improved subsequently. Quitting their working environments implied for them a way out of job insecurity and an atmosphere of low morale.

## 1.4 Our Model of Occupational Transition After Plant Closure and Hypotheses

How plant closure affects workers' lives is subject to complex processes. To reduce the complexity we suggest a model that focuses on the main causal mechanisms. The model consists in an illustration of how some main determinants are linked to a limited number of outcomes and how different aspects of the outcome are related among them. The model is presented in Fig. 1.1.

On the side of the determinants – or moderator variables – we have three main drivers: (i) individuals' characteristics, (ii) individuals' actions, and (iii) labor market context. The individuals' characteristics that we expect to be linked with post-displacement outcomes are the workers' education, sex, age, tenure, nationality, civil status, occupation, and their social network. The individuals' actions that may affect the transition are job search strategy, training, geographic mobility, accepting temporary employment, and household coping strategies. The regional rate of unemployment is probably the best indicator for overall labor market context but also labor market institutions and the skill regime importantly affect occupational transitions. Together with other factors such as employers' preferences or labor market policies – which are not examined in detail in this study – these factors shape the displaced workers' job opportunities.

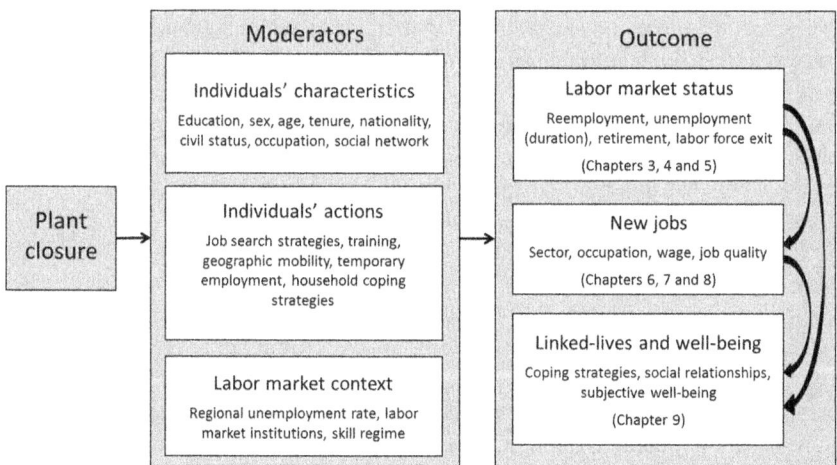

**Fig. 1.1** Model of occupational transition after plant closure

## 1.4 Our Model of Occupational Transition After Plant Closure and Hypotheses

Schematically, we can distinguish four different labor market statuses: reemployed, unemployed, retired, and labor force exit. Unemployment duration is at the same time an outcome and a determinant: we analyze the factors that determine unemployment duration and discuss how it affects other outcomes. For the category of the reemployed, we assess the sectors, occupations, wages and quality of their new jobs. In order to understand the impact of plant closure on workers' sociability and well-being we examine workers' household coping strategies, changes in their social relationships and changes in life satisfaction.

We assume that there is not only a causal relationship between plant closure and the outcome measures but that some of the outcome measures of interest are also causally linked. More precisely, we expect that labor market status 2 years after displacement is linked to the characteristics of the new jobs displaced workers have or will take on, to their sociability and well-being. The characteristics of the new job in turn are also assumed to affect workers' sociability and well-being. To give a concrete example, workers who experienced long unemployment spells are likely to experience an occupational downgrading once they returned to a job. To give another example, workers reemployed in insecure jobs risk seeing their well-being drop because of a latent feeling of uncertainty.

Based on the discussion of the literature presented above our main hypotheses are as follows:

H1. Our first hypothesis refers to workers' reemployment prospects. We expect that the rising demand for high-skilled workers and the importance of education as a signal for unobserved characteristics lead low- and mid-educated workers to encounter more difficulties in finding a job than highly educated workers. Furthermore, we predict that older workers have more difficulty in returning to the active labor force than younger workers. Referring to the theory of the transferability of specific skills, we assume that reemployment is more difficult for older workers because they typically have higher tenure and thus more firm- and sector-specific skills.

H2. Our second hypothesis addresses early retirement. In line with our hypothesis that older workers encounter difficulties in finding a new job, we expect older workers to retire early in order to avoid long-term unemployment. We thus assume that older workers are rather pushed than pulled into early retirement and that they tend to take this pathway involuntarily.

H3. Our third hypothesis examines job search strategies. The labor market literature suggests that a large number of jobs are found through informal contacts. Moreover, authors have argued that jobs encountered through the social network are found within a shorter time, are better paid and of better quality. We therefore predict that displaced workers who find their new jobs through social contacts experience advantages in terms of job quality as compared to those who find their jobs through other channels.

H4. Our fourth and fifth hypotheses highlight workers' reemployment sector. Switzerland's vocational training system is highly standardized at the industry level with common training protocols and skill certification procedures. With respect to workers' reemployment sectors we expect that workers with vocational education – which in Switzerland most often means apprenticeships – disproportionately find new jobs in the same sector they were employed in before job loss.

H5. If workers nevertheless change sector, we hypothesize that push rather than pull mechanisms are at work. More specifically, we expect sectoral changes to be triggered by the experience of long-term unemployment. Furthermore, we predict that workers who change sector in order to avoid long-term unemployment particularly often accept low-end jobs in the service sector.

H6. Our sixth hypothesis analyzes wages. We predict that workers with a large amount of firm-specific skills, – in particular high-tenured, low-qualified and sector or occupation changing workers – are most negatively affected by wage losses. Once these workers lose their job, they are unlikely to receive financial returns from a new employer to the skills that are specific to their pre-displacement firm and thus experience wage losses upon reemployment.

H7. Our seventh hypothesis explores job quality. Research has shown that long-term unemployed workers have the highest risk of occupational and social downgrading. The longer workers search for a job, the less likely they are to return to a job and the lower tends to be its quality. We therefore expect that those workers who experience long unemployment spells are most prone to see their job quality drop upon reemployment. Such a scenario is particularly likely for older workers since they tend to face strong barriers to reemployment after job loss.

H8. Our eight and final hypothesis scrutinizes workers' subjective well-being. We assume that changes in workers' social relationships drive changes in their well-being most strongly, more strongly than changes in their financial situation. We particularly highlight the effect of plant on marital relationships. Previous literature has shown that job loss is likely to lead to persistent tensions between spouses. Plant closure thus may leave long-lasting scars in workers' social lives even after returning to employment.

**Open Access** This chapter is distributed under the terms of the Creative Commons Attribution 4.0 International License (http://creativecommons.org/licenses/by/4.0/), which permits use, duplication, adaptation, distribution and reproduction in any medium or format, as long as you give appropriate credit to the original author(s) and the source, a link is provided to the Creative Commons license and any changes made are indicated.

The images or other third party material in this chapter are included in the work's Creative Commons license, unless indicated otherwise in the credit line; if such material is not included in the work's Creative Commons license and the respective action is not permitted by statutory regulation, users will need to obtain permission from the license holder to duplicate, adapt or reproduce the material.

# References

Addison, J. T., & Portugal, P. (1989). Job displacement, relative wage changes, and duration of unemployment. *Journal of Labor Economics, 7*(3), 281.

Allen, J., & Van der Velden, R. (2001). Educational mismatches versus skill mismatches: Effects on wages, job satisfaction, and on-the-job search. *Oxford Economic Papers, 53*(3), 434–452.

Andersen, J. G. (2002). Coping with long-term unemployment: Economic security, labour market integration and well-being. Results from a Danish panel study, 1994–1999. *International Journal of Social Welfare, 11*, 178–190.

Appelqvist, J. (2007). *Wage and earnings losses of displaced workers in Finland.* Government Institute for Economic Research Finland (VATT), Helsinki, Discussion Paper, No. 422.

Artazcoz, L., Benach, J., Borrell, C., & Cortès, I. (2004). Unemployment and mental health: Understanding the interactions among gender, family roles, and social class. *American Journal of Public Health, 94*(1), 82–88.

Arulampalam, W. (2001). Is unemployment really scarring? Effects of unemployment experiences on wages. *The Economic Journal, 111*(475), F585–F606.

Atkinson, T., Liem, R., & Liem, J. H. (1986). The social costs of unemployment: Implications for social support. *Journal of Health and Social Behavior, 27*(4), 317–331.

Autor, D. H., & Dorn, D. (2009). *Inequality and specialization: The growth of low-skilled service jobs in the United States* (IZA discussion papers no. 4290). Cambridge, MA: National Bureau of Economic Research.

Becker, G. S. (1962). Investment in human capital: A theoretical analysis. *Journal of Political Economy, 70*(5), 9–49.

Berger, S., & Piore, M. (1980). *Dualism and discontinuity in industrial societies.* New York: Cambridge University Press.

Berman, E., Bound, J., & Griliches, Z. (1994). Changes in the demand for skilled labor within U.S. manufacturing: Evidence from the annual survey of manufactures. *The Quarterly Journal of Economics, 109*, 367–397.

Black, S. E., & Spitz-Oener, A. (2010). Explaining women's success: Technological change and the skill content of women's work. *Review of Economics and Statistics, 92*(1), 187–194.

Blanchard, O. J., & Diamond, P. (1994). Ranking, unemployment duration, and wages. *The Review of Economic Studies, 61*(3), 417–434.

Bonoli, G. (2003). Two worlds of pension reform in Western Europe. *Comparative Politics, 35*(4), 399–416.

Bonoli, G., & Hinrichs, K. (2012). Statistical discrimination and employers' recruitment. *European Societies, 14*(3), 338–361.

Brand, J. E. (2006). The effects of job displacement on job quality: Findings from the Wisconsin Longitudinal Study. *Research in Social Stratification and Mobility, 24*(3), 275–298.

Brand, J. E. (2015). The far-reaching impact of job loss and unemployment. *Annual Review of Sociology, 41*, 359–375.

Brand, J. E., & Simon Thomas, J. (2014). Job displacement among single mothers: Effects on children's outcomes in young adulthood. *American Journal of Sociology, 119*(4), 955–1001.

Browning, M., & Crossley, T. F. (2009). Shocks, stocks, and socks: Smoothing consumption over a temporary income loss. *Journal of the European Economic Association, 7*(6), 1169–1192.

Burda, M. C., & Mertens, A. (2001). Estimating wage losses of displaced workers in Germany. *Labour Economics, 8*(1), 15–41.

Burgess, P. L., & Low, S. A. (1998). How do unemployment insurance and recall expectations affect on-the-job search among workers who receive advance notice of layoff. *Industrial and Labor Relations Review, 51*(2), 241–252.

Carlsson, M., & Rooth, D. (2007). Evidence of ethnic discrimination in the Swedish labor market using experimental data. *Labour Economics, 14*, 716–729.

Carrington, W. J. (1993). Wage losses for displaced workers: Is it really the firm that matters? *The Journal of Human Resources, 28*(3), 435.

Cha, Y., & Morgan, S. L. (2010). Structural earnings losses and between-industry mobility of displaced workers, 2003–2008. *Social Science Research, 39*(6), 1137–1152.

Chan, S., & Stevens, A. H. (2001). Job loss and employment patterns of older workers. *Journal of Labor Economics, 19*(2), 484–521.

Charles, K. K., & Stephens, M. J. (2004). Job displacement, disability, and divorce. *Journal of Labor Economics, 22*(2), 489–522.

Clark, A. E. & D'Angelo, E. (2013). *Upward social mobility, well-being and political preferences: evidence from the BHPS*. Centre for Economic Persomance (CEP) Discussion Paper, No. 1252. London: CEP.

Clark, A. E., Diener, E., Georgellis, Y., & Lucas, R. E. (2008). Lags and leads in life satisfaction: A test of the baseline hypothesis. *The Economic Journal, 118*(529), F222–F243.

Clark, A. E., & Oswald, A. J. (1996). Satisfaction and comparison income. *Journal of Public Economics, 61*, 359–381.

Couch, K. A. (2001). Earning losses and unemployment of displaced workers in Germany. *Industrial and Labor Relations Review, 54*(3), 559–572.

Couch, K. A., & Placzek, D. W. (2010). Earnings losses of displaced workers revisited. *American Economic Review, 100*(1), 572–589.

Daniel, K., & Heywood, J. S. (2007). The determinants of hiring older workers: UK evidence. *Labour Economics, 14*(1), 35–51.

Davies, R. B., Elias, P., & Pen, R. (1994). The relationship between a husband's unemployment and his wife's participation in the labour force. In D. Gallie, C. Marsh, & C. Vogler (Eds.), *Social change and the experience of unemployment* (pp. 154–187). Oxford: Oxford University Press.

De Coulon, A., Falter, J.-M., Flückiger, Y., & Ramirez, J. (2003). Analyse der Lohn- unterschiede zwischen der schweizerischen und der ausländischen Bevölkerung. In H.-R. Wicker, R. Fibbi, & W. Haug (Eds.), *Migration und die Schweiz* (pp. 275–301). Zürich: Seismo.

De Graaf-Zijl, M., Van den Berg, G. J., & Heyma, A. (2011). Stepping stones for the unemployed: The effect of temporary jobs on the duration until (regular) work. *Journal of Population Economics, 24*(1), 107–139.

De Witte, H. (2005). Job insecurity: Review of the international literature on definitions, prevalence, antecedents and consequences. *SA Journal of Industrial Psychology, 31*(4), 1–6.

Desmet, R., Jousten, A., & Perelman, S. (2005). *The benefits of separating early retirees from the unemployed: Simulation results for Belgian wage earners* (IZA discussion paper series no. 1571). London: Centre for Economic Policy Research.

Dieckhoff, M. (2011). The effect of unemployment on subsequent job quality in Europe: A comparative study of four countries. *Acta Sociologica, 54*(3), 233–249.

Dolan, P., Layard, R., & Metcalfe, R. (2011). *Measuring subjective well-being for public policy*. Richmond: Office for National Statistics. Crown copyright.

Dorn, D., & Sousa-Poza, A. (2005). The determinants of early retirement in Switzerland. *Swiss Journal of Economics and Statistics, 141*(2), 247–283.

Dorn, D., & Sousa-Poza, A. (2010). "Voluntary" and "involuntary" early retirement: An international analysis. *Applied Economics, 42*(4), 427–438.

Elder, G. H. (1994). Time, human agency, and social change: Perspectives on the life course. *Social Psychology Quarterly, 57*(1), 4–15.

Eliason, M. (2011). Income after job loss: The role of the family and the welfare state. *Applied Economics, 43*(5), 603–618.

Eliason, M. (2012). Lost jobs, broken marriages. *Journal of Population Economics, 25*, 1365–1397.

Eliason, M., & Storrie, D. (2003). *The echo of job displacement* (William Davidson institute working paper no. 618). Göteborg: Department of Economics, Göteborg University.

Eliason, M., & Storrie, D. (2006). Lasting or latent scars? Swedish evidence on the long term effects of job displacement. *Journal of Labor Economics, 24*(4), 831–856.

Eriksson, S., & Rooth, D. (2014). Do employers use unemployment as a sorting criterion when hiring? Evidence from a field experiment. *American Economic Review, 104*(3), 1014–1039.

# References

Ernst Stähli, M., Le Goff, J.-M., Levy, R., & Widmer, E. (2009). Wishes or constraints? Mothers' labour force participation and its motivation in Switzerland. *European Sociological Review, 25*(3), 333–348.

Estevez-Abe, M. (2005). Gender bias in skills and social policies: The varieties of capitalism perspective on sex segregation. *Social Politics: International Studies in Gender, State & Society, 12*(2), 180–215.

Fallick, B. C. (1993). The industrial mobility of displaced workers. *Journal of Labor Economics, 11*(2), 302–323.

Fallick, B. C. (1996). A review of the recent empirical literature on displaced workers. *Industrial and Labor Relations Review, 50*(1), 5–16.

Farber, H. S. (1994). The analysis of interfirm worker mobility. *Journal of Labor Economics, 12*, 554–593.

Farber, H. S. (1997). The changing face of job loss in the United States, 1981–1995. *Brookings Papers on Economic Activity. Microeconomics, 1997*(1997), 55–142.

Farber, H. S. (1998). *Mobility and stability: The dynamics of job change in labor markets* (Working paper no. 400). Princeton: Industrial Relations Section, Princeton University.

Farber, H. S. (2005). What do we know about job loss in the United States? Evidence from the displaced workers survey, 1984–2004. *Federal Reserve Bank of Chicago, 2Q*, 13–28.

Feather, N. T. (1997). Economic deprivation and the psychological impact of unemployment. *Australian Psychologist, 32*(1), 37–45.

Fernández-Macías, E. (2012). Job polarization in Europe? Changes in the employment structure and job quality, 1995–2007. *Work and Occupations, 39*(2), 1–26.

Ferrer-i-Carbonell, A., & Frijters, P. (2004). How important is methodology for the estimates of the determinants of happiness? *The Economic Journal, 114*(497), 641–659.

Fibbi, R., Kaya, B., & Piguet, E. (2003). Le passeport ou le diplôme? *Forum suisse pour l'étude des migrations et de la population, 31*.

Flückiger, Y. (2002). Le chômage en Suisse: Causes, évolution et efficacité des mesures actives. *Aspects de La Sécurité Sociale, 4*, 11–21.

Fox, G. L., & Chancey, D. (1998). Sources of economic distress: Individual and family outcomes. *Journal of Family Issues, 19*(6), 725–749.

Franzen, A., & Hangartner, D. (2006). Social networks and labor market outcomes: The non-monetary benefits of social capital. *European Sociological Review, 22*(3), 252–268.

Gallie, D. (2003). The quality of working life: Is Scandinavia different? *European Sociological Review, 19*(1), 61–79.

Gallie, D., Kostova, D., & Kuchar, P. (2001). Social consequences of unemployment: An east–west comparison. *Journal of European Social Policy, 11*(1), 39–54.

Gallie, D., Paugam, S., & Jacobs, S. (2003). Unemployment, poverty and social isolation: Is there a vicious circle of social exclusion? *European Societies, 5*(1), 1–32.

Gangl, M. (2003). Labor market structure and re-employment rates: Unemployment dynamics in West Germany and the United States. *Research in Social Stratification and Mobility, 20*(03), 185–224.

Gangl, M. (2004). Institutions and the structure of labour market matching in the United States and West Germany. *European Sociological Review, 20*(3), 171–187.

Gardner, J., & Oswald, A. J. (2007). Money and mental wellbeing: A longitudinal study of medium-sized lottery wins. *Journal of Health Economics, 26*(1), 49–60.

Gebel, M. (2009). Fixed-term contracts at labour market entry in West Germany: Implications for job search and first job quality. *European Sociological Review, 25*(6), 661–675.

Gerfin, M., Lechner, M., & Steiger, H. (2005). Does subsidised temporary employment get the unemployed back to work? An econometric analysis of two different schemes. *Labour Economics, 12*(6), 807–835.

Gibbons, R., & Katz, L. F. (1991). Layoffs and lemons. *Journal of Labor Economics, 9*(4), 351–380.

Goos, M., & Manning, A. (2007). Lousy and lovely jobs: The rising polarization of work in Britain. *The Review of Economics and Statistics, 89*(1), 118–133.

Granovetter, M. S. (1995 [1974]). *Getting a job. A study of contacts and careers*. Chicago: University Press.

Green, F. (2008). Temporary work and insecurity in Britain: A problem solved? *Social Indicators Research, 88*(1), 147–160.

Green, F., & McIntosh, S. (2007). Is there a genuine under-utilization of skills amongst the over-qualified? *Applied Economics, 39*(4), 427–439.

Greenaway, D., Upward, R., & Wright, P. (2000). Sectoral transformation and labour-market flows. *Oxford Review of Economic Policy, 16*(3), 57–75.

Gruber, J. (1997). The consumption smoothing benefits of unemployment insurance. *The American Economic Review, 87*(1), 192–205.

Hakim, C. (2006). Women, careers, and work-life preferences. *British Journal of Guidance & Counselling, 34*(3), 279–294.

Hamermesh, D. S. (1989). What do we know about worker displacement in the U.S.? *Industrial Relations, 28*(1), 51–59.

Hansen, H.-T. (2005). Unemployment and marital dissolution: A panel data study of Norway. *European Sociological Review, 21*(2), 135–148.

Hansson, R. O., Dekoekkoek, P. D., Neece, W. M., & Patterson, D. W. (1997). Successful aging at work: Annual review, 1992–1996: The older worker and transitions to retirement. *Journal of Vocational Behavior, 51*(2), 202–233.

Haynes, M., Upward, R., & Wright, P. (2002). Estimating the wage costs of inter- and intra-sectoral adjustment. *Weltwirtschaftliches Archiv, 138*(2), 229–253.

Helliwell, J. F., & Putnam, R. D. (2004). The social context of well-being. *Philosophical Transactions of the Royal Society of London. Series B, Biological Sciences, 359*, 1435–1446.

Hipp, L., Bernhardt, J., & Allmendinger, J. (2015). Institutions and the prevalence of nonstandard employment. *Socio-Economic Review, 13*(2), 351–377.

Ichino, A., Schwerdt, G., Winter-Ebmer, R., & Zweimüller, J. (2007). *Too old to work, too young to retire?* (CEPR discussion paper no. 6510). München: CESifo, Center for Economic Studies & Ifo Institute for economic research.

Jackman, R., & Layard, R. (1991). Does long-term unemployment reduce a person's chance of a job? A time-series test. *Economica, 58*(229), 93.

Jackson, M., Goldthorpe, J. H., & Mills, C. (2005). Education, employers and class mobility. *Research in Social Stratification and Mobility, 23*, 3–33.

Jacobson, L. S., LaLonde, R. J., & Sullivan, D. G. (1993). Earning losses of displaced workers. *The American Economic Review, 83*(4), 685–709.

Jahoda, M. (1982). *Employment and unemployment: A social-psychological analysis*. Cambridge: Cambridge University Press.

Jolkkonen, A., Koistinen, P., & Kurvinen, A. (2012). Reemployment of displaced workers – The case of a plant closing on a remote region in Finland. *Nordic Journal of Working Life Studies, 2*(1), 81–100.

Judge, T. A., Piccolo, R. F., Podsakoff, N. P., & Rich, B. L. (2010). The relationship between pay and job satisfaction: A meta-analysis of the literature. *Journal of Vocational Behavior, 77*, 157–167.

Kahneman, D., Krueger, A. B., Schkade, D., & Schwarz, N. (2004). Toward national well-being accounts. *The American Economic Review, 94*(2), 429–434.

Kalleberg, A. L. (2009). Precarious work, insecure workers: Employment relations in transition. *American Sociological Review, 74*(1), 1–22.

Kaufmann, V., Bergman, M., & Joye, D. (2004). Motility: Mobility as capital. *International Journal of Urban and Regional Research, 28*, 745–756.

Kletzer, L. G. (1989). Returns to seniority after permanent job loss. *The American Economic Review, 79*(3), 536–543.

Kletzer, L. G. (2001). *Job loss from imports: Measuring the costs*. Washington, DC: Institute for International Economics.

Knuth, M., & Kalina, T. (2002). Early exit from the labour force between exclusion and privilege: Unemployment as a transition from employment to retirement in West Germany. *European Societies, 4*(4), 393–418.

## References

Korpi, T. (2001). Good friends in bad times? Social networks and job search among the unemployed in Sweden. *Acta Sociologica, 44*(2), 157–170.

Kriechel, B., & Pfann, G. A. (2002). *On heterogeneity among displaced workers* (Working paper). Maastricht: ROA.

Kriechel, B., & Pfann, G. A. (2005). The role of specific and general human capital after displacement. *Education Economics, 13*(2), 223–236.

Kriechel, B., & Pfann, G. A. (2011). *Workforce reorganization and the worker* (IZA discussion paper series no. 5794). Bonn: IZA.

Kroft, K., Lange, F., & Notowidigdo, M. J. (2013). Duration dependence and labor market conditions: Evidence from a field experiment. *The Quarterly Journal of Economics, 128*(3), 1123–1167.

Kuhn, P. J. (Ed.). (2002). *Losing work, moving on: International perspectives on worker displacement*. Kalamazoo: W.E. Upjohn Institute for Employment Research.

Lalive, R. (2008). How do extended benefits affect unemployment duration? A regression discontinuity approach. *Journal of Econometrics, 142*(2), 785–806.

Larsen, C. A. (2008). *Networks versus economic incentives* (Center for comparative welfare studies working paper no 59). Aalborg: Department of Economics, Politics and Public Administration, Aalborg University.

Lazear, E. P. (1990). Pensions and deferred benefits as strategic compensation. *Industrial Relations, 29*(2), 263–280.

Leana, C. R., & Feldman, D. C. (1995). Finding new jobs after a plant closing: Antecedents and outcomes of the occurrence and quality of reemployment. *Human Relations, 48*(12), 1381–1401.

Lee, D., & Wolpin, K. I. (2006). Intersectoral labor mobility and the growth of the service sector. *Econometrica, 74*(1), 1–46.

Liu, Y., & Grusky, D. B. (2013). The payoff to skill in the third industrial revolution. *American Journal of Sociology, 118*(5), 1330–1374.

Longhi, S., & Brynin, M. (2010). Occupational change in Britain and Germany. *Labour Economics, 17*(4), 655–666.

Mach, A., & Oesch, D. (2003). Collective bargaining between decentralization and stability: A sectoral model explaining the Swiss experience during the 1990s. *Industrielle Beziehungen, 10*(1), 160–182.

Machin, S., & Manning, A. (1999). The causes and consequences of long-term unemployment in Europe. In O. Ashenfelter & D. Card (Eds.), *Handbook of labor economics* (1st ed., Vol. 3, pp. 3085–3139). Amsterdam/New York: Elsevier.

Margolis, D. N. (1999). Part-year employment, slow reemployment, and earnings losses: The case of worker displacement in France. In J. C. Haltiwanger, J. I. Lane, J. R. Spletzer, J. J. M. Theeuwes, & K. R. Troske (Eds.), *The creation and analysis of employer-employee matched data* (pp. 375–416). Bingley: Emerald Group Publishing Limited.

Marsden, P. V., & Gorman, E. H. (2001). Social networks, job changes, and recruitment. In I. Berg & A. L. Kalleberg (Eds.), *Sourcebook of labor market: Evolving structures and processes* (pp. 467–502). New York: Kluwer Academic/Plenum Publishers.

McKee-Ryan, F., Song, Z., Wanberg, C. R., & Kinicki, A. J. (2005). Psychological and physical well-being during unemployment: A meta-analytic study. *The Journal of Applied Psychology, 90*(1), 53–76.

Mills, R. J., Grasmick, H. G., Morgan, C. S., & Wenk, D. (1992). The effects of gender, family satisfaction, and economic strain on psychological well-being. *Family Relations, 41*(4), 440–445.

Moen, P. (1980). Measuring unemployment: Family considerations. *Human Relations, 33*(3), 183–192.

Mouw, T. (2003). Social capital and finding a job: Do contacts matter? *American Sociological Review, 68*(6), 868.

Näswall, K., & De Witte, H. (2003). Who feels insecure in Europe? Predicting job insecurity from background variables. *Economic and Industrial Democracy, 24*(2), 189–215.

Nätti, J., Happonen, M., Kinnunen, U., & Mauno, S. (2005). Job insecurity, temporary workers and trade union membership in Finland 1977–2003. In H. De Witte (Ed.), *Job insecurity, union involvement and union activism* (pp. 11–47). Hampshire: Ashgate.

Neal, D. (1995). Industry-specific human capital: Evidence from displaced workers. *Journal of Labor Economics, 13*(4), 653–677.

Newman, K. (1999). *Falling from grace: Downward mobility in the age of affluence*. Berkeley: University of California Press.

Ng, T. W. H., & Feldman, D. C. (2008). The relationship of age to ten dimensions of job performance. *The Journal of Applied Psychology, 93*(2), 392–423.

Nickell, S. (2001). Introduction. *Oxford Bulletin of Economics and Statistics, 63*(Special Issue), 617–628.

Oberholzer-Gee, F. (2008). Nonemployment stigma as rational herding: A field experiment. *Journal of Economic Behavior & Organization, 65*(1), 30–40.

OECD. (2002). Taking the measure of temporary employment. In *OECD employment outlook* (pp. 127–185). Paris: OECD Publishing.

OECD. (2008). *Education at a glance 2008*. Paris: OECD Publishing.

OECD. (2009). Employment outlook: How do industry, firm and worker characteristics shape job and worker flows? In *OECD employment outlook* (pp. 117–163). Paris: OECD.

Oesch, D. (2013). *Occupational change in Europe. How technology and education transform the job structure*. Oxford: Oxford University Press.

Oesch, D., & Lipps, O. (2013). Does unemployment hurt less if there is more of it around? A panel analysis of life satisfaction in Germany and Switzerland. *European Sociological Review, 29*(5), 955–967.

Oesch, D., & Rodriguez Menes, J. (2011). Upgrading or polarization? Occupational change in Britain, Germany, Spain and Switzerland, 1990–2008. *Socio-Economic Review, 9*(3), 503–531.

Oesch, D., & von Ow, A. (2015). *Do informal contacts increase labor market inequality? Social ties, job access and wages for the unemployed* (LIVES working paper No 38).

Park, D. C. (1994). Aging, cognition, and work. *Human Performance, 7*(3), 181–205.

Parrado, E., Caner, A., & Wolff, E. N. (2007). Occupational and industrial mobility in the United States. *Labour Economics, 14*(3), 435–455.

Payne, J., & Payne, C. (1993). Unemployment and peripheral work. *Work, Employment & Society, 7*(4), 513–534.

Pinquart, M., & Sörensen, S. (2000). Influences of socioeconomic status, social network, and competence on subjective well-being in later life: A meta-analysis. *Psychology and Aging, 15*(2), 187–224.

Pissarides, C. A. (1992). Loss of skill during unemployment and the persistence of employment shocks. *The Quarterly Journal of Economics, 107*(4), 1371–1391.

Podgursky, M., & Swaim, P. (1987). Job displacement and earnings loss: Evidence from the displaced worker survey. *Industrial and Labor Relations Review, 41*(1), 17–29.

Pransky, G. S., Benjamin, K. L., Savageau, J. A., Currivan, D., & Fletcher, K. (2005). Outcomes in work-related injuries: A comparison of older and younger workers. *American Journal of Industrial Medicine, 47*, 104–112.

Pries, M. J. (2004). Persistence of employment fluctuations: A model of recurring job loss. *Review of Economic Studies, 71*(1), 193–215.

Rege, M., Telle, K., & Votruba, M. (2007). *Plant closure and marital dissolution* (Statistics Norway, Research Department, Discussion Papers No. 514). Kongsvinger: Statistics Norway.

Rider, C. I., & Roberts, P. W. (2011). *Organisational failure, educational prestige, and the diminution of cumulative career advantage* (Working paper).

Rose, M. (2003). Good deal, bad deal? Job satisfaction in occupations. *Work, Employment and Society, 17*(3), 503–530.

Ruhm, C. J. (1991). Are workers permanently scarred by job displacements? *The American Economic Association, 81*(1), 319–324.

# References

Sauer, S. J., Thomas-Hunt, M. C., & Morris, P. A. (2010). Too good to be true? The unintended signaling effects of educational prestige on external expectations of team performance. *Organization Science, 21*(5), 1108–1120.

Sheldon, G. M. (2007). *Migration, Integration und Wachstum: Die Performance und wirtschaftliche Auswirkung der Ausländer in der Schweiz.* Bericht im Auftrag der Eidgenössischen Ausländerkommission.

Silverstein, M. (2008). Meeting the challenges of an aging workforce. *American Journal of Industrial Medicine, 51,* 269–280.

Spence, M. (1973). Job market signaling. *The Quarterly Journal of Economics, 87*(3), 355–374.

Spitz-Oener, A. (2006). Technical change, job tasks, and rising educational demands: Looking outside the wage structure. *Journal of Labor Economics, 24*(2), 235–270.

Stevens, A. H. (1997). Persistent effects of job displacement: The importance of multiple job losses. *Journal of Labor Economics, 15*(1), 165–188.

Strandh, M. (2000). Different exit routes from unemployment and their impact on mental well-being: The role of the economic situation and the predictability of the life course. *Work, Employment & Society, 14*(3), 459–479.

Stutzer, A., & Frey, B. S. (2008). Stress that doesn't pay: The commuting paradox. *Scandinavian Journal of Economics, 110*(2), 339–366.

Sverke, M., Hellgren, J., & Näswall, K. (2002). No security: A meta-analysis and review of job insecurity and its consequences. *Journal of Occupational Health Psychology, 7*(3), 242–264.

Sweet, S., & Moen, P. (2011). Dual earners preparing for job loss: Agency, linked lives, and resilience. *Work and Occupations, 39*(1), 35–70.

Veenhoven, R., Ehrhardt, J., Ho, M., & de Vries, A. (1993). *Happiness in nations: Subjective appreciation of life in 56 nations 1946–1992.* Rotterdam: Erasmus University Rotterdam.

Velling, J., & Bender, S. (1994). Berufliche Mobilität zur Anpassung struktureller Diskrepanzen am Arbeitsmarkt. *Mitteilung aus der Arbeitsmarkt- und Berufsforschung, 3,* 212–231.

Weder, R., & Wyss, S. (2010). *Arbeitslosigkeit unter niedrig Qualifizierten: Die Rolle der Globalisierung* (SECO Publikation Arbeitsmarktpolitik No. 29). Bern: SECO.

West, M., Nicholson, N., & Rees, A. (1990). The outcomes of downward managerial mobility. *Journal of Organizational Behavior, 11*(2), 119–134.

Winefield, A. H. (2002). Unemployment, underemployment, occupational stress and psychological well-eing. *Australian Journal of Management, 27*(Special Issue), 137–148.

Winkelmann, R., & Winkelmann, L. (1998). Why are the unemployed so unhappy? Evidence from panel data. *Economica, 65*(257), 1–15.

Wrenn, K. A., & Maurer, T. J. (2004). Beliefs about older workers' learning and development behavior in relation to beliefs about malleability of skills, age-related decline, and control. *Journal of Applied Social Psychology, 34*(2), 223–242.

Wyss, S. (2009). *Stellenverlust und Lohneinbusse durch die Globalisierung ?* University of Basel, Wirtschaftswissenschaftliches Zentrum der Universität Basel Working Paper No. 05/09

Wyss, S. (2010). *Erhöht die Importkonkurrenz das Arbeitslosigkeitsrisiko der Niedrigqualifizierten?* University of Basel, Wirtschaftswissenschaftliches Zentrum der Universität Basel Working Paper No. 01/10

Young, C. (2012a). Losing a job: The nonpecuniary cost of unemployment in the United States. *Social Forces, 91*(2), 609–633.

Young, C. (2012b). *Unemployment insurance and job search activity: Evidence from random audits.* Stanford University, Unpublished Working Paper.

# Chapter 2
# A Tailor-Made Plant Closure Survey

In Switzerland there is no data publicly available for workers who lost their job because their plant shut down. For this reason, we ran our own survey. This chapter presents this survey including its design and the procedure we chose to collect data. The chapter is organized as follows: we first discuss whether using plant closure data may alleviate the problem that unemployment is a selective phenomenon and that particular groups of workers are more prone to lose their job than others. Next, we present out sampling strategy and discuss how potential survey bias may threaten the validity of our data. We address our data collection procedure and explain how we linked survey data to register data. We go on to analyze potential bias in the data that we collected and describe the construction of a control group. We then present the institutional and labor market context of our study. Finally, we discuss the main limits of our study.

## 2.1 Plant Closure Data as a Way to Avoid Selection Bias

Job loss is a typical non-random phenomenon: workers with particular characteristics such as lower levels of education have a higher probability of losing their job (Balestra and Backes-Gellner 2016: 17). A non-random selection into unemployment would be less a cause for concern if we could control for all of the workers' characteristics that are relevant for reemployment. But important characteristics such as motivation, work performance or social skills are usually not observed by researchers and thus cannot be controlled for. If workers with unobserved characteristics that hinder reemployment are overrepresented in the group of the displaced workers, the negative effect of job loss on average workers will be overestimated. In such a case the results would be affected by selection bias.

It has been argued that a strategy to address this bias is the use of plant closure data (Brand 2006). If the workers of a company are displaced because of economic failure, the reason for job loss cannot be attributed to the workers themselves; it may thus be exogenous to them. In other words, if the whole workforce of a company is displaced, it may be reasonable to assume that the employer did not dismiss workers based on their performance, motivation or other individual characteristics (Gibbons and Katz 1991: 352). Accordingly, observable and unobservable characteristics are likely to be similarly distributed among workers displaced by plant closure and among workers not displaced – as would be the case in an experiment with random attribution to treatment.

However, more recent research argues that even with plant closure data there may still be a selection bias at work. In fact, workers may self-select into firms with a higher propensity to close down. Belonging to the workforce of a non-profitable plant does not seem to be completely random as a comparison of wages between displaced and non-displaced workers suggests (Hijzen et al. 2010: 254–5). Confronted with a choice, highly qualified workers are likely to avoid employment in a plant with economic difficulties.

Moreover, there may be selection out of the sample. Well-informed and entrepreneurial workers will try to quit the company before the actual shutdown (Eliason and Storrie 2009b: 1397). It has been suggested that those workers with the best labor market prospects have the highest probability of "leaving the sinking ship" early. A study based on Austrian administrative data provides evidence for this assumption: workers with higher incomes had a higher probability of leaving the company up to a year before it closed down (Schwerdt 2011: 99). Moreover, those who left the company one to two quarters before the closure had significantly better labor market outcomes than workers from non-closing plants *ceteris paribus* (Schwerdt 2011: 100).

For our study, we sampled those workers who were employed in one of the five plants at the moment of the announcement of the plant closure. The announcement took place between 3 and 9 months before the actual displacement – except in Plant 2 (Biel), where there was no advance notice. In the light of the finding by Schwerdt (2011) that workers might "leave the sinking ship" up to one year before the plant closed down, we may be confronted with selection out of the sample.

## 2.2 Sampling

To constitute a sample of workers displaced by plant closure, we would ideally draw a random sample of all workers who experienced this situation within a specific period and geographical space. However, in Switzerland there is no systematic account of workers affected by plant closure. Although the Swiss Labour Force Survey records involuntary job loss, no distinction is made between displacement because of plant closure and dismissal for just cause. For this reason we conducted our own survey.[1]

---

[1] The project team consisted of five people. The principal investigator, Daniel Oesch, launched the project, was responsible for the acquisition of funding, supervised the project at all stages, con-

Our survey was conducted among the workforces of five recently closed plants. We defined three criteria for the selection of the companies and then proceeded with convenience sampling, i.e. chose the plants that agreed to participate in our survey. The selection criteria were the following: (1) The plants had to have closed down about 1–2 years before the survey was conducted. This strategy aimed at capturing long-term unemployment and the exhaustion of unemployment insurance benefits.[2] Using this strategy implies that our data is right-censored, i.e. that some of the workers have not experienced exit from unemployment at the moment when we conducted the survey. (2) We targeted medium-sized and large plants with more than 100 employees. The rationale behind this choice was to avoid reverse causality: in the case of small firms, closure may be caused by the workers' performance, which would blur our analysis of the cause effect of plant closure on workers' ensuing lives. (3) We focused on the manufacturing sector. In this sector plant closures are particularly frequent, which points to its outstanding social relevance (Cha and Morgan 2010: 1141).

Based on these three criteria we made an inventory of closed plants through a screening of the national and regional online press and a short survey among the cantonal employment offices. We identified ten plants, contacted them by mail and telephone, and succeeded in persuading five plants to participate in the survey. For two plants, access to the workers' addresses was given by the plant's management. In two other plants, the access was provided by the cantonal employment offices that accompanied the closing process and in one plant by the works council.

Plant 1 was part of a multinational corporation with headquarters in Switzerland and was active in the sector of machine tool manufacturing. Between October 2009 and August 2010 it relocated its production site from an industrial area outside Geneva to another part of Switzerland and abroad and subsequently displaced 169 workers. Fifteen production workers remained in the factory to provide the plant's machine repair service. A small number of workers helped to assemble the machines in the new production site in Switzerland but without being continuously employed there and five workers went abroad to work at the new production site. In addition, employees in the research and development department and the administration continued to operate on the site. The closure of the production department was announced about 4 months in advance.

---

ducted data analysis and published results. The author of this study, Isabel Baumann, was involved in all stages of the project, prepared and managed the survey, collected the data, conducted data analysis, and published results. The student assistants, Jessica Garcia and Lorenza Visetti, were responsible for the data entry and coding process and Jessica Garcia conducted telephone interviews with a particular group of survey participants. Katrina Riva was responsible for authoring a data documentation codebook that describes the content and structure of the dataset used for this study – which will be made publicly available on the platform DARIS. Certain tasks were outsourced such as the printing and the sending of the questionnaire. In addition, numerous colleagues helped us with some of the tasks.

[2] In Switzerland, workers are normally entitled to unemployment benefits of 18 months (that is, after having worked for at least 18 months (AVIG 2012, Art. 27, Ziff. 2).

Representatives of the employees or trade unions and the employer negotiated a redundancy plan. The plan included the set-up of an outplacement center with particular structures to promote the reemployment of workers with disabilities. Workers had the right to leave the plant immediately if they found a new job. They received a termination payment of at least CHF 10,000 and additional benefits depending on their tenure and age. Workers who had to move house or commute at least 40 km longer distances were entitled to an additional payment of CHF 3500. An early retirement plan allowed female workers to retire at 61 and male workers at 62, 3 years before the regular retirement age, on condition that they signed up for unemployment benefits.[3] Swiss residents were guaranteed a replacement rate of 70 % of their former wage. For French residents – who were numerous in this plant – the early retirement plan covered up to 60 % of their former wage. In addition, the plant continued to pay the contributions to the company's old-age pension fund until the regular retirement age in order to avoid a reduction in pension benefits.

Plant 2 was a Swiss company located in the agglomeration of the city of Biel and active in the printing sector. At the end of November 2009 the company announced that it was unable to pay the salaries. The cantonal employment office then informed the workforce that the plant would be closed down completely because of insolvency. The 262 employees – who had accepted wage cuts 1 year earlier in order to prevent a closure of the plant – became unemployed almost overnight. Not only was there no redundancy plan, but the workers lost money since the plant was incapable of reimbursing overtime and the workers' shares of the retirement fund.

Plant 3 was part of a multinational corporation with headquarters outside Switzerland. Located outside a small town in North-Western Switzerland, it produced various kinds of chemicals. Due to shift-work and weekend-work supplements, the pre-displacement wages paid by Plant 3 were high compared with other firms in the region. The closure was announced about 4 months in advance. In January 2009 its 430 workers were displaced. About 15 workers, who were responsible for tidying up and cleaning the plant, continued to be employed for another 2 years. The sector to which Plant 3 belonged had been experiencing turbulences for many years and high turnover was observed at the intermediate management level of Plant 3 during the years before the closure.

The plant offered a redundancy plan containing termination pay. For a 25-year old worker with 5 years of tenure the termination pay was CHF 8250 and for a 45-year old worker with 20 years of tenure CHF 22,000. While workers had the opportunity to leave the plant before the official end of their contract, those who remained until the end received a premium of CHF 70 for each day worked. The company mandated an outplacement center to provide workers with support for their job search and allowed workers to use its services during their working time. If workers had to move house for their new job and had to commute at least 30 km more than before, they received financial support up to CHF 4000. Older workers at

---

[3] The Swiss unemployment insurance entitles workers who become unemployed at the age of 62 to receive unemployment benefits up to their regular retirement age.

2 years from the official retirement age had the option of early retirement. They received pension benefits that corresponded to at least 70 % of their former wage or at least CHF 55,000 per year.

Plant 4 was a Swiss company producing printing machines in the Canton of Bern. When it closed down, 324 workers lost their job in three phases between October 2009 and August 2010. The displacement was announced 5–9 months in advance. Nearly a hundred of the workers affected were relocated to another plant together with the machines on which they were specialized. About 50 displaced workers were employed in a firm that started operating on the production site of Plant 4. However, this firm also closed down about 2 years later.

The plant agreed to a redundancy plan after negotiating with the trade union. For workers who earned less in their new job the company paid the difference for 6–24 months, a measure aimed at encouraging workers to accept lower paid jobs more readily. This measure was, however, little used. In contrast, almost all workers who were eligible for the early retirement benefits included in the redundancy plan accepted the offer. Workers were enabled to take to early retirement from the age of 56.5 years. Workers aged up to 57 were paid their full salary up to age 58 and then received a flat rate of CHF 4000 per month until they retired regularly. Workers aged between 58 and 59 also received a flat rate of CHF 4000 per month until their regular retirement. Workers who were 60–63 at the moment of displacement were paid 90 % of their former salary and those over 63 were paid 100 % of their salary up to the regular retirement age.

Plant 5 produced metal and plastic components and employed about 205 workers in an industrial zone in North-Western Switzerland. It had been sold to a multinational corporation with headquarters in Switzerland about 2 years before this corporation closed the plant. The displacement took place between September 2009 and March 2010 and was announced about 6 months in advance. There was some limited turnover before the closure was officially announced.

The plant offered a redundancy plan including termination pay depending on workers' tenure and age. A 25-year old worker with 5 years of tenure received CHF 11,000 and a 45-year old with 20 years of tenure CHF 33,000. The plan also included the setting-up of an external outplacement center which employees were permitted to use within official working hours. The workers were given priority in the event of vacancies in other plants of the company, but this option was rarely taken up. Workers who found a new job could negotiate to leave the plant before the official displacement date. If workers had to move house or commute longer distances to their new job they received financial support. Finally, the redundancy plan offered the option of early retirement for workers from age 58. Early retirement benefits were calculated based on workers' tenure and were disbursed in the form of payments to the company's old-age pension fund.

None of the five plants offered a training program funded by the companies. However, the workers who enrolled in the public employment offices were entitled, like any unemployed job seeker in Switzerland, to participate in active labor market measures such as training and internships.

**Table 2.1** Information on the five manufacturing plants included in the survey

| Plant | Sector | Workers displaced | Refused address transmission | Inactive address | Active addresses | Official dis-placement dates |
|---|---|---|---|---|---|---|
| Plant 1 (Geneva) | Metal products | 169 | 0 (0%) | 20 (11%) | 149 | 01.10 |
| Plant 2 (Biel) | Printing | 262 | 3 (1%) | 30 (11%) | 229 | 12.09 |
| Plant 3 (NWS 1) | Chemicals | 430 | 6 (1%) | 67 (16%) | 357 | 01.09 |
| Plant 4 (Bern) | Machinery | 324 | 19 (6%) | 17 (5%) | 288 | 10.09–08.10 |
| Plant 5 (NWS 2) | Metal & plastic | 205 | 8 (4%) | 17 (8%) | 180 | 09.09–03.10 |
| Total | | 1390 | 36 (3%) | 151 (11%) | 1203 | |

In order to access the workers' postal addresses we had to receive their consent. By means of a letter we informed the workers about our study and asked if they refused to participate. 4% of the total population (n=53) refused to give access to their address.[4] In addition, about 10% of the addresses (n=133) turned out to be invalid because the workers had moved or – in a few cases – were deceased. From an original population of 1389 workers, this left us with a survey population of 1203 individuals, as presented in Table 2.1.[5]

## 2.3 Survey Bias

Biases typically associated with data collection are nonresponse bias and measurement error. Nonresponse bias occurs when survey participants differ from nonparticipants in a way that is relevant for the phenomenon under study (Dillman et al. 2009: 17). If the group of nonrespondents were to be composed completely at random, this would reduce the statistical power of the results but not induce systematic bias. Unfortunately, nonresponse is often non-random: individuals not participating in a survey are likely to be less interested in the topic, to have less time to participate

---

[4]The main reasons for refusal were (i) that workers did not feel concerned by our study, for instance because they were hired on a temporary basis, (ii) that they did not speak the language, or (iii) that they were frustrated with their situation. Note that refusals were very low where the process was managed by the works council (0%), but significantly higher where workers were contacted by the plant's former management (4% and 6% refusals respectively).

[5]For these workers we signed an agreement with the data providers – firm managements, cantonal employment offices and workers' council – guaranteeing the workers' data protection.

2.3 Survey Bias 41

or to have lower literacy in the language of the questionnaire (Groves and Couper 1998; Stoop 2005). For Switzerland, earlier findings show that immigrant groups from non-EU countries are usually underrepresented in surveys (Laganà et al. 2011; Lipps et al. 2013).

It is thus important to understand the mechanism behind nonresponse and, if possible, to correct for it. Dillman et al. (2009: 16) introduced the tailored survey design method, an approach that strategically uses survey design to reduce potential bias. A first possibility to address nonresponse bias is to repeatedly contact the population that is surveyed. This measure alone, however, may not be sufficient to reach individuals belonging to subgroups with traditionally low participation rates such as particular immigrant groups. A possible strategy to win the participation of these groups is to alter the survey protocol, for instance by using a shorter questionnaire (Peytchev et al. 2009: 786).

A second technique is the use of a mixed-mode approach (Dillman et al. 2009). Taken on their own, different survey modes each have their advantages and disadvantages. For instance, an Internet survey may be particularly suited for reaching younger cohorts while its coverage is limited, notably among older cohorts (Schräpler 2001: 13; Täube and Joye 2002: 77; Kempf and Remington 2007). Used in combination, these different modes may be a powerful method to increase the respondents' representativeness. A third strategy is the use of financial incentives that encourage respondents to reciprocate by completing the survey. By motivating particularly those respondents with a tendency not to answer survey questionnaires, incentives have proved to reduce nonresponse bias (Dillman et al. 2009: 249). Research in survey methodology indicates that unconditional incentives are more effective than incentives contingent on completing a survey (Harrison 2010: 519; Lipps 2010: 84). In addition, cash and vouchers appear to be more effective than noncash incentives (Harrison 2010).

Once the fieldwork is completed and the researchers have doubts about the representativeness of their sample, an ex-post method to deal with nonresponse bias is to build nonresponse adjustment weights. In order to use this procedure, it is imperative to know at least one characteristic of all individuals (respondents and nonrespondents) in the sample (Corbetta 2003: 227). The more characteristics there are available, the more sophisticated the weighting becomes.[6] Finally, if other data sources are available, they may provide helpful information about the nonrespondents. Particularly helpful seems to be administrative data since it tends to be comparatively reliable (Corbetta 2003: 196). It is thus valuable for the study's quality to have at least some measures for the nonrespondents.

Another problem that impairs data quality and that typically occurs in data collection is measurement error (Antonakis et al. 2010: 1095). Measurement errors may have random or systematic causes (Phillips 1981: 400). They are random if

---

[6] After the identification of the under- and overrepresented groups based on the known characteristics a weighting coefficient is calculated for each respondent (Little and Vartivarian 2005). This weighting coefficient is attributed to every individual while statistical operations are carried out.

they have no systematic pattern and if the data measured sometimes over- and sometimes underestimates the true value of a variable.

Social desirability may systematically bias respondents' answers (Bound et al. 2001: 3746, 3784). In this context, it has been shown that working hours are regularly overstated. This finding has been explained by the positive connotation of hard work. Similarly, retrospective questions are systematically error-prone. A study assessing the validity of retrospective data by comparing it with longitudinal data finds large differences. Subjective psychological states are remembered with particular inaccuracy, while other measures such as reading skills, height or weight are reported more correctly (Henry et al. 1994: 100). This is likely to be a result of most respondents' imperfect memory, the fact that they can only report what they were aware of at the time (Hardt and Rutter 2004: 260–1). However, while it is uncontested that longitudinal studies are the best way to examine changes over time, cross-sectional assessments of past events may be the second-best option (Hardt and Rutter 2004: 261).

A technique to evaluate and reduce potential measurement error is to use multiple indicators for the variables measured (Bound et al. 2001: 3740). Particularly appropriate for the validation of survey data is information stemming from registers, for instance from the public administration or from employers (Corbetta 2003: 196). Even this data may, however, not be completely free from error.

## 2.4 Data Collection

The strategies that we used to handle survey bias are the combination of our own survey with administrative data. The main features of our survey design were multiple contact attempts, mixed modes, incentives and weighting. Our data collection instrument was a questionnaire with about 60, mainly closed-ended questions. Many of the questions were adopted from established surveys such as the Swiss Household Panel or the Swiss Labour Force Survey.

The questionnaire was structured into seven parts: the first part contained questions on the workers' job in the plant from which they were displaced. The second part was about the job search and the third about the workers' new job if they had found one. The fourth part asked questions on workers' well-being and social life and the fifth part questions on their household. In a sixth part workers were asked to indicate their socio-demographic information. In the last part we asked for their consent to access register data, further contacts and whether they wished to be informed about the results of the study. Since the target group consists of individuals living in both the German- and French-speaking regions of Switzerland, the questionnaire was drawn up in two languages. It was first cross-examined by survey experts. Then four workers of the survey population completed a test questionnaire. Their feedback on the intelligibility and other features of the questionnaire was incorporated in the questionnaire.

2.4 Data Collection

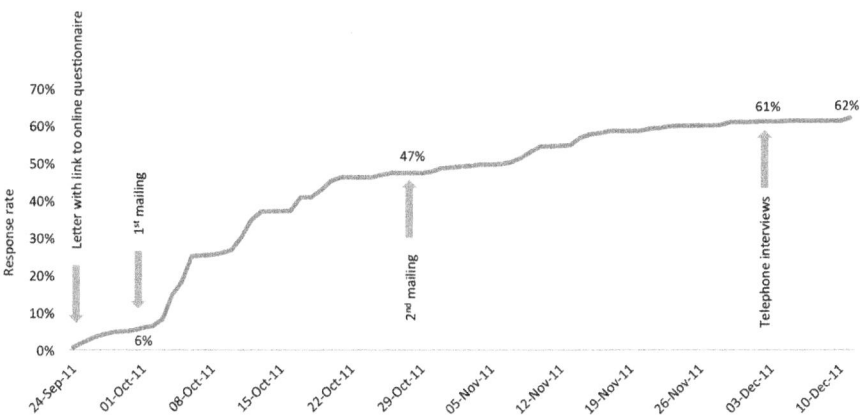

**Fig. 2.1** Timeline of the survey with response rate and contact attempts

The survey was started at the end of September 2011 and completed in December 2011 (see Fig. 2.1). We first sent out a pre-notice letter that presented the purpose of our study and announced the imminent questionnaire. A Web link given in the letter provided workers with access to the online version of the questionnaire and allowed them to start participating in the survey immediately. A recommendation letter issued by the Swiss State Secretariat of Economic Affairs (SECO) accompanied the pre-notice letter.[7] The purpose of this letter was to enhance the survey's legitimacy by showing governmental support. One week later, the workers received the paper-and-pencil version of the questionnaire. This mailing was accompanied by an unconditional financial incentive in the form of a voucher for 10 Swiss Francs (about 8 €) for Migros, Switzerland's biggest retail company. About 1 month later, at the beginning of November, those workers who had not yet participated received the paper-and-pencil questionnaire a second time. The control of response was possible since our survey was not anonymous. An individual identification number affixed on every questionnaire allowed us to track responses back to the participants.

This strategy also allowed us to evaluate the respondents' representativeness while the survey was still running. Since previous research from Switzerland found an underrepresentation of particular immigrant groups, we analyzed nonresponse bias according to national origin. Information about the nationality of the whole survey population was not available in our data. We therefore created a proxy for national origin on the basis of workers' surnames. Thereby, we distinguished between four groups: (1) Switzerland, France and Germany, (2) Spain and Portugal, (3) Italy, and (4) other countries, notably ex-Yugoslavia and Turkey. When taking this proxy – an admittedly rough indicator for immigration background – and looking at the response rate of these four groups, we observed differences in nonresponse rates as predicted by previous research: Group 1 had a response rate of 66 %, Group 2 56 %, Group 3 55 % and Group 4 40 %. Accordingly, in order to increase

---

[7] This institution also partially funded our study.

the response rate of Group 4 we drew a sample of this group and succeeded in completing the survey questionnaire with 15 individuals from non-EU member countries by telephone. This measure led to a final response rate of 52% for Group 4, similar to those of the other proxy immigrant groups.

Of all the respondents 76% used the paper-and-pencil questionnaire, 21% responded online and 3% by telephone.[8] It is not surprising that paper-and-pencil was the most frequently used mode since we had workers' postal addresses at our disposal, but not their email addresses. The repeated contact attempts seem to have been worthwhile. The access to the online questionnaire at the start of the survey resulted in a response rate of 6%. After the first mailing of the paper-and-pencil questionnaire the response rate rose to 47%. The second mailing led to an increase in responses of another 14 percentage points and the telephone interviews contributed one more percent. Figure 2.1 shows the timeline of our survey. Whether the use of incentives helped improve the response rate cannot be tested since a control group without incentives would have been needed.

The overall response rate of the survey was 62%, which is equal to 748 workers. Almost two out of three displaced workers thus responded to our questionnaire, a relatively high response rate as compared to an earlier plant closure study for Switzerland which had response rates between 20 and 31% depending on the company (see Weder and Wyss 2010: 9–13). Workers' motivation to participate in this study may be due to a number of factors such as multiple contacts, mixed modes of surveying, financial incentives and an official recommendation letter from the State Secretariat for Economic Affairs. In addition, workers possibly felt strongly concerned by the topic of the survey and were interested in the goals of the study (Sweet and Moen 2011: 9). Comments that we received with the questionnaires let us assume that the workers were relieved to be able to inform us about their experiences after plant closure. After completing the survey, we adjusted for nonresponse by weighting the data provided by the respondents. We used a technique that is based on a "missing at random" assumption (see Baumann et al. 2016).[9]

Very important for our study was the fact that we were able to link the survey data to register data from the public unemployment insurance. The unemployment

---

[8] In addition to the non-EU immigrants, we conducted seven telephone interviews with workers who called because they did not want to participate in the survey. We were able to persuade them to give us some basic information about themselves. We therefore conducted a total of 22 telephone interviews.

[9] In this case, subgroups based on variables available for respondents and nonrespondents are created, assuming that non-participation happened at random within these subgroups. Accordingly, we created subgroups based on information that we received from the address providers for all displaced workers. Since the same information is not available for all plants in our sample, different variables are taken into account for each plant when constructing the individual-level weights. This type of nonresponse adjustment is most effective when the available variables used to construct the subgroups (e.g. sex, age, nationality, occupation) are correlated to the variable of interest in the study (e.g. reemployment prospects). The literature on job displacement suggests that this is the case: sex, occupation, age and nationality seem to affect reemployment chances (e.g. Farber 1997; Chan and Stevens 2001; Kletzer 2001; Jolkkonen et al. 2012). Our method to construct weights thus appears relevant.

## 2.4 Data Collection

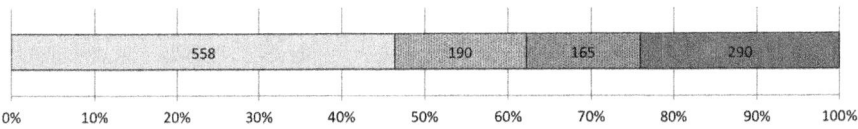

**Fig. 2.2** Proportions of available survey and register data. Note: The numbers in the figure indicate the size (n) of each group of workers. Total N = 1203

register data contains numerous variables on the workers' unemployment history. However, it is only available for a limited number of workers since access to this information depends on several preconditions. First, a worker must have registered with the unemployment insurance, secondly access was possible only if there was no explicit refusal by the workers[10] and thirdly the workers had to be identifiable in the unemployment insurance database on the basis of ambiguous indicators, that is to say name and address. Workers who did not apply for unemployment benefits because they found a job right away, went into retirement or preferred to avoid the stigma of living on benefits are not covered by this data source.

In total, we gained access to the unemployment register data of 355 workers. 190 of these 355 workers also participated in the survey; for these 190 workers, we have information from two sources on certain measures such as pre-displacement income. The other 165 (of the 355) did not participate in the survey; the data available on these nonparticipants increased the number of workers for whom we have relevant information to 913 workers or 76% of the total survey population (Fig. 2.2). For the post-displacement labor market status – one of our main outcome variables – we have information for 884 workers, which is equal to 74% of the total survey population.

Finally, our database also includes basic information such as birth date, occupation or nationality that we received from the workers' former employers. Plant register data is available for all displaced workers (N = 1203), but the amount and type of information vary across plants: while we received important information such as occupation or age from some plants, we obtained information only on the displacement date from others.

In Table 2.2 we present the descriptive statistics of our study. We distinguish between plant, survey and register data. In addition, we created variables that contain the maximum available information by combining the three data sources.[11] The combined dataset reveals that about 16% of the workers in our sample are female and 84% male. 8% worked before the displacement as managers, 5% as

---

[10] In order to receive the workers' agreement we included a question in our survey that was formulated in such a way that the respondents had to inform us if they did not wish us to access their data. 144 respondents – about 20% of the respondents – refused access.

[11] We prioritize register data before survey data and survey data before plant data whenever more than one data source was available. For the construction of the wage variable, we prioritized survey data for workers with monthly wages over CHF 10,500 because for administrative reasons wages above this amount are not assessed.

**Table 2.2** Descriptive statistics for different types of data (in %)

|  |  | Plant data | Survey data | Register data | Combined data |
|---|---|---|---|---|---|
| Sex | Female | 17.1 | 17.2 | 18.0 | 15.7 |
|  | Male | 82.9 | 82.8 | 82.0 | 84.3 |
| ISCO 1-digit occupation (before displacement) | Managers | 10.9 | 4.9 | 2.8 | 8.1 |
|  | Professionals | 5.5 | 9.9 | 6.7 | 5.2 |
|  | Technicians | 21.7 | 17.9 | 13.7 | 19.4 |
|  | Clerks | 5.0 | 11.5 | 10.9 | 8.3 |
|  | Craft workers | 25.0 | 25.6 | 27.1 | 25.9 |
|  | Machine operators | 29.9 | 24.3 | 32.4 | 29.6 |
|  | Elementary occupations | 2.0 | 6.0 | 6.4 | 3.5 |
| Age (at displacement) | <25 | 14 | 7.1 | 5.1 | 8.2 |
|  | 25–29 | 6.3 | 3.5 | 6.8 | 5.4 |
|  | 30–34 | 6.8 | 6.3 | 8.5 | 6.7 |
|  | 35–39 | 9.2 | 7.7 | 7.9 | 8.2 |
|  | 40–44 | 13.4 | 11.7 | 11.6 | 11.9 |
|  | 45–49 | 14.3 | 17.3 | 18.6 | 16.5 |
|  | 50–54 | 13.4 | 14.7 | 17.5 | 15.0 |
|  | 55–59 | 10.2 | 14.8 | 11.8 | 11.9 |
|  | >59 | 12.3 | 17.0 | 12.1 | 16.3 |
| Education | Does not know/refusal | – | 4.0 | 5.1 | 4.5 |
|  | Mandatory education or less | – | 9.5 | 18.3 | 13.3 |
|  | Pre-apprenticeship | – | 3.6 | 3.7 | 3.4 |
|  | Upper secondary education | – | 53.4 | 59.2 | 54.1 |
|  | Higher vocational education | – | 17.3 | 7.1 | 14.7 |
|  | University of applied sciences or university | – | 12.2 | 6.6 | 10.1 |
| Nationality | Switzerland | 76.4 | 74.4 | 69.4 | 71.6 |
|  | Germany | 6.5 | 3.9 | 3.4 | 4.2[a] |
|  | France | 0.6 | 7.6 | 0.1 | 5.3 |
|  | Italy | 5.4 | 4.6 | 5.3 | 8.0 |
|  | Portugal | 1.0 | 1.3 | 1.1 |  |
|  | Spain | 2.2 | 1.3 | 3.1 |  |
|  | Other EU countries | 1.0 | – | 0.6 |  |
|  | Kosovo and Albania | 1.3 | 0.6 | 1.0 | 10.9[b] |
|  | Ex-Yugoslavia | 3.7 | 3.1 | 9.55 |  |
|  | Turkey | 1.4 | 2.6 | 4.5 |  |
|  | Asia | 0.6 | – | 1.7 |  |
|  | N max | 1203 | 748 | 355 | 1203 |

[a]Germany and Austria
[b]Non-EU countries. Although Croatia has been a member of the European Union since 2013, it is included in this category

professionals, 19 % as technicians or associate professionals, 8 % as clerks or sales workers, 26 % as craft workers, 29 % as machine operators or assemblers and 4 % in elementary occupations. Regarding the age structure, 14 % were aged under 30, 43 % were between 30 and 50, and 43 % over 50. With respect to education, 17 % have less than upper secondary education, 69 % have upper secondary education, 10 % have a tertiary degree and about 4 % refused to answer. Finally, the large majority of the workers are Swiss citizens (72 %), 4 % are German and 5 % French citizens, 8 % come from other European Union countries and 11 % from non-EU countries. Overall, the median worker in our sample is a prime-aged male production worker.[12]

In addition to the survey and register data we collected some qualitative data. We interviewed the head of the human resource department of Plants 3 (NWS 1), 4 (Bern) and 5 (NWS 2), the chairperson of the works council of Plant 1 (Geneva) and the trade unionist who represented workers' interests in the insolvency process of Plant 2 (Biel). The conversations covered the closure procedure and the details of the redundancy plan (if one was negotiated). Over the period of our study, we had regular exchanges with some of the displaced workers about their experience when we tested the questionnaire and by telephone when they had questions about it. Moreover, in June 2013 we presented and discussed the results of the study to the survey participants in Bern and Geneva. These events not only provided a useful reality check of the results but also gave us another valuable opportunity to learn how workers lived through the displacement.

## 2.5 Identifying the Presence of Bias in Our Data

The crucial issue is whether our survey design and the use of register data helped us to avoid the main biases outlined above. Nonresponse bias is present when individual characteristics relevant for the outcome variables of our study – for example reemployment – also determine the likelihood of participating in the survey. A proper nonresponse analysis requires the availability of characteristics for all workers – participants and nonparticipants. Since our dataset only partially fulfills this requirement, we first analyze nonresponse with the available characteristics and then analyze the propensity to participate using variables that are available for all respondents plus the nonrespondents for whom we have register data.

Figure 2.3 presents a logistic regression analysis predicting the likelihood of participating in the survey. For this analysis we use only data that is available for both survey participants and nonparticipants. As independent variables we use nationality, sex, age and occupation. The variable "nationality" is a proxy that we constructed on the basis of the workers' surnames. The other variables were provided

---

[12] The dataset is publicly available from FORSbase service at FORS Center: https://forsbase.unil.ch/project/study-public-overview/13181/0/The dataset is called "Situation professionnelle deux ans après des licenciements collectifs dans le secteur industriel – 2011".

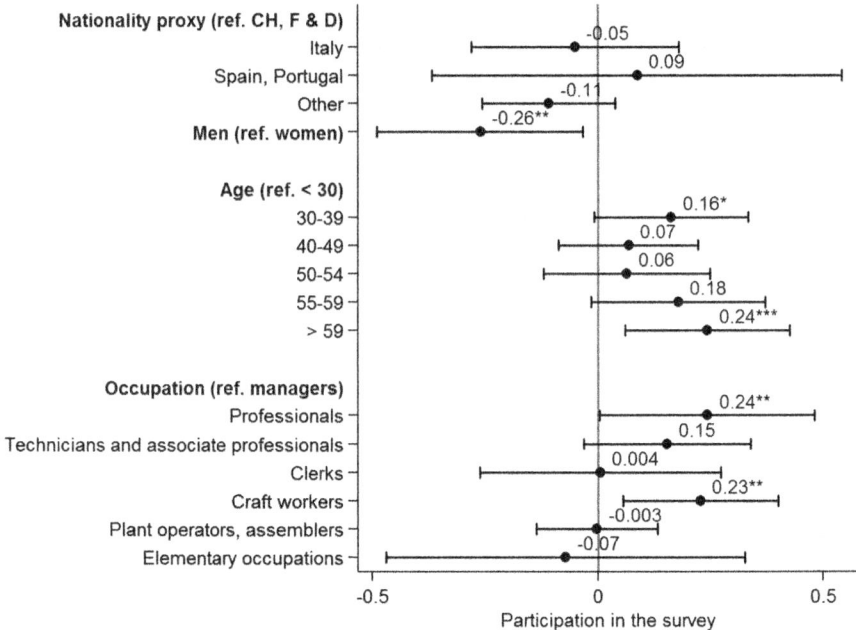

**Fig. 2.3** Average Marginal Effects (AME) for a binomial logistic regression for participation in the survey. N = 350. Note: Significance levels: * p < 0.1, ** p < 0.05, *** p < 0.01. This analysis is based on data from only one plant (Plant 3) because the same variables were not available for the other plants. Reading example: As compared to workers with Swiss, French or German nationality, workers with Italian nationality are 5 percentage points less, workers with Spanish and Portuguese nationality 9 percentage points more and workers with other nationality 11 percentage points less likely to participate in the survey

by the plants. However, not all plants provided us with complete information: Only Plant 3 (NWS 1) provided us with the variables sex, age and occupation. Since the nationality proxy is based on workers' names, this information is available for workers from all plants. Accordingly, we base Fig. 2.3 solely on data from Plant 3. Since logistic regression estimates cannot be interpreted as relative risks, we indicate the average marginal effects which specify the effect size (Mood 2010: 80).

Our analysis shows that there are no statistically significant differences in participation in the survey with respect to nationality. In contrast, we observe that men are 26 percentage points likely than women to answer the survey questionnaire – a finding that confirms earlier results on nonresponse in surveys in Switzerland (Joye and Bergman 2004: 79). We also find significant differences with respect to age, workers aged 30–39 or over 55 being 16–24 percentage points more likely to participate in the survey than workers in their twenties. With respect to occupation, the analysis shows that that professionals and craft workers are 23–24 percentage points more likely to participate in the survey than managers.

In order to evaluate the effect of our strategies to circumvent nonresponse bias – repeated contact attempts, mixed methods, weighting and using register data – we

2.5 Identifying the Presence of Bias in Our Data

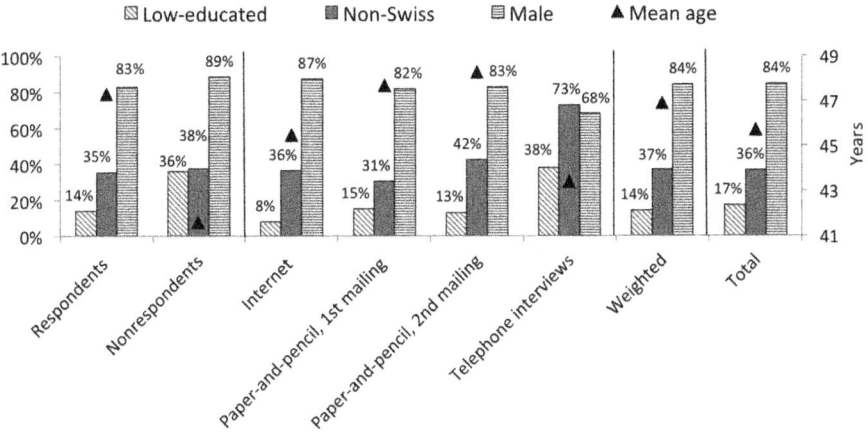

**Fig. 2.4 Respondents' characteristics by survey mode, weight and response.** Note: The low-educated include individuals with less than upper secondary education. N Respondents = 748, N Nonrespondents = 165, N Internet = 157, N Paper-and-pencil 1st mailing = 398, N Paper-and-pencil 2nd mailing = 165, N Telephone interviews = 22, N Weighted = 748, N Total = 1203. Z-tests reveal that respondents and nonrespondents are significantly different for the following characteristics: Male (p < 0.03), Non-Swiss (p < 0.02), Low-educated (p < 0.00). A t-test reveals that respondents and nonrespondents differ according to age (p < 0.00)

would ideally compute a similar model as presented in Fig. 2.3 for different worker subgroups. But since these worker subgroups are small, an analysis by means of a logistic regression is difficult. For this reason, we proceed with a descriptive analysis, comparing the socio-demographic characteristics of different worker subgroups. The analysis of the nonrespondents relies on the register data available for 165 nonrespondents.

Accordingly, Fig. 2.4 illustrates the characteristics – the proportion of low-educated, non-Swiss and male workers and the mean age – of the nonrespondents and subgroups of respondents according to different survey modes, weighted data and the total (respondents and nonrespondents combined). Among the respondents 14 % are low-educated, 35 % are non-Swiss and 83 % are male, and they have a mean age of 47.3 years. In contrast, among the nonrespondents there are more than twice as many low-educated workers (36 %), and slightly more workers have a foreign nationality (38 %) or are male (89 %). In addition, nonrespondents have a significantly lower mean age (41.6) than respondents. Thus, there seem to be substantial differences between respondents and nonrespondents, regarding their age and their level of education.

Did the use of a mixed-mode approach and multiple contact attempts reduce the differences between respondents and nonrespondents? Participants who responded on the Internet were somewhat younger (45.5), less likely to be low-educated (8 %), and more likely to be male (87 %) as compared to participants who answered the questionnaire on paper. The workers who responded after the first or the second mailing by means of the paper-and-pencil questionnaire are similar: they have a mean age of 47.7 and 48.3, 15 % and 13 % respectively are low-educated, and 82 % and 83 % respectively are male. They differ only regarding the proportion of workers with foreign nationality, 31 % and 42 % respectively being non-Swiss. In contrast, differences are noteworthy with respect to respondents who answered the questionnaire by telephone: this specifically targeted group is younger (43.4), more likely to be low-educated (38 %), much more likely to have a foreign nationality (73 %) and much less likely to be male (68 %).

If we examine the weighted survey data we find that it is very similar to the unweighted survey data (respondents): the mean age is 46.9, 14 % are low-educated, 37 % are non-Swiss and 84 % are male. Accordingly, the weighted sample strongly differs from the group of the nonrespondents, most of all in terms of age and education. This suggests that the nonrespondents' weights did not strongly adjust for nonresponse and thus failed in their purpose. The quality of the nonresponse weights depends on the available data (Groves and Peytcheva 2008). In our case, the sociodemographic variables most strongly affecting nonresponse such as age, education, nationality and sex were not available for all workers and therefore we could not appropriately correct for nonresponse. Finally, if we collapse the respondents and the nonrespondents into one group (total), the mean age is 45.7, 17 % are low-educated, 36 % have a foreign nationality and 84 % are male.

Our results suggest that the use of telephone interviews and the register data provided the highest contribution to the nonresponse adjustment. In contrast, the other two survey modes of Internet and paper-and-pencil, as well as the weighting did not contribute, even though the former two helped to substantially increase the response rate.

We now turn to the evaluation of the measurement error by comparing the survey data with the register data. We use the register data as "true" values since they rely on official documents and recordings. The difference between these two types of data and the survey data is thus considered as the measurement error. For all the analysis we only use those cases in our database for which both register and survey data are available. Following Bound et al. (1994), we report the mean pre-displacement wage[13] for both datasets and the difference between the survey and the register mean, which is defined as mean measurement error. However, since in the register data the workers' wage is top-censored at CHF 10,500 for policy reasons, we limit the analysis of the measurement error to wages up to this amount in both databases.

The mean wage of the survey data is CHF 6283 with a standard deviation of CHF 1580. For the register data we observe a mean wage of CHF 6268 with a standard deviation of CHF 1593. The box-and-whisker plot in Fig. 2.5 complements these results by indicating the distribution of the data. The horizontal line in the middle of the gray box represents the median (50 % percentile), the lower hinge of the box the 25th percentile and the higher hinge the 75th percentile. The two boxes are almost identical, suggesting that the distribution of the wages is highly similar. The single

---

[13] We use a wage measure that includes a 13th monthly salary for both survey and register data.

2.5 Identifying the Presence of Bias in Our Data

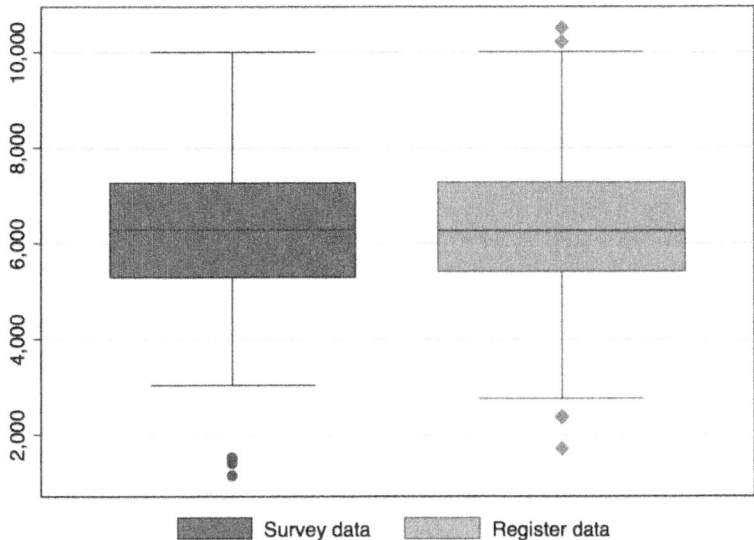

**Fig. 2.5** Box-and-whisker plot for pre-displacement wages according to survey and register data. N = 150

exceptions are some outliers which are represented by the dots located outside of the whiskers[14] in Fig. 2.5.

The mean of the measurement error – the difference between the survey data wage mean and the register data wage mean – is CHF 103 with a standard deviation of CHF 1054. Thus, on average the measurement error is less than 2 %, which indicates that our survey measured the pre-displacement wage accurately. The distribution of the measurement error is presented graphically in Fig. A.1 in the Annex. The illustration shows that most errors lie close to zero, but that we are confronted with a small number of large errors. This finding is expressed by the large standard deviation of the measurement error.

These findings lead us to the question whether the error in measurement substantially influences the outcomes of our study. In order to test this question we run two OLS-regressions where we measure the effect of age, sex, nationality and education on workers' pre-displacement wage, first based on survey data and then based on register data. Again, we only use those cases in our database for which we have both survey and register data at hand. The results are presented in Table A.1 in the Annex. We find statistically significant effects for exactly the same characteristics, in particular an advanced age, sex and tertiary education. Regarding the size of the effect we find differences that are mostly small except for some characteristics such as tertiary education, where they are of the order of about 15 % and thus noteworthy. Overall, Table A.1 suggests, however, that measurement error does not constitute a major problem of our survey.

---

[14] The whiskers represent the short horizontal lines above and below the colored box.

It is worthwhile to improve the quality of the data within the bounds of possibility. One approach is to drop outliers, another to replace survey data with register data whenever both data sources are available (what we call "combined data"). Both approaches involve some problems. Dropping outliers relies on having a precise definition of when a value is an outlier. It also reduces the sample size and thus the statistical power of the analysis. Likewise, by replacing survey data with register data, we assume that register data is more reliable than survey data, which may not always be true. In the case of our study, we have the additional problem that we have two data sources for a maximum of only 190 workers and thus cannot assess measurement error for all workers who responded to the survey.

## 2.6 Constructing a Non-experimental Control Group

Scholars studying job displacement have pointed out that the causal effects of job loss can only be fully understood if displaced workers are compared with non-displaced workers (see e.g. Jacobson et al. 1993). The analysis of wage losses requires information about the counterfactual earning path since the workers' earnings would probably have increased if they had not been displaced (Fallick 1996: 9). Likewise, the reemployment prospects of displaced workers must be compared with those of non-displaced workers among whom – about 2 years later – some may have lost their job or gone into early retirement. Inclusion of a control group in a job displacement study thus allows us not only to compare outcomes before and after displacement, but also to compare the outcomes of displaced workers with the hypothetical situation in which they had remained in their former job.

The study of causal effects ideally builds on data from randomized experiments.[15] Since randomized experiments often cannot be implemented in the social sciences, quasi-experimental techniques have been developed (Dehejia and Wahba 1999: 1053). One of these is difference-in-difference, an approach that aims at comparing the evolution of outcomes between two groups, one of which has undergone a particular treatment while the other has not (Angrist and Pischke 2010: 14). The idea behind this technique is that a potential difference in the outcomes can be attributed to the treatment – the so-called treatment effect (Caliendo and Kopeinig 2008: 32–4).[16]

---

[15] Random attribution to the treatment or the control group theoretically provides researchers with two identical groups regarding the individuals' observed and unobserved characteristics. This setting allows comparison between the outcome of the treated and the non-treated individuals. Thereby the outcome of the control group simulates the counterfactual – the outcomes that hypothetically would have been observed if the treated individuals had remained untreated. In the absence of the treatment it is assumed that the outcome would be the same for both groups.

[16] The parameter that is estimated is the average treatment effect on the treated (ATT). It is defined as the difference between expected outcome values with and without treatment for those who actually received a treatment. It is given by $\beta = E\,[Y(1)-Y(0) \mid Z=1]$, $Y(0)$ standing for the outcome without, $Y(1)$ for the outcome with treatment, and $Z$ for the treatment.

## 2.6 Constructing a Non-experimental Control Group

The post-hoc construction of a control group proceeds by pairing the individuals in the sample – the treated individuals – with untreated individuals who are similar on observable characteristics (Brand 2006: 277). This procedure is called matching and simulates a random attribution of individuals to either the treatment or the control group. Accordingly, this technique is based on the assumption that the control group is different from the treated group only with respect to the treatment.

Since exact matches on relevant characteristics such as age, education or occupation are hard to find, Rosenbaum and Rubin (1985: 34) introduced the propensity score matching method. The propensity score is a function that describes the individuals' propensity to experience the treatment event given their characteristics (Rosenbaum and Rubin 1983: 43). Propensity score matching is used in particular when the matching is based on multiple covariates and when the sample is small. Since the estimation of the propensity score relies on *observable* covariates, this technique involves the strong assumption that the attribution to the treatment was based on observables (Dehejia and Wahba 1999: 1053).[17]

For our study, we construct a control group of non-displaced workers. The control group provides us with counterfactual information and thus with more precise estimations of the change in wages and the employment rate which workers experience as a consequence of plant closure. We construct the control group on the basis of data from the Swiss Household Panel (SHP). This database contains information on almost 10,000 individuals from about 4000 households and offers a large range of variables relevant for the study of the labor market. We use two waves of data from 2009 – the year when (most of) the workers in our sample were displaced – and 2011 – the year when the treated individuals were surveyed.

Using data from the SHP may raise methodological issues. First, the sampling is done at the level of the household and not the individuals. Second, attrition in the SHP does not occur randomly (Voorpostel 2010: 372). Individuals who remain longer in the sample, and thus are less prone to attrition, are more likely to be female, married, older and higher-educated individuals. Accordingly, we need to keep in mind that the SHP consists of a selected group of people.

We chose a binary model distinguishing between displacement by plant closure (treatment) and no displacement (no treatment). Our specification includes workers who were employed in 2009, which results in a number of observations of 4601. A more in-depth description of the control groups can be found in the dissertation which is the basis for this book (Baumann 2015).

---

[17] Formally, the matching estimator can be described as $Pr(Z=1 \mid X)$, rather than x as is the case in other matching techniques. X is the vector of covariates for a particular individual and Z indicates whether the individual was exposed ($z=1$) or unexposed ($z=0$) to the treatment. The treated and the controls are selected in such a way that they have the same distribution of x. The matching process relies on two further assumptions (Caliendo and Kopeinig 2008: 35). First, the covariates that are included in the model are chosen based on the conditional independence assumption (CIA). Second, the common support assumption affirms that the individuals' (pre-treatment) characteristics do not perfectly predict attribution to the treatment. This condition guarantees that individuals with the same characteristics can be in both the treatment and the control group.

## 2.7 Limits

Our sampling strategy is convenience sampling, an approach that has its limitations (Lohr 1999: 5). In particular, the data are not generated by a known probability mechanism such as random sampling and therefore do not allow inferences from the sample to the entire population (Western and Jackman 1994: 412; Berk 2004: 51). Focusing on the manufacturing sector, our results are probably not generalizable to other sectors. For instance, workers in this sector are on average somewhat more likely to have completed an apprenticeship than in other sectors.

However, within the manufacturing sector the composition of the workforce of the plants in our sample is similar to that of other firms. This suggests that our results can be generalized for manufacturing workers. Nevertheless, since we sampled only from closed plants in the manufacturing sector, inference on the entire manufacturing sector has to be made with caution and accordingly the significance level should be read with reservations. A more conservative interpretation of our findings would be that they are the results of a case study. However, since no database was available from which we could have drawn a random sample, a procedure corresponding to the standards of the art would have been very costly, both in terms of time and money. In addition, our survey follows an established tradition of plant closure studies which analyze single firms (Kriechel and Pfann 2005; Trotzier 2005; Jolkkonen et al. 2012).

A problem that is linked to the sampling method and the incomplete randomness of experiencing a plant closure is treatment effect heterogeneity (Cha and Morgan 2010: 1141; Burda and Mertens 2001: 22–24). Treatment effect heterogeneity describes the problem that individuals differ not only in terms of socio-demographic characteristics and therefore in their propensity to experience a treatment (pre-treatment heterogeneity), but also in how they are affected by a particular treatment (Brand and Simon Thomas 2014). If treatment effect heterogeneity is at work, average treatment effects can vary widely depending on the socio-demographic composition of the treated and simple averages do not have a straightforward interpretation. Solutions to this problem require data on treated and non-treated individuals which can be linked by means of propensity score matching. However, since it is impossible in the large Swiss surveys to identify workers who have experienced plant closure, we were not able to assess potential treatment effect heterogeneity.

A third limit of this study is the absence of proper longitudinal data. Our use of retrospective measures to assess workers' occupational situation and life satisfaction before they lost their job is definitely valuable in order to examine within-individual changes. However, it is clearly only a second-best solution (Hardt and Rutter 2004). It is widely accepted in the literature that retrospective measures are biased. Some measures can be assessed more correctly than others by retrospective assessment. Unfortunately, accuracy seems to be comparatively low for psychosocial indicators such as subjective well-being – an important measure in our study (Henry et al. 1994). Accordingly, data reliability could be significantly enhanced if repeated survey waves and thus panel data on displaced workers in Switzerland were available.

## 2.8 The Institutional Context of the Swiss Labor Market

Several institutions affect how displaced workers experience the occupational transition after job loss: the employment protection legislation shaping the procedure of dismissal, the unemployment insurance, the retirement regulations, the skill regime and the overall labor market situation. Although the employment legislation regarding individual dismissals in Switzerland is comparatively weak and termination pays are not required,[18] plant closures are regulated more strictly (OECD 2013: 78, 85). Plant closures are a form of collective dismissal that is legally defined as a displacement of more than 10 % of the workforce for reasons not related to individual workers.[19] Firms that undertake a collective dismissal are obliged to announce the layoff at least 1 month in advance to their personnel and to the cantonal employment office. At the same time, the company has to inform its workforce about the number of displaced workers, as well as the reason and the date of displacement. Furthermore, the company has to offer the workers the opportunity to negotiate a potential redundancy plan and a strategy to avoid displacements. Consequently, plant closures in Switzerland are usually accompanied by collective negotiations over redundancy plans. However, in 2009 and 2010 there was not yet a legal – although there was an informal – obligation for the companies to offer a redundancy plan.[20]

While employment protection in Switzerland is low, the unemployment insurance is comparatively generous (Schwab and Weber 2010). All employed workers are compulsorily enrolled in the unemployment insurance. Workers who contributed at least 12 (18) months within the preceding 24 months are entitled to a benefit period of 12 (18) months. The replacement rate is 70 % of the last six salaries (80 % for workers with low income and job seekers with children). For workers aged over 54, a contribution period of 24 months provides them with access to unemployment benefits for 24 months. Workers who become unemployed 4 years or less before their regular pension age are entitled to a total benefit period of two and a half years. Workers under the age of 25 receive unemployment benefits for a maximum of 10 months. Additionally, all workers who receive unemployed benefits are monitored and have access to a range of active labor market measures.

In Switzerland the legal retirement age is 65 for men and 64 for women. A full pension requires a contribution of at least 44 years for men and 43 for women (OECD 2011: 310–1). The pension system has a redistribution part, a savings part – both mandatory –, and a voluntary provision. Early retirement is possible 2 years before the official retirement age but implies a reduction of 7 % of pension benefits for each year of early retirement. Thus the governmental pension system offers little

---

[18] During the first year of employment, the notice period of dismissal is 1 month, during the second to the ninth year 2 months and thereafter 3 months.

[19] See Swiss Code of Obligations Art. 335d-k.

[20] This legislation changed in June 2013: Art. 335i in the Code of Obligation now requires that plants employing more than 250 and displacing more than 30 workers negotiate a redundancy plan.

incentive to retire early. However, if redundancy plans with early retirement schemes are available, this option may be convenient.

In 2011, 35% of the residents of Switzerland aged 25–64 held a tertiary degree, 50% an upper secondary or post-secondary non-tertiary degree, and 15% had less than upper secondary education (OECD 2014). As compared to other countries, the share of individuals with tertiary education is higher than in Germany (28%) or Austria (19%) but lower than in the UK (39%) or the US (42%). The share of individuals with upper secondary education is higher in Germany (58%) and Austria (63%) and lower in the US (46%) and the UK (37%) than in Switzerland.

Among the young people finishing compulsory school, about two-thirds enroll in vocational education and training (VET) (SERI 2015: 4). Most VET programs consist in a dual vocational education combining workplace-based training with school-based general education; a minority of young people attend exclusively school-based VET programs (Fuentes 2011). After 3 or 4 years, students graduate from their VET program with a standardized certificate. Students who have additionally completed a Federal Vocational Baccalaureate may enroll in tertiary-level professional education and training (PET) which prepares them for specialized technical and managerial positions. The VET and PET training systems are strongly oriented towards the demand for skills in the labor market. Both systems are collectively organized by the state, the cantons and employers' organizations and trade unions; vocational schools and host companies monitor the quality of the training. Switzerland's educational system is also standardized with respect to tertiary education. About a quarter of all young people graduating from compulsory school enroll in such training (Helbling and Sacchi 2014: 2). A school-leaving exam (Matura – comparable to the Abitur in Germany) provides access to tertiary education institutions for all students.

Referring to the classification of educational systems developed by Allmendinger (1989), Switzerland's vocational training system is highly standardized on a national level. It comprises both training protocols that set the quality standards of the educational system and a procedure of skill certification in a similar way as in Germany (see Dieckhoff 2008: 94). Allmendinger (1989: 240) argued that standardized certificates serve employers as screening devices for workers' skills before they hire them, in contrast to non-standardized educational systems where workers have to be screened on-the-job. As a consequence, in less standardized educational systems newly hired workers are more likely to lose their job again. In Switzerland in contrast new job matches are likely to be relatively stable and occupational transitions comparatively smooth.

In terms of the skill production regime typology developed by Estevez-Abe et al. (2001), Switzerland corresponds approximately to the firm- and industry-specific type, characterized by a large proportion of workers with vocational training. The classification of Switzerland in the specific-skill regime contradicts Estevez-Abe et al. (2001: 8) insofar that those authors expect the workers to only invest in firm-specific skills if employment protection is high – which is not the case in Switzerland. Nevertheless, since low employment protection is cushioned by relatively generous unemployment benefits, a high proportion of workers in Switzerland seem to be willing to invest in specific skills. In line with the argument by those authors, high unemployment benefit replacement rates and long benefit entitlement durations may provide displaced workers with the conditions to find a new job that matches their skills.

## 2.9 Aggregate Unemployment

The plant closures that we sampled occurred in the context of a rather low but rising unemployment rate in Switzerland. At the beginning of the financial crisis, in 2008, the unemployment rate was 3.4%.[21] It then increased to 4.3% in 2009 and to 4.5% in 2010 and fell to 4.0% in 2011. Four of the plants in our sample were located in German-speaking regions where the unemployment rates were close to the national average. One plant in contrast was located close to Geneva in French-speaking Switzerland where unemployment rates were higher in this period at about 7%.

Regional differences in aggregate unemployment – which seem to be stable over time – are a much-debated issue among Swiss scholars (Flückiger et al. 2007: 57). First, it has been observed that unemployment levels are generally higher in French- or Italian-speaking cantons than in German-speaking cantons (Flückiger et al. 2007: 60; Brügger et al. 2007). This result is due to both higher inflows and lower outflows of unemployed workers in the Latin (French and Italian-speaking) regions. A possible explanation for this pattern may be cultural differences in attitudes toward work as residents of the Latin-speaking regions consider work less important and are more favorable in votes to restrict working time than those of German-speaking regions (Brügger et al. 2009). Second, the demographic structure of the active population varies by canton (de Coulon 1999). Third, cantonal tax policies and the presence of foreign workers seem to contribute to the differences (Feld and Savioz 2000).

These factors may explain one of the main findings of this study, namely that workers from Plant 1, located in French-speaking Geneva, were substantially less likely to return to employment than workers in Plants 2–5, located in German-speaking Switzerland. More precisely, due to its proximity to the French border – and thus the greater competition among job seekers – and the higher prevalence of older workers, workers from Plant 1 may have experienced much more difficulty in finding a new job than workers from other plants (Flückiger and Vasiliev 2002: 407).

It should also be noted that deindustrialization progressed slowly over the period of our study: in relative terms the share of manufacturing employment decreased from 19.3% in 2008 to 18.2% in 2012. In absolute terms manufacturing employment was rather stable after 2009. Measured in full-time equivalents, manufacturing employment decreased from 661,000 in 2008 to 629,000 in 2009 and 626,000 in

---

[21] Rates according to the ILO definition of unemployment and based on the Swiss Labour Force Survey.

2010, before recovering in 2011 and 2012, when the figure increased again to 633,000 and 636,000.[22]

Although Switzerland does not belong to the European Union, its economy and labor market do not constitute a case *sui generis* as is often assumed. In fact, the Swiss economy shares many common features with Austria and Southern Germany, in particular a strong reliance on vocational education, a resilient manufacturing sector and low levels of unemployment. As an illustration, in 2011 the unemployment rates in the adjacent *Bundesländer* of Austria and Germany were lower than in Switzerland – with below 3.5 % in Western Austria (comprising Oberösterreich, Salzburg and Tirol), 3.3 % in Bavaria and 3.6 % in Baden-Württemberg.[23] It may thus be expected that a survey on plant closure in Salzburg, Stuttgart or Munich would produce comparable results to the ones presented here.

In this chapter we have discussed how we collected our data and the extent to which we are confronted with survey bias. In a nutshell, our analysis led to two main findings: first, the use of a mixed-mode approach – and in particular telephone interviews – helped to decrease nonresponse bias. Second, although our data does not seem immune to measurement error, the use of different sources, i.e., register data, improves the quality of the data. Overall, applying a tailor-made survey design substantially contributed to addressing survey bias.

**Open Access** This chapter is distributed under the terms of the Creative Commons Attribution 4.0 International License (http://creativecommons.org/licenses/by/4.0/), which permits use, duplication, adaptation, distribution and reproduction in any medium or format, as long as you give appropriate credit to the original author(s) and the source, a link is provided to the Creative Commons license and any changes made are indicated.

The images or other third party material in this chapter are included in the work's Creative Commons license, unless indicated otherwise in the credit line; if such material is not included in the work's Creative Commons license and the respective action is not permitted by statutory regulation, users will need to obtain permission from the license holder to duplicate, adapt or reproduce the material.

# References

Allmendinger, J. (1989). Educational systems and labor market outcomes. *European Sociological Review, 5*(3), 231–250.
Angrist, J. D., & Pischke, J. (2010). Economics: How better research design is taking the con out of econometrics. *Journal of Economic Perspectives, 24*(2), 3–30.
Antonakis, J., Bendahan, S., Jacquart, P., & Lalive, R. (2010). On making causal claims: A review and recommendations. *The Leadership Quarterly, 21*(6), 1086–1120.
Balestra, S., & Backes-Gellner, U. (2016). *When a door closes, a window opens? Long-term labor market effects of involuntary separations* (German Economic Review, (advanced online access) 1–21.

---

[22] Source: Swiss Federal Office of Statistic, BESTA/STATEM statistics. Data for third semester.
[23] Source: Eurostat (accessed on May 5, 2015): http://appsso.eurostat.ec.europa.eu/nui/show.do

# References

Baumann, I. (2015). *Labor market experience and well-being after firm closure. Survey evidence on displaced manufacturing workers in Switzerland.* Dissertation, Supervisor: Oesch, D. Université de Lausanne.

Baumann, I., Lipps, O., Oesch, D., & Vandenplas, C. (2016). How to survey displaced workers in Switzerland: Ways of addressing sources of bias. In M. Oris, D. Joye, C. Roberts, & M. Ernst Stähli (Eds.), *Surveying vulnerabilities, surveying vulnerable populations.* New York/Heidelberg/Dordrecht/London: Springer.

Berk, R. A. (2004). *Regression analysis: A constructive critique.* London: Sage Publications.

Bound, J., Brown, C., Duncan, G. J., & Rodgers, W. L. (1994). Evidence on the validity of cross-sectional and longitudinal labor market data. *Journal of Labor Economics, 12*(3), 345–368.

Bound, J., Brown, C., & Mathiowetz, N. (2001). Measurement error in survey data. In J. J. Heckman & E. Leamer (Eds.), *Handbook of econometrics* (Vol. 5, pp. 3705–3843). Amsterdam: Elsevier Science & Technology.

Brand, J. E. (2006). The effects of job displacement on job quality: Findings from the Wisconsin Longitudinal Study. *Research in Social Stratification and Mobility, 24*(3), 275–298.

Brand, J. E., & Simon Thomas, J. (2014). Job displacement among single mothers: Effects on children's outcomes in young adulthood. *American Journal of Sociology, 119*(4), 955–1001.

Brügger, B., Lalive d'Epinay, R., & Zweimüller, J. (2007). *Regionale Disparitäten der Arbeitslosigkeit: Kulturelle Grenzen und Landesgrenzen* (SECO Publikation Arbeitsmarktpolitik No. 23). Bern: Staatssekretariat für Wirtschaft SECO.

Brügger, B., Lalive, R. & Zweimüller, J. (2009). *Does culture affect unemployment? Evidence from the Röstigraben* (CESifo working paper No. 2714).

Burda, M. C., & Mertens, A. (2001). Estimating wage losses of displaced workers in Germany. *Labour Economics, 8*(1), 15–41.

Caliendo, M., & Kopeinig, S. (2008). Some practical guidance for the implementation of propensity score matching. *Journal of Economic Surveys, 22*(1), 31–72.

Cha, Y., & Morgan, S. L. (2010). Structural earnings losses and between-industry mobility of displaced workers, 2003–2008. *Social Science Research, 39*(6), 1137–1152.

Chan, S., & Stevens, A. H. (2001). Job loss and employment patterns of older workers. *Journal of Labor Economics, 19*(2), 484–521.

Corbetta, P. (2003). *Social research: Theory, methods and techniques.* London/Thousand Oaks: SAGE Publications.

De Coulon, A. (1999). Disparité régionale du chômage: Population étrangère et courbe de Beveridge en Suisse. *Schweizerische Zeitschrift für Volkswirtschaft und Statistik, 135*(2), 165–185.

Dehejia, R. H., & Wahba, S. (1999). Causal effects in nonexperimental studies: Reevaluating the evaluation of training programs. *Journal of the American Statistical Association, 94*(448), 1053–1062.

Dieckhoff, M. (2008). Skills and occupational attainment: A comparative study of Germany, Denmark and the UK. *Work Employment Society, 22*(1), 89–108.

Dillman, D. A., Smyth, L., & Leani, C. (2009). *Internet, mail, and mixed-mode surveys: The tailored design method.* Bingley: Emerald Group Publishing Limited.

Eliason, M., & Storrie, D. (2009). Job loss is bad for your health – Swedish evidence on cause-specific hospitalization following involuntary job loss. *Social Science & Medicine, 68*(8), 1396–1406.

Estevez-Abe, M., Iversen, T., & Soskice, D. (2001). Social protection and the formation of skills. A reinterpretation of the welfare state. In P. A. Hall & D. Soskice (Eds.), *Varieties of capitalism. The institutional foundations of comparative advantage* (pp. 145–183). Oxford: Oxford University Press.

Farber, H. S. (1997). The changing face of job loss in the United States, 1981–1995. *Brookings Papers on Economic Activity. Microeconomics, 1997*(1997), 55–142.

Feld, L. P., & Savioz, M. R. (2000). Cantonal and regional unemployment in Switzerland: A dynamic macroeconomic panel analysis. *Schweizerische Zeitschrift für Volkswirtschaft und Statistik, 136*(3), 463–483.

Flückiger, Y., & Vasiliev, A. (2002). Les raisons des différences de chômage entre Genève et le reste de la Suisse. *Swiss Journal of Economics and Statistics, 138*(4), 387–410.

Flückiger, Y., Kempeneers, P., & Bazen, S. (2007). Regionale Unterschiede bei der Arbeitslosigkeit: Ein revidierter Ansatz. *Die Volkswirtschaft, 7/8,* 57–61.

Fuentes, A. (2011). *Raising education outcomes in Switzerland* (OECD Economics department working papers, no. 838). Paris: OECD Publishing.

Gibbons, R., & Katz, L. F. (1991). Layoffs and lemons. *Journal of Labor Economics, 9*(4), 351–380.

Groves, R. M., & Couper, M. P. (1998). *Nonresponse in household interview survey.* Hoboken: Wiley.

Groves, R. M., & Peytcheva, E. (2008). The impact of nonresponse rates on nonresponse bias: A meta-analysis. *Public Opinion Quarterly, 72*(2), 167–189.

Hardt, J., & Rutter, M. (2004). Validity of adult retrospective reports of adverse childhood experiences: Review of the evidence. *Journal of Child Psychology and Psychiatry, and Allied Disciplines, 45*(2), 260–273.

Harrison, C. H. (2010). Mail survey and paper questionnaires. In P. V. Marsden & J. D. Wright (Eds.), *Handbook of survey research* (pp. 499–526). Bingley: Emerald Group Publishing Limited.

Helbling, L., & Sacchi, S. (2014). Scarring effects of early unemployment among young workers with vocational credentials in Switzerland. *Empirical Research in Vocational Education and Training, 6*(12), 1–22.

Henry, B., Moffitt, T. E., Caspi, A., Langley, J., & Silva, P. A. (1994). On the "Remembrance of Things Past": A longitudinal evaluation of the retrospective method. *Psychological Assessment, 6*(2), 92–101.

Hijzen, A., Upward, R., & Wright, P. (2010). The income losses of displaced workers. *The Journal of Human Resources, 45*(1), 243–269.

Jacobson, L. S., LaLonde, R. J., & Sullivan, D. G. (1993). Earning losses of displaced workers. *The American Economic Review, 83*(4), 685–709.

Jolkkonen, A., Koistinen, P., & Kurvinen, A. (2012). Reemployment of displaced workers – The case of a plant closing on a remote region in Finland. *Nordic Journal of Working Life Studies, 2*(1), 81–100.

Joye, D., & Bergman, M. M. (2004). Carrières professionnelles: Une analyse biographique. In E. Zimmerman & R. Tillmann (Eds.), *Vivre en Suisse 1999–2000: Une année dans la vie des ménages et familles en Suisse* (pp. 77–92). Bern: Peter Lang.

Kempf, A. M., & Remington, P. L. (2007). New challenges for telephone survey research in the twenty-first century. *Annual Review of Public Health, 28,* 113–126.

Kletzer, L. G. (2001). *Job loss from imports: Measuring the costs.* Washington, DC: Institute for International Economics.

Kriechel, B., & Pfann, G. A. (2005). The role of specific and general human capital after displacement. *Education Economics, 13*(2), 223–236.

Laganà, F., Elcheroth, G., Penic, S., Kleiner, B., & Fasel, N. (2011). National minorities and their representation in social surveys: Which practices make a difference? *Quality & Quantity, 47*(3), 1287–1314.

Lipps, O. (2010). Effects of different incentives on attrition and fieldwork effort in telephone household panel surveys. *Survey Research Methods, 4*(2), 81–90.

Lipps, O., Laganà, F., Pollien, A., & Gianettoni, L. (2013). Under-representation of foreign minorities in cross-sectional and longitudinal surveys in Switzerland. In J. Font & M. Méndez (Eds.), *Surveying ethnic minorities and immigrant populations: Methodological challenges and research strategies* (pp. 241–267). Amsterdam: University Press.

Little, R., & Vartivarian, S. L. (2005). Does weighting for nonreponse increase the variance of survey means? *Survey Methodology, 31,* 161–168.

Lohr, S. L. (1999). *Sampling: Design and analysis.* Pacific Grove: Duxbury Press.

Mood, C. (2010). Logistic regression: Why we cannot do what we think we can do, and what we can do about it. *European Sociological Review, 26*(1), 67–82.

# References

OECD. (2011). *Pensions at a glance 2011: Retirement-income systems in OECD and G20 countries*. Paris: OECD Publishing.

OECD. (2013). *OECD employment outlook 2013*. Paris: OECD Publishing.

OECD. (2014). *Education at a glance 2014: OECD indicators*. Paris: OECD Publishing.

Peytchev, A., Baxter, R. K., & Carley-Baxter, L. R. (2009). Not all survey effort is equal: Reduction of nonresponse bias and nonresponse error. *Public Opinion Quarterly, 73*(4), 785–806.

Phillips, L. W. (1981). Assessing measurement error in key informant reports: A methodological note on organizational analysis in marketing. *Journal of Marketing Research, 18*(4), 395–415.

Rosenbaum, P. R., & Rubin, D. B. (1983). The central role of the propensity score in observational studies for causal effects. *Biometrika, 70*(1), 41–55.

Rosenbaum, P. R., & Rubin, D. B. (1985). Constructing a control group using multivariate matched sampling methods that incorporate the propensity score. *The American Statistician, 39*(1), 33–38.

Schräpler, J.-P. (2001). *Respondent behaviour in panel studies. A case study of the German Socio-Economic Panel (GSOEP)* (DIW-discussion paper 244). Berlin: DIW.

Schwab, M., & Weber, B. (2010). Die Schweizer Arbeitslosenversicherung im internationalen Vergleich. *Die Volkswirtschaft, 5*, 39–42.

Schwerdt, G. (2011). Labor turnover before plant closure: "Leaving the sinking ship" vs. "Captain throwing ballast overboard". *Labour Economics, 18*(1), 93–101.

SERI. (2015). *Facts and figures. Vocational and professional education and training in Switzerland 2014*. Biel: State Secretariat for Education, Research and Innovation SERI.

Stoop, I. (2005). *The hunt for the last respondent: Nonresponse in sample survey*. The Hague: Social and Cultural Planning Office of the Netherlands.

Sweet, S., & Moen, P. (2011). Dual earners preparing for job loss: Agency, linked lives, and resilience. *Work and Occupations, 39*(1), 35–70.

Täube, V. G., & Joye, D. (2002). Determinants of internet use in Switzerland. In W. Glatzer (Ed.), *Rich and poor: Disparities, perceptions, concomitants* (pp. 73–86). Dordrecht: Kluwer Academic Publishers.

Trotzier, C. (2005). Vingt ans de trajectoire après un licenciement collectif: Ouvrières et ouvriers. *Revue Économique, 56*(2), 257–275.

Voorpostel, M. (2010). Attrition patterns in the Swiss household panel by demographic characteristics and social involvement. *Swiss Journal of Sociology, 36*(2), 359–377.

Weder, R., & Wyss, S. (2010). *Arbeitslosigkeit unter niedrig Qualifizierten: Die Rolle der Globalisierung* (SECO Publikation Arbeitsmarktpolitik No. 29). Bern: SECO.

Western, B., & Jackman, S. (1994). Bayesian inference for comparative research. *The American Political Science Review, 88*(2), 412–423.

# Chapter 3
# Reemployment or Unemployment

Previous research on displaced workers' labor market prospects shows that workers with a higher educational level are substantially more likely to return to employment than low-educated workers. There seem to be two main reasons for this finding. First, the demand for high-skilled labor is rising as a consequence of the automation of production processes and technological change that is skill-biased in favor of highly educated workers. Second, education is an important signal to employers about workers' unobserved abilities such as their ability to learn. We therefore hypothesize that low- and mid-educated workers encounter more difficulties in finding a job than highly educated workers (hypothesis H1, see Sect. 1.4).

With respect to reemployment after job loss, studies also show that older workers experience much greater difficulties in returning to the active labor force than younger workers. This phenomenon may be due to older workers' longer firm tenure which goes along with a skills profile that contains a large amount of firm-specific skills not readily transferable to a new firm. Accordingly, we expect older workers to have more difficulty in returning to the active labor force than younger workers (hypothesis H1).

We begin our empirical analysis with the question whether displaced workers managed to return to the active labor force within the time that passed between their job loss and our survey. We assess this question based on our combined data and then compare the finding with the counterfactual outcome of a control group of non-displaced workers. We then identify the socio-demographic and contextual factors that potentially favor or inhibit workers' reemployment and discuss how this result compares with findings from earlier studies and different contexts. We conclude by discussing the implications of our results for our hypotheses.

## 3.1 Labor Market Status Two Years After Displacement

Figure 3.1 shows that at the moment of the survey – on average 23 months after job displacement – 66% of the workers were again working as employees and 3% were self-employed or worked in a family company. 8% of the workers went into early retirement and 3% retired regularly. 14% were unemployed still receiving unemployment benefits, but 3% were unemployed the entitlement having been expired. Finally, 2% of the workers did training or childcare and 1% were unable to work because of disability. If we group these categories into broader categories, 69% of workers were back in employment, 11% retired, 17% were still or again unemployed and 3% had dropped out of the labor force.

How do these results compare with the findings from other plant closure studies? A survey conducted in 2007 in Switzerland finds reemployment rates between 72% and 92% and unemployment rates between 8% and 28% – depending on the company – 1-6 years after job loss (Weder and Wyss 2010: 27). The authors do not, however, consider workers exiting the labor force into retirement or training. To compare their findings with our results, we thus have to reproduce their analysis by excluding the retired and labor force dropouts. This approach provides us with a reemployment rate of 80% and an unemployment rate of 20% – and thus similar results. However, since the study by Weder and Wyss was conducted in the context of the boom phase of 2002–2006 and displacements taking place in phases of macroeconomically favorable conditions tend to lead to substantially higher reemployment rates (Kletzer 2001: 44), it would have been unsurprising if we had observed lower reemployment than their study.

Moreover, the response rate of the survey conducted by Weder and Wyss was about 30% and thus more than 30 percentage points lower than the response rate in our own survey. Since survey response is not a random phenomenon – more

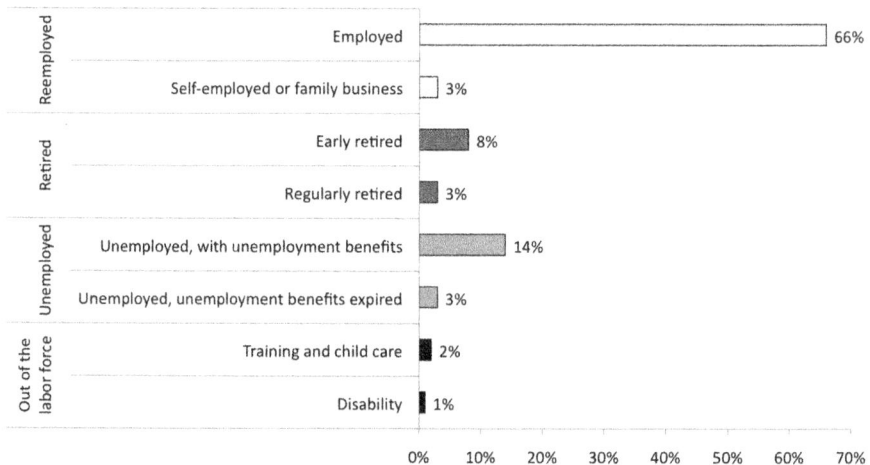

**Fig. 3.1** Displaced workers' labor market status about 2 years after job loss. N=887

## 3.1 Labor Market Status Two Years After Displacement

motivated and better-educated individuals being more likely to participate – a higher response rate leads to observations that are more representative for the entire survey population. In the case of a low response rate it is likely that only the most motivated and highly educated workers answered the survey. Accordingly, we would again expect the reemployment rate of the study by Weder and Wyss to be higher than in our survey.

Comparing our results with a Finnish study, our reemployment rate is slightly higher. More precisely, Jolkkonen et al. (2012: 88) find for Finland that 61 % of the displaced manufacturing workers were back in employment, 14 % were still unemployed, 19 % in training and 5 % had left the labor force. Yet, this study assessed workers' labor market status only 10 months after displacement and the workers thus had less time to find a job than those in our study before they were surveyed. At the same time, in the Finnish study the unemployment rate is lower but the proportion of workers in training is much higher than in our study. This difference is perhaps due to a substantially larger proportion of unemployed workers participating in active labor market programs in Finland than in Switzerland.

Considering the results by Kletzer (2001: 31) based on the US Displaced Worker Survey, our analysis provides higher average reemployment rates. For manufacturing workers displaced between 1979 and 1999, the author reports a reemployment rate of 64 %. Displaced manufacturing workers in the US thus seem to face slightly more difficulties in returning to a job than those in Switzerland. This result becomes more pronounced by the fact that Kletzer's analysis measures workers' reemployment rate within up to 5 years after while our analysis includes workers up to 2 years after job loss.

What explains the comparatively high reemployment rate of our study? First, this outcome may be due to the differences between studies with respect to workers' tenure. Since in the US displaced workers have by definition tenure of at least 3 years (Devens 1986: 40), workers in the study conducted by Kletzer (2001) are likely to be more strongly attached to their pre-displacement firms. Because of their higher share of firm-specific skills they may experience greater difficulties in finding a new job than the workers with lower tenure in our sample.

Second, it is possible that among the workers in Kletzer's sample some individuals were laid off for just cause instead of being displaced because of plant closure. Although the Displaced Worker Survey distinguishes between various reasons for job loss, it is plausible that self-reported data underestimates the share of workers who were fired, because survey respondents are reluctant to admit failure (Kuhn 2002: 15). If potential future employers know that workers were laid off for just cause, they seem to refrain from hiring them. Gibbons and Katz (1991) described this phenomenon as the "lemon effect of layoffs". According to this idea, employers avoid hiring workers laid off individually because they fear that they were displaced because of unfavorable characteristics such as low productivity. In contrast, workers displaced together with the entire workforce are not assumed to be individually responsible for their job loss.

Three additional explanations probably account even better for our finding (see Oesch and Baumann 2015). In absolute terms, employment in Switzerland's

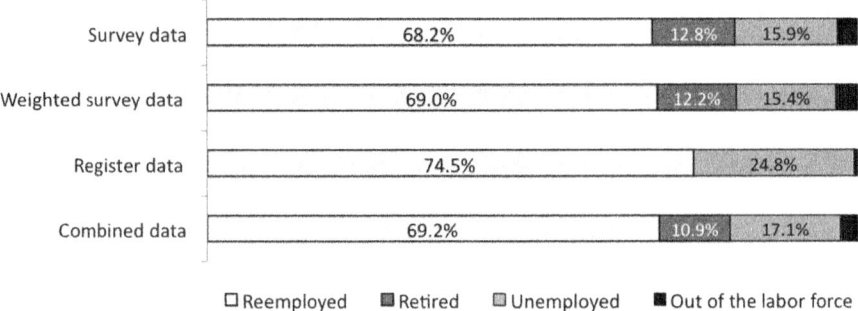

**Fig. 3.2** Labor market status 2 years after displacement calculated for four different data subsets. Note: Survey data N=742, Weighted survey data N=742, Register data N=322, Combined data N=887

manufacturing sector was stagnating rather than decreasing over the period under study. This possibly led to the more robust reemployment prospects of workers displaced from a manufacturing plant in Switzerland as compared to other countries. Moreover, Switzerland's labor market was not strongly affected by the economic crisis of 2008. Even though the national unemployment rate rose between 2008 and 2010 before falling again in 2011, the unemployment rate was never higher than 4.5 % at the national level or 7.2 % in any of the districts studied here. Workers who were not able to find a job in manufacturing thus may have had job opportunities in other sectors. Finally, Switzerland's educational system provides a standardized certification of vocational training. Accordingly, workers with upper secondary education – who represent the majority of the workforce – acquire industry- rather than merely firm-specific skills during their apprenticeship. If workers lose their job, they seem to transit relatively smoothly to other companies in the same sector.

We now turn to a robustness test of the results presented in Fig. 3.1 by comparing the outcome for different data subsets. In Fig. 3.2 we present the workers' labor market status based on (1) survey data only, (2) weighted survey data only, (3) register data only, and (4) survey and register data combined. A Pearson chi$^2$ test reveals that the results for the datasets (1), (2) and (4) are not significantly different from one another. But as is clearly visible from Fig. 3.2, dataset (3) leads to substantially different results: reemployment and unemployment are more frequent here than in the other datasets (for reemployment: 74.5 % as compared to 68.2 %, 69 % and 69.2 %). This is not surprising since workers going into retirement or exiting the labor force less frequently request unemployment benefits, and since the register data does not indicate whether workers have transited from unemployment to retirement. For this reason, we are unable to identify the retired based on register data. Another noteworthy feature of our database is that the combined data contains a slightly larger proportion of reemployed and unemployed workers than the survey data; in contrast, the proportion of retired workers is slightly smaller. This result

3.1 Labor Market Status Two Years After Displacement 67

**Table 3.1** Probability of being employed, retired, unemployed or out of the labor force in 2011 for the treatment and the control group in our sample and a control group based on the Swiss Household Panel (in %)

| Labor market status in 2011 | Treatment group (workers displaced in 2009) | Control group (workers in the SHP not displaced in 2009) | Average treatment effect on the treated (Difference) |
|---|---|---|---|
| Employed | 69% | 93% | −24 percentage points |
| Retired | 11% | 4% | +7 percentage points |
| Unemployed | 17% | 1% | +16 percentage points |
| Out of the labor force | 3% | 2% | +1 percentage point |
| N | 887 | 4265 | |

Note: The approach used is radius caliper matching with a radius of 0.001. The radius chosen is narrow, which implies that the workers in our control group are thus highly similar to the workers in the treatment group. Tests with other radiuses revealed similar results (ATT between −20% and −25% for reemployment). The results were consistent with and without bootstrapping (with up to 999 replications)

stems from the combination of the survey data with the register data – a data sub-set from which retired workers are missing.

In order to gauge the causal effect of plant closure on workers' labor market prospects, we run a difference-in-difference analysis, comparing the displaced workers' outcome with the counterfactual outcome of non-displaced workers. Very likely, not all of the workers would have been employed in 2011 if their plant had not closed down. Some would have been in full-time training, stopped working in order to care for their children or gone into retirement. Some would probably have been unemployed because they quit their job and did not find a new job or had been displaced individually.

The control group is constructed based on data from the Swiss Household Panel and represents workers who did not lose their job in 2009. We create a control group that is similar to the displaced workers in terms of their age, education and sex by matching them by means of propensity score matching. We follow the workers in our control group who were not displaced in 2009 – the year when most of the workers in our sample lost their job – through 2011 and assess their labor market situation at that moment – the year when we interviewed the workers in our sample. We measure the Average Treatment Effect on the Treated (ATT), which represents the difference in the chance of being employed in 2011 between workers who experienced a plant closure in 2009 and those who did not lose their job in that year.

Table 3.1 presents the results of our analysis. In the treatment group, 69% of the workers were (re-)employed in 2011 while this was the case for 93% of the workers in the control group. The remaining 7% of the workers in the control group comprise 1% who were unemployed, 2% who were out of the labor force and 4% who were retired. Accordingly, workers who were displaced in 2009 because of plant closure were 24 percentage points less likely to be employed in 2011, 7 percentage points more likely to be retired, 16 percentage points more likely to be unemployed and 1 percentage point more likely to be out of the labor force. We can thus maintain that job displacement has a strong causal effect on the workers' labor market situation.

However, since the control group does not correspond to the treatment group in terms of education and sex as discussed in Chap. 2, we test the robustness of the unemployment level of the control group by comparing it to the average unemployment rate in Switzerland. The unemployment rate as defined by the International Labor Organization (ILO) for workers aged 15–65 was 4.2 % in 2009, 4.7 % in 2010 and again 4.2 % in 2011 (OECD Statistics). As Table 3.1 above shows, the unemployment rate of our constructed control group was 1 % during this period and thus lower than the average Swiss unemployment rate. The lower unemployment rate of the control group is partially due to the fact that we observe individuals who were employed in 2009 while the average Swiss unemployment rate includes workers who finished their education or training. In addition, the average Swiss unemployment rate includes workers from all sectors and not only from the manufacturing sector. Nevertheless, it is possible that with the estimate we computed for our control group we underestimate the counterfactual, the unemployment probability that the displaced workers would have had if they had not lost their job.

## 3.2 Labor Market Status by Socio-demographic Characteristics

We now turn to the analysis of the labor market status by socio-demographic characteristics. We start in Table 3.2 with a descriptive analysis. Pearson chi$^2$ tests indicate that the labor market status differs significantly by sex, education, collar (blue-/white-collar), age, nationality, civil status and plant. Women have a higher reemployment rate than men, but the same unemployment rate. The difference between the sexes results from the larger proportion of men going into retirement. More precisely, in contrast to women, men went much more often into *early* retirement (2 % of women versus 11 % of men). One possible explanation is that the women in our sample are on average younger (42) than the men (46). Another reason for this difference may be that because of non-standard employment patterns over women's life course their occupational pension savings are more modest and they thus are less likely to be able to afford early retirement.

The reemployment rates do not vary strongly according to educational levels: while 72 % of the workers with a tertiary degree found a new job, this was the case for 70 % of workers with upper secondary education and for 66 % of workers without upper secondary education. However, the difference is larger with respect to the unemployment rate. While only 13 % of the workers with tertiary education were unemployed, 22 % of the workers without upper secondary education were unemployed. If we add the workers who left the labor force, workers without upper secondary education were twice as likely to be either unemployed or out of the labor force as workers with tertiary education (27 % versus 13 %).

## 3.2 Labor Market Status by Socio-demographic Characteristics

**Table 3.2** Labor market status by sex, education, collar, age, nationality and plant (in %)

|  | Reemployed | Retired | Unemployed | Out of labor force | N |
|---|---|---|---|---|---|
| **Sex** | | | | | |
| Women | 75 | 4 | 17 | 5 | *151* |
| Men | 68 | 12 | 17 | 2 | *735* |
| **Education** | | | | | |
| Less than upper secondary education | 66 | 7 | 22 | 5 | *148* |
| Upper secondary education | 70 | 10 | 18 | 3 | *482* |
| Tertiary education | 72 | 15 | 13 | 0 | *223* |
| **Collar** | | | | | |
| Blue-Collar | 68 | 9 | 19 | 3 | *544* |
| White-Collar | 71 | 14 | 13 | 2 | *328* |
| **Age** | | | | | |
| <30 | 86 | 0 | 7 | 7 | *97* |
| 30–39 | 90 | 0 | 8 | 2 | *133* |
| 40–49 | 87 | 0 | 12 | 1 | *252* |
| 50–54 | 82 | 0 | 15 | 3 | *130* |
| 55–59 | 53 | 14 | 30 | 3 | *110* |
| >59 | 12 | 51 | 34 | 3 | *150* |
| **Nationality** | | | | | |
| Switzerland | 71 | 12 | 15 | 3 | *594* |
| France | 40 | 9 | 49 | 2 | *57* |
| Germany or Austria | 82 | 13 | 5 | 0 | *39* |
| Italy, Portugal or Spain | 62 | 19 | 14 | 4 | *77* |
| Non-European Union countries | 77 | 0 | 21 | 2 | *106* |
| **Plant** | | | | | |
| Plant 1 (Geneva) (6.9%; 21 months) | 44 | 8 | 46 | 2 | *102* |
| Plant 2 (Biel) (5.5%; 22 months) | 70 | 4 | 22 | 4 | *177* |
| Plant 3 (NWS 1) (3.3%; 34 months) | 80 | 8 | 9 | 4 | *240* |
| Plant 4 (Bern) (2.5–2.9%; 15–24 months) | 61 | 28 | 10 | 1 | *221* |
| Plant 5 (NWS 2) (4.6–5.0%; 20–25 months) | 82 | 1 | 15 | 2 | *147* |
| Total | 69 | 11 | 17 | 3 | |

Note: N(total)=887, N(sex)=886, N(education)=853, N(collar)=872, N(age)=865, N(nationality)=881, N(plant)=887. The rows add up to 100%. For every plant we indicate in brackets the unemployment rate at the district level in the month after the displacement and the number of months between the displacement and the survey. Pearson chi$^2$ tests and Fisher's exact tests indicate significant relationships at the level $p<0.01$ between employment status on the one hand and sex, education, collar, age, nationality, plant on the other

An analysis of more detailed educational categories (not shown) reveals that workers with a pre-apprenticeship were the least often reemployed (55% as compared to 69–73% for the other educational categories) and by far the most often unemployed (35% as compared to 11–18%). But the sample size of this group is small (n=29) and therefore the results have to be read with caution. Interestingly, the analysis also shows that workers with tertiary *vocational* education had the highest reemployment (73%) and the lowest unemployment rate (11%). Workers with a university degree instead had a slightly lower reemployment rate (71%) and a higher unemployment rate (15%).

The type of collar did not make a large difference regarding reemployment, but with respect to unemployment. Among the white-collar workers (managers, professionals, technicians and clerks) 71% found a new job while this was the case for 68% of the blue-collar workers (craft workers, machine operators and assemblers and elementary occupations). Regarding unemployment, 13% of the white-collar workers were without a job, as against 19% of the blue-collar workers. If we combine those in unemployment and those out of the labor force, the contrast is stronger: while 22% of the blue-collar workers were inactive, this was the case for only 15% of the white-collars. There is also a substantial difference regarding retirement: 14% for white-collars versus 9% for blue-collars. This difference is entirely due to early retirement: 11% of the white-collars and only 6% of the blue-collars retired early.

If we look into more detailed occupational groups we find that workers in elementary occupations (59%) and clerks (62%) had the lowest reemployment and the highest unemployment rates (22% and 23%). In contrast, managers (79%), plant operators (72%) and technicians (72%) had the highest reemployment and the lowest unemployment rates (3%, 17% and 14%). This result confirms that the type of collar did not importantly affect reemployment: white-collars (comprising managers, technicians and clerks) and blue-collars (comprising plant operators and elementary occupations) are represented among the occupations with both the highest and lowest reemployment rate.

The strongest differences exist between age categories. While among workers aged 16–50 over 82% were reemployed 2 years after the survey, this was the case for only 53% of those aged 55–59 and for only 13% of those over 60. This difference may be partly explained by the fact that workers in this age group have the possibility of retiring. Indeed, 15% of the 55–59 year olds and 49% of the 60–64 year olds retired. However, a large proportion of the older workers who were not reemployed at the moment of the survey were unemployed: 30% of the 55–59 year olds and 36% of the 60–64 year olds.

If we look at nationality, we find that workers from Germany and Austria had the highest reemployment (82%) and the lowest unemployment rate (5%). Workers from non-European Union countries – such as citizens from Turkey or Kosovo – had the second highest reemployment (75%) but also the second highest unemployment rate (21%). This result is due to the fact that almost none of them retired or quit the labor force. The Swiss as well as the Italian, Portuguese and Spanish have intermediate rates of reemployment (71% and 62% respectively) and unemployment (15% and 14% respectively). Citizens from these Southern countries of the European Union went more often into retirement than other workers (19%). Finally, the French workers have a particularly low reemployment rate (40%) and a very high unemployment rate (49%). This result may be due to the fact that the plant in Geneva employed a large number of French citizens living in neighboring France – and these workers encountered particular difficulties in finding a job. This may be due both to a more adverse economic situation in the Geneva area and to the functioning of the French unemployment insurance system which enables workers to transit into early retirement from a much lower age than in Switzerland while being formally unemployed.[1]

Large differences in the reemployment rates can also be identified between the workers of the five different plants. One explanation may be the differences in regional unemployment rates. In the month after the displacement the unemployment rate was only 2.5–2.9% in the district where Plant 4 (Bern) was located, while it was 6.9% in the district where Plant 1 (Geneva) was located. The particularly high level of unemployment in Plant 1 may also be due to the fact – mentioned above – that a large share of its workers were cross-border workers from France, where the labor market prospects were generally gloomier.

## 3.3 Determinants of Reemployment

We now analyze the net influence of an array of socio-demographic and contextual factors on the likelihood of being reemployed by means of a multinomial logistic regression. Our dependent variable is the post-displacement labor market status. We distinguish between three outcomes: (i) reemployed, (ii) retired, and (iii) unemployed or out of the labor force.[2] We combine the unemployed and labor force dropouts in one category because most of the labor force dropouts have tried to search for a job and we thus assume that they quit the labor force because they were not successful in finding a job. As independent variables we use education, age, tenure, nationality and district unemployment rate. We estimate a model with the covariates education, age, tenure, nationality, district unemployment, duration since displacement, sex, civil status, collar, and plant. Since in nonlinear models – such as logistic regressions – the coefficients are only able to indicate the significance and the direction of the effect, we calculate the average marginal effects (AME), which provide us additionally with information about the size of the effect (Bornmann and

---

[1] Although the benefits for older unemployed workers were becoming less favorable in the aftermath of the crisis, in 2008 unemployed workers were exempted from job search from the age of 57.5 (Source: Droit Finances: http://droit-finances.commentcamarche.net/, Pole Emploi: www.pole-emploi.fr)

[2] In order to test the robustness of our results, we complemented the multinomial with binomial logistic regression models with the same independent variables, distinguishing between being (i) reemployed and (ii) unemployed or out of the labor force. Since the retirees are excluded from this analysis the sample size is smaller (N–581). The outcomes were basically the same.

Williams 2013: 567). Since our data are nested at the plant level, we use clustered standard errors.

Figure 3.3 indicates that education matters for job prospects even if we control for all other covariates. Workers with upper secondary education have 6 percentage points better reemployment prospects than workers without. Tertiary education proves to be even more important with an advantage of 8 percentage points as compared to less than upper secondary education. Our hypothesis H1 that more highly educated workers have better chances on the labor market thus seems to be supported.[3]

However, age has an even stronger effect on the chance of being reemployed than education. Workers aged over 55 have significantly lower prospects than those under 30. More precisely, workers aged 55–59 have a 28 percentage points lower and workers aged over 59 a 50 percentage points lower chance of finding a job. The importance of age also becomes evident if we consider the pseudo $R^2$ (not shown): no other independent variable affects the model fit of our data more strongly than age.[4]

In a life-course perspective, a situation where young workers experience the most detrimental effects is the worst, the argument being that if workers experience hardship at a young age, they will suffer cumulative disadvantages over their lifetime. At the same time, our result implies that even if job loss happens late in workers' so far continuous careers, they are not immune to calamity.

Our findings for tenure are not certain. Although workers with intermediate tenure (6–10 years) are slightly but significantly less likely to be reemployed than workers with a tenure of under 2 years, this result does not correspond to the prediction based on labor market theory. We therefore cannot adequately interpret this result.

With respect to nationality, we find that French workers have significantly lower reemployment prospects than workers with Swiss nationality, the difference amounting to 6 percentage points. This finding is probably not due to workers' nationality *per se,* but to the country in which they live – the local labor market situation. We therefore tested an additional model where we inserted a control for "country of residence".[5] Indeed, this variable picks up the effect of French nationality, workers

---

[3] We also ran an analysis with more detailed educational categories. We found that as compared to workers without upper secondary education, all higher educational levels provide statistically significant positive effects – with the exception of pre-apprenticeship, which is a short form of apprenticeship. The best reemployment prospects were found for workers with a degree from a university of applied sciences.

[4] We also tested models using age squared and tenure squared but the results were basically the same. In addition, we created more detailed age variables. Using an age variable with 12 categories (instead of 6 categories as shown in Table 3.2) resulted in significantly lower reemployment prospects for workers over the age of 53 (significant at $p<0.1$), over the age of 57 (significant at $p<0.01$) and over the age of 61 (significant at $p<0.01$) as compared to workers aged 33 to 36.

[5] The results are included in Figure 3.3 since the inclusion of the country of residence substantially decreases our sample size. 26% of the workers living in France are of Swiss nationality ($n=16$). The negative effect of living in France remains if we compute the model only for Plant 1.

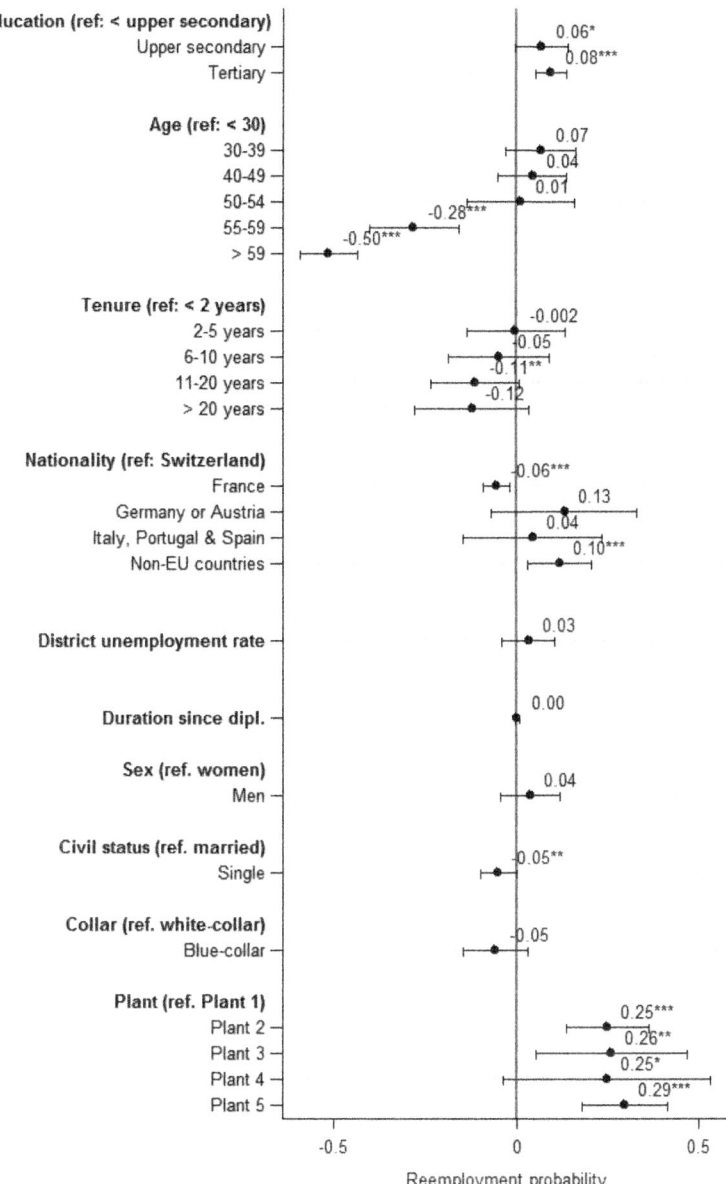

**Fig. 3.3** Average marginal effects (*AME*) for a multinomial logistic regression for being reemployed. N=664. Note: The dependent variable is multinomial and differentiates between three outcomes: (i) employed, (ii) unemployed or out of the labor force and (iii) retired. Only the AME for (i) relative to (ii) are shown. The second outcome – (iii) as compared to (ii) – is mainly determined by age and therefore of minor interest here. Significance levels: * p<0.1, ** p<0.05, *** p<0.01. Standard errors are clustered at the plant level. We tested whether there is collinearity between education and occupation. The correlation between education and collar is −0.46 (and −0.51 between education and ISCO 1-digit occupational groups). However, although the correlation is rather high, the result for collar barely changes if we drop education from the regression analysis. Finally, we also tested whether the negative effect of age remains if we include a measure for change of occupation. The age effect indeed remained significant. Reading example: As compared to workers with less than upper secondary education, workers with upper secondary education are 6 percentage points and workers with tertiary education 8 percentage points more likely to be reemployed

who live in France having 18 percentage points lower reemployment prospects than workers living in Switzerland.

Returning to our analysis of the effect of nationality on workers' reemployment prospects, we find moreover that workers from non-EU countries have a significantly higher chance of being reemployed than Swiss workers of 10 percentage points. As discussed earlier, this result primarily reflects the low probability of workers with a non-EU nationality transiting into retirement but not their low likelihood of being unemployed.

The district unemployment rate does not seem to have an impact on workers' reemployment chances if we control for plants. The district unemployment rate only becomes significant if we construct categories. Under this condition, workers who live in a district with an unemployment rate of over 6 % are significantly less likely to find a job than those in a district with less than 3 % unemployment.[6] For the other categories, the effect is not significant.

With respect to civil status, our analysis shows that workers who are single are 5 percentage points less likely to find a job than those who are married or have a partner. A plausible explanation may be that workers with a partner (and possibly children – a variable that we cannot control for, for lack of information) were more strongly under pressure to return to employment than workers without family obligations. In addition, single workers are probably more likely to retire early since they are more flexible than married partners who tend to retire together (Rice et al. 2011).

The reemployment prospects are in all models significantly worse for the workers of Plant 1 (Geneva), even after controlling for the district unemployment rate and the workers' nationality. Accordingly, the labor market context of Geneva makes it much more difficult for unemployed workers to find their way back into employment. As discussed above, a potential reason for this result may be that a large share of the workers in Plant 1 live in France. Yet, even if we include the variable "country of residence" in the analysis, we still find that workers of Plant 1 (Geneva) have a significantly lower chance of finding a new job than workers of Plants 2 (Biel) and 5 (NWS 2). Thus, the potential explanation mentioned earlier does not seem to turn out to be correct: the effect we find for Plant 1 is apparently not due to the fact that a large proportion of workers in this plant live in France. An alternative explanation may be that workers of Plant 1 have had fewer incentives to search for a job because of a particularly favorable redundancy plan. Although the redundancy plans in Plants 3 (NWS 1), 4 (Bern) and 5 (NWS 2) also provided a financial compensation for job loss, we learned that workers in Plant 1 received their termination pay in the form of a higher wage for their last 3 months in the plant. As the unemployment benefits are based on the last 6 monthly wages, this measure led to comparatively higher unemployment benefits for workers in Plant 1 (Geneva). This may have indirectly contributed to the lower reemployment rate in Plant 1 as workers in this plant felt less pressure to find a job and possibly had a

---

[6] We also entered the district unemployment in a quadratic form. However, the square term did not reveal a significant effect.

3.3 Determinants of Reemployment

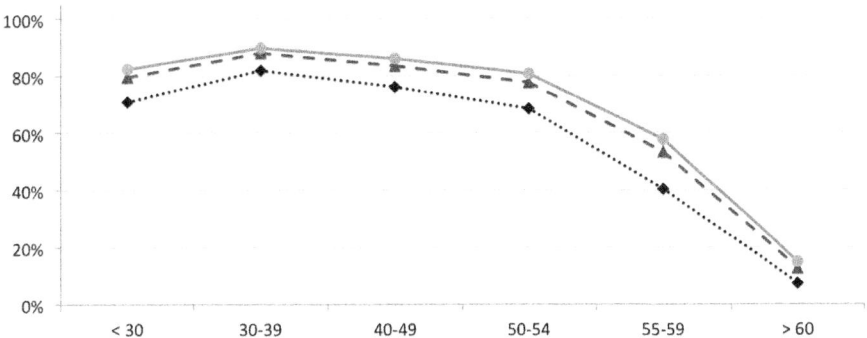

**Fig. 3.4** Predicted probability for a blue-collar Swiss married man to be reemployed (as compared to being unemployed or out of the labor force) by age and educational groups (Based on analyses conducted for Fig. 3.3). N=664

higher reservation wage than the workers in the other plants. However, the differences between the plants do not seem to be solely due to the specificities of the redundancy plans. The plant with the highest reemployment prospects – even after controlling for covariates – was not Plant 2 (Biel) without a redundancy plan but Plant 5 (NWS 2), where a redundancy plan existed.

This finding is again interesting in terms of the life-course paradigm which highlights the relevance of contextual factors. Our result shows that, depending on the geographic context with its specific features such as local institutions or culture, outcomes can be strongly divergent. In order to test whether our results are driven more strongly by some plants, we ran Model 5 for each plant separately (not shown).[7] Since the number of observations in these analyses is small, the standard errors are in some cases very large and the results thus not very robust. However, the analyses seem to confirm the finding that older workers are less likely to be reemployed than younger workers – the result being mainly driven by Plants 1 (Geneva) and 5 (NWS 2) and to a lesser extent by Plant 3 (NWS 1).

Figure 3.3 reveals that education and age play an important role in displaced workers' reemployment. In order to illustrate these findings, we graphically present the probability for a blue-collar Swiss married man (the modal category) to be reemployed, holding collar, nationality and civil status constant and varying only education and age. With respect to the effect of education, Fig. 3.4 shows that workers who have no upper secondary education have the lowest reemployment chances across all age cohorts. Interestingly, the difference between workers with upper secondary and tertiary education is very small, but the size of the difference is consistent across age groups. The finding that education has a positive impact on workers' reemployment prospects confirms our hypothesis H1. The effect is, however, less strong than we expected. One reason for this outcome may be that the education variable does not appropriately measure what we intended to assess, namely

---

[7] The result for Plant 2 did not achieve convergence and thus revealed no result.

workers' skills. Probably, the availability of information about work experience or attended continuous training throughout workers' career would allow us to assess their skill profile more precisely. A broader, more encompassing measure of workers' skills may have provided us with more explanatory power.

With respect to the effect of education, our results are in line with earlier research. Wyss (2009) finds for Switzerland that low-educated workers have a probability of being unemployed of 26%, workers with an intermediate level of education a probability of 23% and highly qualified workers a substantially lower probability of 4%. Tertiary education thus protects workers best by far from unemployment. This last result stands in contrast to our study where both upper secondary *and* tertiary education reduce the risk of unemployment. For the US, Kletzer (2001: 49–51) finds that manufacturing workers with a college degree (tertiary education) have a 13 percentage points higher reemployment rate than workers with a high school degree (upper secondary education). The study finds that the educational level more strongly affects the reemployment prospects of younger workers (under 45) than of older workers. This finding contradicts our results – at least for male Swiss blue-collar workers – where the educational level matters more for older than for younger workers (see Fig. 3.3). Overall it thus seems that in the US the workers' level of education plays a slightly more important role than in Switzerland.

With respect to the effect of age, Fig. 3.4 confirms that age can been singled out as the most important factor determining whether workers are reemployed or unemployed 2 years after their displacement. This finding conforms to other displaced worker studies. The Swiss study by Wyss (2009: 40–1) reports for workers over 55 a likelihood of over 20% of remaining in unemployment, whereas workers between 46 and 55 only have a 3% likelihood and those under 46 a less than 1% likelihood. Jolkkonen et al. (2012: 88) find for Finland that the workers' disadvantage in terms of reemployment starts from the age of 40. The most severe handicap is however experienced by workers over 50. A US study by Farber (1997: 93) based on the Displaced Worker Survey finds that workers over the age of 55 have about 20 percentage points lower reemployment prospects than younger workers. This result has been confirmed by the same author in a later study where he shows that for workers over 55 the proportion of the reemployed oscillates between 40% and 60% and for younger workers between 60% and 80%, depending on the business cycle (Farber 2005: 18–9).

Other studies from Switzerland have come to similar conclusions about older job seekers' vulnerability in the labor market. A recent report by the OECD (2014aPlease fix "a" or "b" for OCED (2014)., b: 19) shows that the reemployment rate of workers between 55 and 64 is comparatively low for Switzerland and below the average of the European Union. As mentioned above, Wyss (2009: 40–1) reports that an advanced age is one of the main disadvantages after job loss in Switzerland. A qualitative study in which Swiss employers were interviewed about their hiring practices finds that employers clearly target young workers when they have a lack of skilled personnel (Trageser and Hammer 2012: 363).

Our finding that older workers suffer most from plant closure contradicts one strand of the international literature which argues that labor market institutions are biased primarily against young workers (Allmendinger 1989; Blanchflower and Freeman 2000; Gangl 2002; Breen 2005). A possible explanation for our contrasting result may be that in Switzerland young workers are comparatively well integrated into the labor market. With its weak employment protection and a highly standardized vocational training system that signals workers' productivity, employers in Switzerland may be less reluctant to hire young workers than in other contexts. It thus seems that the age-bias in Switzerland rather disadvantages older workers but not the young.

Yet, the scope of the negative age effect on workers' reemployment prospects may not have been fully assessed by the international job displacement literature since analyses often do not include workers over 60. For instance, the study by Eliason and Storrie (2006) based on Swedish data and the study by Jacobson et al. (1993) based on administrative data from Pennsylvania include only workers up to age 50. The study by Couch (2001) using German longitudinal data examines workers up to age 55. In our study in contrast, workers over age 54 constitute 28% – and thus a large proportion – of the sample.

Theoretically, our finding is not easy to explain. It is possible that factors that we do not observe in our models explain older workers' difficulties. For instance, older workers may be less productive than younger workers. However, this view does not seem to hold, as studies have shown that age *per se* does not provide reliable information about workers' productivity. A study from Austria that measures productivity at the firm level claims that there is no link between age and productivity (Mahlberg et al. 2013: 11). A Dutch study shows that although *physical* productivity decreases after the age of 40, *cognitive* productivity is not affected by age (van Ours 2010: 457). If, however, older workers are not hired because they are physically less productive, only older workers in physically demanding occupations – blue-collar occupations – would face hurdles when trying to return to employment. In other words, we would have to find a difference between blue- and white-collar workers in our data. However, this is not the case and we find no evidence that older workers' encounter less difficulty in finding a new job if they have an occupation that foremost demands cognitive skills.

An alternative explanation may be that generous welfare provisions cause the age effect by making it interesting for older workers to wait for retirement by remaining unemployed for a while. However, this assumption does not seem to hold: First, unemployment benefits for workers over 55 are limited to a maximum of 2 years and there are few incentives to retire early in Switzerland. Accordingly, without early retirement plan as contained in some redundancy plans, it would be difficult to remain without working until regular retirement age. Second, further analyses show that unemployed workers over 54 made strong efforts to apply for jobs: 26% of them applied for 50–100 jobs and 46% for over 100 jobs (see Fig. A.2 in the Annex). As compared to younger unemployed workers, those over 54 put the greatest effort into the job search. Third, the unemployed aged between 55 and 59 experience a stronger decrease in overall life satisfaction (−3.4 points on an 11-point scale) as compared to the unemployed on average (−2.8 points). This finding suggests that older workers' unemployment is involuntary.

With respect to the explanatory factors collar, nationality and sex, our results contrast with other earlier findings: unlike Fallick (1996: 7), Kletzer (2001) and Jolkkonen et al. (2012: 88), we could not identify a substantial effect of the workers' collar on their reemployment prospects. Similarly, in contrast to studies from the US by Hamermesh (1989: 54) and Farber (1997: 93), nationality and sex do not seem to play a central role in the context of our study.

## 3.4 Conclusion

In sum, in this chapter we have shown that about two-thirds of the displaced workers were back in employment about 2 years after displacement. 17 % of the workers were still or again unemployed at that moment, 3 % out of the labor force and 11 % retired. Reemployment is most strongly determined by workers' age. Workers aged over 55 encounter much more difficulty in finding a job than younger workers. Our hypothesis H1 that older workers face barriers after job loss can thus clearly be confirmed. With respect to education, workers with higher levels of education do have an advantage in terms of reemployment, as our hypothesis H1 predicted. However, education seems to make a less strong difference than age.

Comparing the displaced workers to a control group based on the Swiss Household Panel shows that displaced workers have a significantly and much higher risk of being unemployed 2 years after job loss. The experience of plant closure thus does have a clearly negative impact on workers' career prospects. However, as discussed in Chap. 2, the control and the treatment group are alike in terms of age but not in terms of education and sex. The control group contains a larger share of women and of workers with higher levels of education. Our estimation of the counterfactual outcome may therefore overestimate the employment rates and underestimate the unemployment rates since our analysis suggests that a tertiary-level of education positively affects workers' employment prospects. At the same time, since the control and treatment group are alike with respect to age, the variable that affects career outcomes most strongly, the counterfactual outcome may not be too strongly miscalculated.

How do these results contribute to the previous literature on labor market transitions after plant closure? First, these results indicate which worker subgroups are the most likely to experience a relatively smooth transition after job displacement: the younger and the better-educated workers. At the same time, they show which workers are the most vulnerable in the aftermath of plant closure: older workers. Second, it seems that following plant closures in the Swiss manufacturing sector, most workers are able to find a job. With the exception of the two oldest age cohorts, we find little evidence for the bleak expectation held by some scholars that displaced industrial workers are condemned to long-lasting unemployment.

In this chapter we have provided evidence for the scope of the impact plant closure has on workers' employment prospects. This finding allows policy makers to anticipate the extent of support that workers may need after non-self-inflicted job loss. Moreover, showing which groups of workers are the most vulnerable to long-term unemployment helps to develop more targeted assistance that is more effective in eventually bringing them back to employment.

**Open Access** This chapter is distributed under the terms of the Creative Commons Attribution 4.0 International License (http://creativecommons.org/licenses/by/4.0/), which permits use, duplication, adaptation, distribution and reproduction in any medium or format, as long as you give appropriate credit to the original author(s) and the source, a link is provided to the Creative Commons license and any changes made are indicated.

The images or other third party material in this chapter are included in the work's Creative Commons license, unless indicated otherwise in the credit line; if such material is not included in the work's Creative Commons license and the respective action is not permitted by statutory regulation, users will need to obtain permission from the license holder to duplicate, adapt or reproduce the material.

## References

Allmendinger, J. (1989). Educational systems and labor market outcomes. *European Sociological Review, 5*(3), 231–250.

Blanchflower, D. G., & Freeman, R. B. (2000). The declining economic status of young workers in OECD countries. In D. G. Blanchflower & R. B. Freeman (Eds.), *Youth employment and joblessness in advanced countries*. Chicago: Chicago University Press.

Bornmann, L., & Williams, R. (2013). How to calculate the practical significance of citation impact differences? An empirical example from evaluative institutional bibliometrics using adjusted predictions and marginal effects. *Journal of Informetrics, 7*(2), 562–574.

Breen, R. (2005). Explaining cross-national variation in youth unemployment. Market and institutional factors. *European Sociological Review, 21*(2), 125–134.

Couch, K. A. (2001). Earning losses and unemployment of displaced workers in Germany. *Industrial and Labor Relations Review, 54*(3), 559–572.

Devens, R. M., Jr. (1986). Displaced workers: One year later. *Monthly Labor Review, 109*(7), 40–43.

Eliason, M., & Storrie, D. (2006). Lasting or latent scars? Swedish evidence on the long term effects of job displacement. *Journal of Labor Economics, 24*(4), 831–856.

Fallick, B. C. (1996). A review of the recent empirical literature on displaced workers. *Industrial and Labor Relations Review, 50*(1), 5–16.

Farber, H. S. (1997). The changing face of job loss in the United States, 1981–1995. *Brookings Papers on Economic Activity. Microeconomics, 1997*(1997), 55–142.

Farber, H. S. (2005). What do we know about job loss in the United States? Evidence from the displaced workers survey, 1984–2004. *Federal Reserve Bank of Chicago, 2Q*, 13–28.

Gangl, M. (2002). *The only way is up? Employment protection and job mobility among recent entrants to European labour markets* (Working paper of the Mannheimer Zentrum für Europäische Sozialforschung no 48). Mannheim: MZES.

Gibbons, R., & Katz, L. F. (1991). Layoffs and lemons. *Journal of Labor Economics, 9*(4), 351–380.

Hamermesh, D. S. (1989). What do we know about worker displacement in the U.S.? *Industrial Relations, 28*(1), 51–59.

Jacobson, L. S., LaLonde, R. J., & Sullivan, D. G. (1993). Earning losses of displaced workers. *The American Economic Review, 83*(4), 685–709.

Jolkkonen, A., Koistinen, P., & Kurvinen, A. (2012). Reemployment of displaced workers – The case of a plant closing on a remote region in Finland. *Nordic Journal of Working Life Studies, 2*(1), 81–100.

Kletzer, L. G. (2001). *Job loss from imports: Measuring the costs*. Washington, DC: Institute for International Economics.

Kuhn, P. J. (Ed.). (2002). *Losing work, moving on: International perspectives on worker displacement*. Kalamazoo: W.E. Upjohn Institute for Employment Research.

Mahlberg, B., Freund, I., Crespo Cuaresma, J., & Prskawetz, A. (2013). Ageing, productivity and wages in Austria. *Labour Economics, 22*(100), 5–15.

OECD. (2014a). *Schweiz. Bessere Arbeit im Alter*. Paris: OECD Publishing.

OECD. (2014b). *Education at a glance 2014: OECD indicators*. Paris: OECD Publishing.

Oesch, D., & Baumann, I. (2015). Smooth transition or permanent exit? Evidence on job prospects of displaced industrial workers. *Socio-Economic Review, 13*(1), 101–123.

Rice, N. E., Lang, I. A., Henley, W., & Melzer, D. (2011). Common health predictors of early retirement: Findings from the english longitudinal study of ageing. *Age and Ageing, 40*(1), 54–61.

Trageser, J., & Hammer, S. (2012). Altersrücktritt im Kontext der demographischen Entwicklung. *Soziale Sicherheit CHSS, 6*, 361–364.

Van Ours, J. C. (2010). Will you still need me: When I'm 64? *De Economist, 157*(4), 441–460.

Weder, R., & Wyss, S. (2010). *Arbeitslosigkeit unter niedrig Qualifizierten: Die Rolle der Globalisierung* (SECO Publikation Arbeitsmarktpolitik No. 29). Bern: SECO.

Wyss, S. (2009). *Stellenverlust und Lohneinbusse durch die Globalisierung ?* University of Basel, Wirtschaftswissenschaftliches Zentrum der Universität Basel Working Paper No. 05/09

# Chapter 4
# Early Retirement and Exit from the Labor Force

In the light of older workers' difficulties in returning to employment after job displacement it is fundamental to analyze a third pathway older workers may take beside reemployment and unemployment: early retirement. The question here at stake is whether workers are involuntarily pushed out of the labor market and subsequently suffer from social exclusion or whether they experience this option as an alleviation of their critical situation. Some studies have shown that older job seekers choose this pathway primarily as a better alternative to long-term unemployment (Chan and Stevens 2001; Ichino et al. 2007). Other studies found that pull factors such as generous early retirement plans, being financially well off or having an economically inactive spouse may incite older workers to leave the labor force before the official retirement age (Knuth and Kalina 2002: 414).

Starting from the hypothesis H2 (see Sect. 1.4) that push factors better explain the mechanisms underlying older workers' transition into early retirement than pull factors, this chapter analyzes displaced workers' transition into early retirement, focusing on workers over 55 but excluding those workers who reached the official retirement age (that is, 64 for women and 65 for men). We first present the overall probability of retiring early. We then describe the factors that may be linked to the workers' transition into early retirement. In a next step we analyze the effect of explanatory factors by means of a regression analysis. Finally, we discuss whether the early retirement plans, which were provided by the plants, may have affected workers in their decision to retire early. We use well-being measures to help us in our interpretation.

## 4.1 Transition into Early Retirement

Our data reveals that a considerable proportion of workers went into early retirement. Taking workers of all age cohorts together, 8 % retired early, and among the workers aged over 55, the proportion of early retirees is 32 % – almost a

**Table 4.1** Proportion of workers aged 56–64 in early retirement, reemployment and unemployment by different characteristics (in %)

|  | Early-retired | Reemployed | Unemployed |
|---|---|---|---|
| Number of job applications | | | |
| <11 | 27 | 27 | 13 |
| 11–50 | 45 | 33 | 17 |
| 51–100 | 18 | 22 | 26 |
| >100 | 9 | 18 | 44 |
| Pre-displacement gross monthly wage | | | |
| CHF <5000 | 5 | 4 | 8 |
| CHF 5000–5999 | 18 | 4 | 22 |
| CHF 6000–6999 | 28 | 41 | 32 |
| CHF 7000–7999 | 22 | 18 | 18 |
| CHF >7999 | 27 | 33 | 33 |
| Economically active partner | | | |
| Yes | 49 | 85 | 58 |
| No | 51 | 15 | 42 |
| Plant | | | |
| Plant 1 (Geneva) | 4 | 0 | 40 |
| Plant 2 (Biel) | 3 | 28 | 30 |
| Plant 3 (NWS 1) | 15 | 35 | 16 |
| Plant 4 (Bern) | 76 | 17 | 5 |
| Plant 5 (NWS 2) | 1 | 20 | 9 |
| Sex | | | |
| Women | 3 | 12 | 6 |
| Men | 97 | 88 | 94 |
| Total in % | 32 | 31 | 37 |
| *Total N max* | 67 | 65 | 77 |

Note: For each category, every column sums up to 100 %. Regularly retired workers are excluded from the analysis

third – while only 31 % of the workers in this age category were reemployed and 37 % were unemployed.

In a next step we examine whether this pathway was chosen by the workers rather because of push or pull factors. In Table 4.1 we present the descriptive analysis of the proportions *of workers aged 56 to 64* in early retirement, reemployment and unemployment by the number of applications written, pre-displacement wage, presence of an economically active partner, plant and sex.

We find that older workers who retired early are more strongly represented among those who wrote *less* than 50 applications than among those who applied *more* than 50 times. For older workers in unemployment the opposite is the case. This suggests that the early retirees did not search for a job as intensively as the older workers who returned to employment or who still were unemployed.

Regarding the workers' pre-displacement wage, workers who retired early have about the same probability of having an income over CHF 7000 (49 %) as reemployed

4.2 Determinants of Early Retirement

and unemployed older workers (each 51%). In addition, we find that 23% of the workers who retired early had a pre-displacement income of under CHF 6000 while this is true for only 8% of the reemployed. The pattern contradicts the possible expectation that workers with higher wages are more likely to retire early and that workers with lower wages are constraint to carry on working until their official retirement age. With respect to the availability of an economically active partner, the early-retired are much more likely to be *without* a working partner (51%) than the reemployed (14%) and slightly more likely than the unemployed (42%). Thus, having a spouse who is not working may be an incentive for older workers to step back from the active work life.

With respect to the plant we find that among the early retirees most of them were employed in Plant 4 (76%) before displacement. In contrast, workers from Plants 1, 2 and 5 make up together only 8% while workers from Plant 3 represent 15% of all early retirees. If we turn to reemployment it is striking that none of the older workers in Plant 1 in Geneva was reemployed. This finding may be explained by workers being residents of France where they have access to unemployment benefits for an unlimited duration beginning at age 57.5. Evidence for this assumption is provided by the fact that workers from Plant 1 constitute 40% of the unemployed workers. Workers from the other companies represent between 17 and 35% of the reemployed. Finally, women constitute only 3% of the early retirees while they make up 12% of the reemployed. This may indicate that women less often have the opportunity to retire early because of financial reasons.

## 4.2 Determinants of Early Retirement

In order to measure the net effect of the factors discussed above, we continue with a multinomial logistic regression analysis, presented in Fig. 4.1. Our dependent variable is "going into early retirement" as compared to being "reemployed" or "unemployed or out of the labor force". We run a model for going into early retirement, relative to being reemployed. We enter the variables age, sex, education, plant (as a proxy for the redundancy plan), wage and economic activity of the partner. It was not possible to include the number of workers' job applications in the model because this information is available for too small a number of early-retired workers to produce robust results. We restrict our analysis to workers aged 56–64 and exclude workers who retired regularly. In order to test the robustness of the results, we also estimated two types of binomial models where we compare first workers who retired early with workers who were reemployed and second workers who retired early with workers who were reemployed, unemployed or out of the labor force. The results that are similar to the findings from the multinomial analysis.

Our analysis shows that the closer the workers are to the regular retirement age, the higher is the likelihood of retiring early, a result that is entirely plausible as with each year the cuts in pension benefits that workers have to accept when retiring early becomes less burdensome. We find a large and significant effect for sex, men

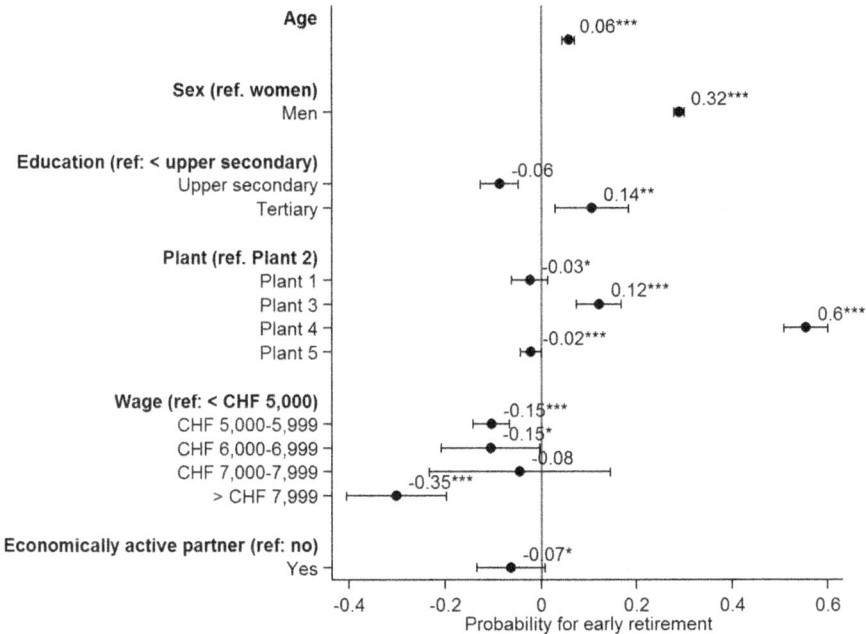

**Fig. 4.1** Average marginal effects (AME) for a multinomial logistic regression for going into early retirement for workers aged 56–64. N=141. Note: The dependent variable is multinomial and differentiates between three outcomes: (i) early-retired, (ii) reemployed and (iii) unemployed or out of the labor force. Only workers aged 56 to 64 are included and the regular retirees are excluded. Standard errors are clustered at the plant level. Significance levels: * $p < 0.1$, ** $p < 0.05$, *** $p < 0.01$. Significance levels: * $p < 0.1$, ** $p < 0.05$, *** $p < 0.01$. Reading example: With each year in age workers' probability of retiring early increases by 6 percentage points

being 32 percentage points more likely than women to retire early relative to being reemployed, unemployed, or out of the labor force. Workers with tertiary education were 14 percentage points more likely to retire early than workers without upper secondary education. For the variable plant we use Plant 2 as reference category since this plant was the only one without a redundancy plan. Workers in Plants 1 and 5 seem to be slightly (2–3 percentage points) less likely to retire early as compared to workers in Plant 2 (reference category). Workers in Plant 3 are 12 and – most noteworthy – workers in Plant 4 60 percentage points more likely to retire early than workers in Plant 2. A possible explanation for these results may be the redundancy plans. Whether they are relevant will be discussed later. With respect to wage we find that workers with an income of CHF 5000–6999 are 15 percentage points less likely to retire early as compared to those with an income below CHF 5000. Interestingly, workers in the highest wage category (CHF>7999) are the least likely to retire early relative to becoming reemployed. This result suggests that workers with higher wages have more enjoyable jobs and continue to work until the regular retirement age. Finally, workers with an economically active partner are 7 percentage points less likely to retire early than workers with a non-active partner.

4.2 Determinants of Early Retirement

**Table 4.2** Retirement-related features of the redundancy plans

| Plant | Early retirement provisions in general | Example for a 60-year-old man with 15 years' tenure and previous gross monthly wage of CHF 6000 |
|---|---|---|
| 1 (Geneva) | *Age limit*: 62 (men), 61 (women) | – |
| | *Benefits*: One-off payment of CHF 20,000 for workers with 36+ years' tenure, 16,000 for 31+ tenure, 13,000 for 26+ tenure and 10,000 for 25+ tenure. 7000 for workers with young children. For French residents: Top-up of unemployment benefits up to 60 % of former wage (without 13th monthly wage). Contribution to old-age pension fund guaranteed. | |
| 2 (Biel) | – (no redundancy plan) | – |
| 3 (NWS 1) | *Age limit*: 60 (men), 59 (women) | CHF 4500/month |
| | *Benefits*: at least 70 % of former wage (13th monthly wage incl.) or at least CHF 4500/month | |
| 4 (Bern) | *Age limit*: 56.5 | $\approx$ CHF 2500/month (90 % of regular pension rate to which he is entitled at age 65, which depends on the years worked and the salary earned) |
| | *Benefits*: 100 % of regular pension for age 63+, 90 % of regular pension for age 60+, CHF 4000/month until age 60, 90 % of regular pension for age 56.5+ | |
| 5 (NWS 2) | *Age limit*: 58 | 1500 CHF/month (¼ of former wage) |
| | *Benefits*: 5/12 of annual salary for 30+ years' tenure, 4/12 for 20+ years', 3/12 for 10+ years, 2/12 for under 10 years | |

When we tested different models introducing all or only a selection of the discussed covariates, we observed that the introduction of the variable plant into the model strongly increases the models' goodness of fit (pseudo $R^2$). This suggests that the differences between plants decisively contribute to the explanation of workers' entry into early retirement. Perhaps workers were incited to retire early by the redundancy plans negotiated between the employees' and employers' representatives, some redundancy plans indeed containing extensive early retirement provisions.

In Table 4.2, we present an overview of the redundancy plans and calculate the benefits for an exemplary worker aged 60 with 15 years of tenure and a pre-displacement wage of CHF 6000. Plant 1 located in Geneva provides men over the age of 62 and women over the age of 61 with early retirement benefits that depend on their tenure. Workers with at least 25 years' tenure received a one-off payment of CHF 10,000 while workers with at least 36 years received CHF 20,000. Moreover, workers received a top-up of their unemployment benefits up to 60 % of their former wage. This measure is of relevance only for workers who live in France and who are subject to the French unemployment benefit system. Workers living in Switzerland do not need this provision since they have a replacement rate of at least 70 % of their former wage if they apply for unemployment benefits. The worker in the example in

Table 4.2 does not receive early retirement provisions in Plant 1 since s/he is below the age limit.

Plant 2 close to Biel did not provide a redundancy plan. In Plant 3 in North-Western Switzerland male workers received early retirement benefits from the age of 60 and female workers from the age of 59. The provisions amounted to 70 % of the former wage inclusive of the 13th monthly wage. This leads for our exemplary worker to a monthly income of CHF 4500. Workers in Plant 4 in the Canton of Bern could request early retirement provisions from the age of 56.5 years. Dependent on their age, they received 90–100 % of the pension benefits that they would have received if they had gone into regular retirement. Since the amount of the regular retirement benefits depends on the requirements of the decentralized pension funds, we can only approximately estimate the amount of the benefits for early-retired workers in Plant 4, which is about CHF 2500.[1] In Plant 5 in North-Western Switzerland received early retirement benefits from the age of 58. The benefits depended on the tenure. For our exemplary worker this scheme results in a monthly income of CHF 1500.

To come back to the results of our regression analysis presented in Fig. 4.1, we contend that the early retirement provisions in the redundancy plan do not offer a clear-cut explanation of the much higher likelihood of retiring early of workers in Plant 4 (Bern) and the slightly higher likelihood of workers in Plant 1 (Geneva) as compared to workers in Plant 2 (Biel). Regarding Plant 4, the early retirement benefits are not as generous as in Plant 3 (NWS 1) but the age limit for receiving early retirement provisions is very low, i.e. 56.5 years. This condition probably led to the early retirement of a large proportion of workers. With respect to Plant 1 the higher propensity to retire early may stem from the fact that almost half of the workforce live in France where the transition into this gateway is facilitated by social security institutions. While in France workers over the age of 50 are entitled to 36 months of unemployment benefits, in Switzerland the maximum duration is 24 months (Schwab and Weber 2010: 40).

Finally, given the generous early retirement provisions, we would have expected workers from Plant 3 to be particularly likely to go into early retirement. This is, however, not the case and we therefore conclude that in addition to the redundancy plan other mechanisms seem to be at work. A possible factor behind the differences may have been how the provisions offered by the redundancy plan were communicated to the workers. For instance, it is conceivable that many older workers in Plant 3 (NWS 1) were not as well informed about their opportunities as workers in Plant 4 (Bern). Another possibility is that there was an effect of conformity motivating workers in Plant 4 to retire early together.[2]

Do our results rather point to the presence of pull or push mechanisms? On the one hand, the impact of age and wage suggest that push mechanisms are at work: as we have seen in the section on reemployment, older workers have much more difficulty in finding a job. Exiting the labor force into early retirement thus may be a

---

[1] This amount has been estimated with the help of Plant 4's former head of human resources.

[2] This assumption relies on qualitative information about the retired workers in this plant that they continued to meet regularly for common activities after job loss.

## 4.2 Determinants of Early Retirement

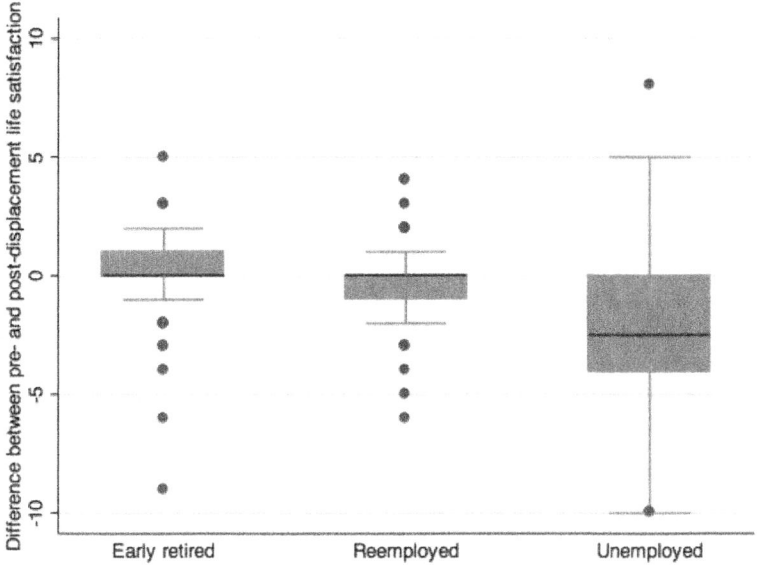

**Fig. 4.2** Change in life satisfaction before and after displacement (in points on an 11-point scale) for workers aged 56–64. N: Early-retired=63, Reemployed= 54, Unemployed=66

smooth pathway after job displacement. The finding that workers with lower wages are more likely to retire early may suggest that high wages do not have a pull effect. Alternatively, it is possible that workers with lower wages had bleaker reemployment prospects than workers with higher wages – probably related to their occupational status – and therefore had to retire early.

On the other hand, the result from the descriptive analysis regarding the number of job applications and the result from the regression analysis that belonging to Plants 1 or 4 has a positive effect on retiring early suggest that pull mechanisms are at work. The fact that the early retirees were less likely to apply *more* than 50 times for a job than workers who were reemployed or unemployed indicates that many of them did not search highly intensively. Moreover, the higher likelihood of retiring for individuals working in a plant with early retirement provisions suggests that, not surprisingly, these benefits had an inciting effect.

Overall, it is therefore difficult to tell whether pull factors are more important than push factors. As a last resort to find out whether one mechanism predominates over the other, we analyze the early retirees' change in subjective well-being between their pre- and post-displacement situation. We compare the outcome for the early retirees with the one for the reemployed and unemployed workers aged 56 to 64. The results are presented in Fig. 4.2.

We assessed workers' life satisfaction on a scale from 0 to 10 where 0 stands for not satisfied at all and 10 for very satisfied. We measure change in life satisfaction between the situation before displacement when workers were still employed and the moment of the survey. We calculate the difference between the two values by simply subtracting one value from the other. A negative value means that workers were more satisfied before displacement than after, and a positive value that they were more satisfied after displacement than before. A value of zero indicates that there was no change.

We find that the early retirees experience an average decrease in life satisfaction by 0.1 points, the reemployed by 0.3 points and the unemployed by 2.6 points. With respect to the distribution of the change in well-being, Fig. 4.2 suggests that for the early retirees the 25- and the 50-percentile levels are at zero change in life satisfaction and the 75-percentile level at 1 point increase. Accordingly, half of all early retirees lie within a very narrow range of almost no change in life satisfaction. At the same time, the dots outside of the whiskers indicate that the early retirees experience strong decreases or intermediate increases in life satisfaction. The pattern of the reemployed older workers is similar: half of the workers experienced either no change in life satisfaction or a decrease in 1 point. In contrast, the unemployed clearly experienced the strongest drop in life satisfaction, the median being a 2.5 points decrease and the 25-percentile level a 4 points decrease. Taken together, these descriptive results show that among the workers over 55, the early retirees were the least negatively affected by plant closure. This suggests that they were rather pulled than pushed out of the active labor force.

## 4.3 Exit from the Labor Force

A small proportion of workers ($n=23$) in our sample quit the labor force for training ($n=9$), childcare ($n=2$), disability ($n=7$) or other unspecified reasons ($n=5$). The theory suggests that there is an interaction effect between sex and civil status explaining labor force dropout, married women being most likely to quit the labor force. However, because of the small number of observation, we can only carry out a very rough analysis and the results are not in line with the theoretical predictions. In fact, among those in *training*, men and – not surprisingly – young workers are overrepresented. If we consider those who do *childcare*, both genders are represented. Among the *disabled*, the majority worked in typically manual occupations (craft workers, machine operators or elementary occupations) and were over 55 at the moment of displacement. In the category of *other situations* no particular sociodemographic pattern is identifiable.

With respect to these workers, it may be interesting to examine if we can find evidence for whether these workers were pushed out of the workforce (e.g. because they could not find a job) or whether they voluntarily quit the labor market. Because of small $n$, we cannot thoroughly analyze this question, but descriptive statistics can still give an idea of their potential motives. Among the labor force dropouts two-thirds searched for a job. This suggests that some of the labor force exits were a consequence of low reemployment prospects. Among the workers in "other" situations one searched for 7–9 months, one for 13–18 months and one for 19–24 months. One worker who does childcare searched for 5–6 months. In contrast, workers who have gone into training did not search longer than 2 months and among workers with disability no one indicated having searched for a job. If we look at the number of job applications that workers who quit the labor force have written, we find that among those who went into training, most of them wrote fewer than six application letters. The same is true for those with disability benefits. In contrast, the two workers in childcare and the workers in "other" situations wrote either 50–100 or more than 100 applications. This shows that the workers in childcare or other situations tried intensively to find a job and exited the labor market only when they were not successful.

Finally, an interesting finding is that workers both with an economically active partner and with an inactive partner tended to leave the labor market. This indicates that not only workers who have a second income – and thus are financially secure – dropped out. Overall, it seems difficult to generalize on the situation of the labor force dropouts. From the small number of observations available we can only maintain that the workers in this group followed individualized strategies and probably had a variety of reasons to quit the labor force.

## 4.4 Conclusion

In this chapter we have shown that although older workers faced considerable barriers to returning to the labor force, the evidence suggests that there were not only push but also pull mechanisms that led workers to choose to retire early. In fact, workers with a non-working partner and with early retirement provisions were more likely to retire early than those with an economically active partner and without provisions. Accordingly, our findings seem to contradict our hypothesis H2.

How do our findings compare with the literature about early retirement? Our outcomes do not completely confirm the results from most continental European countries that workers are involuntary pushed into early retirement. By contrast, they seem to conform to the observation by Dorn and Sousa-Poza (2010: 432) that the pathway into early retirement in Switzerland is often voluntary. Understanding the link between job displacement and retirement is crucial since it may lead to informed policy decisions about how to support older displaced workers and how to promote longer working lives (Tatsiramos 2010: 517). Teyssier and Vicens (2001: 25) contend that facilitating early retirement is a success in addressing old-age poverty, but does not enhance the social integration of workers towards the end of their careers. It thus seems that there is a trade-off between these two concerns. A potential solution would be that in the case of a plant closure early retirement provisions could not exclusively be accessed immediately after the closure but for several years after displacement. This would motivate older workers to first search for a job and only transit into early retirement if they were not able to find one. If – as is the case with most redundancy plans – workers have to decide directly after the plant closure whether to retire early, they are likely to choose the most secure option and accept the early retirement provisions instead of trying to return to the labor force.

This chapter shows that for older workers' who belonged to the age group required for early retirement usually chose this option; there is little evidence that the early-retired workers were forced into this gateway. For policy decisions this finding implies that offering older displaced workers early retirement plans, ideally including financial contributions to the social security system, allows them to overcome job loss without major calamity. If, in contrast, workers over 55 years have to search for a job, they are likely to suffer a difficult occupational transition often encompassing long-term unemployment and – as we will see in the next chapters – reemployment in precarious jobs.

**Open Access** This chapter is distributed under the terms of the Creative Commons Attribution 4.0 International License (http://creativecommons.org/licenses/by/4.0/), which permits use, duplication, adaptation, distribution and reproduction in any medium or format, as long as you give appropriate credit to the original author(s) and the source, a link is provided to the Creative Commons license and any changes made are indicated.

The images or other third party material in this chapter are included in the work's Creative Commons license, unless indicated otherwise in the credit line; if such material is not included in the work's Creative Commons license and the respective action is not permitted by statutory regulation, users will need to obtain permission from the license holder to duplicate, adapt or reproduce the material.

# References

Chan, S., & Stevens, A. H. (2001). Job loss and employment patterns of older workers. *Journal of Labor Economics, 19*(2), 484–521.

Dorn, D., & Sousa-Poza, A. (2010). "Voluntary" and "involuntary" early retirement: An international analysis. *Applied Economics, 42*(4), 427–438.

Ichino, A., Schwerdt, G., Winter-Ebmer, R., & Zweimüller, J. (2007). *Too old to work, too young to retire?* (CEPR discussion paper no. 6510). München: CESifo, Center for Economic Studies & Ifo Institute for economic research.

Knuth, M., & Kalina, T. (2002). Early exit from the labour force between exclusion and privilege: Unemployment as a transition from employment to retirement in West Germany. *European Societies, 4*(4), 393–418.

Schwab, M., & Weber, B. (2010). Die Schweizer Arbeitslosenversicherung im internationalen Vergleich. *Die Volkswirtschaft, 5*, 39–42.

Tatsiramos, K. (2010). Job displacement and the transitions to re-employment and early retirement for non-employed older workers. *European Economic Review, 54*(4), 517–535.

Teyssier, F., & Vicens, C. (2001). La trajectoire des licenciés économiques: Un nouvel equilibre des droits? Résultats d'une approche comparative européenne. *Travail et Emploi, 87*, 9–28.

# Chapter 5
# Job Search Strategies and Unemployment Duration

About 90 % of the reemployed and unemployed workers in our study indicated they had searched for a job. While finding a job after displacement is challenging for all workers, some manage to return quickly to the active labor force whereas others remain unemployed for over a year or even arrive at the end of eligibility for unemployment benefits.[1] These differences may translate into diverging career outcomes and quality of life. In particular, since in modern societies individuals' social status strongly depends on their participation in the economic production system, unemployment, especially if it is extended, may trigger a feeling of failure and a downgrading of workers' social status (Gallie and Paugam 2000: 1).

Earlier studies have suggested that activation of the social network improves job seekers' reemployment prospects, not only in terms of reemployment chances but also of job quality. This leads to our hypothesis H3 (see Sect. 1.4) that workers who found their new job through former colleagues, acquaintances, friends or family manage to return more quickly to jobs of better quality.

In this chapter we analyze the use of different job search strategies and their effect on workers' success to find a job. We then examine how long displaced workers spent on their job search and which factors are most strongly related to short spells of unemployment. Finally, we briefly discuss the transition out of the labor force to training, childcare and disability.

## 5.1 Job Search Strategies

Workers are not passive victims of job loss but can actively try to influence their labor market outcomes (Kalleberg 2009: 14). Activating one's social network, an intensive job search, or increasing the geographical job search radius are assumed

---

[1] Eligibility for unemployment benefits expires in Switzerland for the median unemployed worker after 18 months.

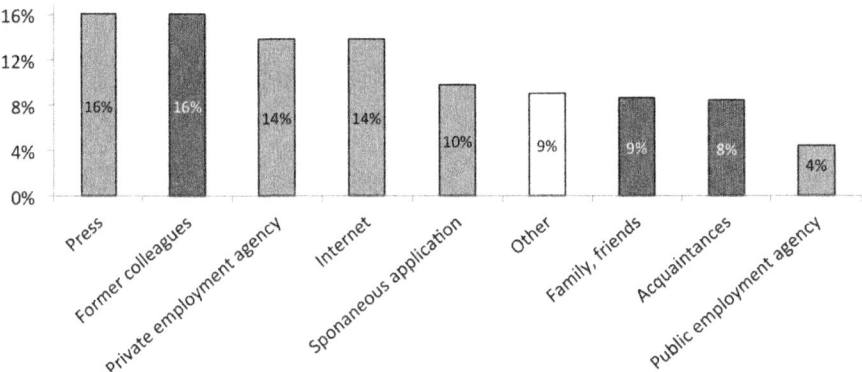

**Fig. 5.1** Information channel for finding new job. Note: N=499. *Dark gray*: informal search methods, *light gray*: formal search methods

to increase the likelihood of a successful job search – everything else being constant (Granovetter 1995 [1974]; Marsden and Gorman 2001: 470; Burgess and Low 1998: 242; Kaufmann et al. 2004).

In order to maintain their financial security while they search for a job, workers can apply for unemployment benefits on condition that they paid into the mandatory unemployment insurance for at least 1 year within the preceding 2 years while they were employed. We find for our sample that the likelihood of applying for benefits depends on the workers' labor market status. Among the still or again *unemployed* workers 98% had applied, but only 66% of the *reemployed* and 73% of the *labor force dropouts*. The difference between the unemployed and the reemployed suggests that the reemployed either anticipated their rapid reemployment or that they found a job even before they became unemployed.

### 5.1.1 The Application Process

With respect to information channels we find that 16% of the workers found their new job through a job offer in the press and the same proportion through their former colleagues (see Fig. 5.1). 14% managed to get back into the active labor force with the aid of a private employment agency and the same proportion found their new job through a job offer in the Internet. 10% of the workers found their job due to a spontaneous application. 9% of the workers found their job because of information provided by family or friends and 8% by acquaintances. The public employment agency directly helped 4% of the workers to find their new job.

A common distinction in the literature is between formal and informal job search methods (Granovetter 1973: 1372). Formal methods represent those where job seekers use formal intermediaries such as agencies or advertisements, while informal methods consist in job search through personal contacts. Among the workers in

## 5.1 Job Search Strategies

our sample who found a new job, 34% of the workers used informal methods such as former colleagues, family, friends or acquaintances (dark gray in Fig. 5.1).

The result on the proportion of jobs found through personal contacts corresponds to the findings from other Swiss and European studies. A literature review shows that across Europe between 31 and 47% of job seekers in Europe find their employment through their social network (Marsden and Gorman 2001: 479). Yet these job seekers are not necessarily unemployed as is the case in our study. However, a Swiss study that focuses on *unemployed* workers' use of their social ties in job search also reveals that about a third of the workers learned about their new job from their personal contacts (Bonoli et al. 2013: 67). Accordingly, this job search strategy seems to be one of the most important instruments to help workers return to the active labor force.

A descriptive analysis of the determinants of the use of different job search channels reveals that workers aged over 55 tend to find their job more frequently (42%) though their social network than workers aged under 30 (28%). The differences are statistically significant, but the relationship is not linear. In contrast, there are no significant differences in the use of personal contacts by nationality, gender or collar.

Granovetter (1995 [1974]: 13–14) – focusing on managers, professionals and technicians – argues that job search through social contacts leads to employment in jobs of better quality. For our data, we find that workers who found their new job through social networks experience a stronger wage loss than workers who found their job through other channels (−6% versus −2%). If we distinguish between jobs found through *colleagues* on the one hand and jobs found through *other contacts* on the other hand, we find that workers who used the first method experienced wage losses of −5% and those who used the second method experienced a decline in wages of −6%. With respect to contract type, risk of job loss or skill mismatch in the new position, finding a job through personal contacts did not seem to have a positive effect on the quality of the new job. The result remains unchanged if we restrict the analysis to the managers, professionals and technicians in our sample (the group of occupations analyzed by Granovetter 1995 [1974]).

Moreover, we find no evidence for a link between job search through the social network and reduced unemployment duration either. Although a larger proportion of the workers who found their job through colleagues, friends or acquaintances were reemployed within less than 1 month (34%) as compared to the workers who found their job through other channels (28%), the opposite is the case if we consider the proportion of workers who found their job within 4 months: 57% of the workers who found their job through the personal network versus 65% of the workers who found their job through other channels.

It may be assumed that workers who are active in associations are more likely to find a job or to find a job within short notice, as they have access to a larger network of individuals. Among the workers in our sample, 77% are member of at least one association. Many are members of several associations (see Fig. 5.2). In fact, 46% are members of a sports club, 37% of a trade union, 28% of a church, 14% of a

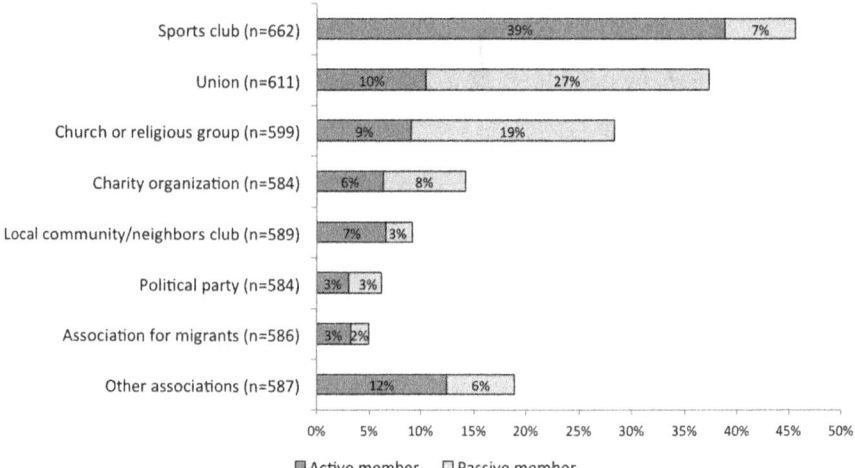

**Fig. 5.2** Membership of associations. N = 677. Multiple answers per respondent possible; lines do not sum up to 100 %. Reading example: 39 % of the respondents indicated being an active member of a sports club, 7 % indicated being a passive member of a sports club

charity organization, 10 % of a neighbors' association, 6 % of a political party, 5 % of a migrant association and 18 % of other types of associations.

A descriptive analysis of the workers' labor market status by membership in an association reveals that workers who are members of at least one association are not more likely to be reemployed than workers who are not members of any association. With respect to the unemployed, there is a small difference: among the individuals who did not belong to any association 19 % were unemployed, while among the workers who were members only 15 % were unemployed. The differences may stem from age differences as we find that among the non-members 10 % retired but among the members 13 % went into retirement. The difference is, however, not significant. Turning to the duration of job search, we find that the differences between the non-members and members in associations are even smaller. Accordingly, membership of an association does not seem to be linked to the success of job search.

Figure 5.3 illustrates the number of job applications workers had written by their labor market status at the moment of the survey. In all labor market status categories we find workers who have written over 100 applications. While it is less surprising that 44 % of the unemployed and 13 % of the reemployed sent out over 100 applications, it is interesting that this was also the case for 36 % of the labor force dropouts and 6 % of the retired workers. This shows that some of the labor force dropouts and retirees tried hard to find a job but probably were not successful and therefore quit the labor market. At the same time, 43 % of the labor force dropouts and 22 % of the retirees applied less than six times and thus quit the labor market without making much effort to search for a job. Unsurprisingly, we find from Fig. 5.3 that the unemployed applied more frequently for jobs than the reemployed. One reason for this

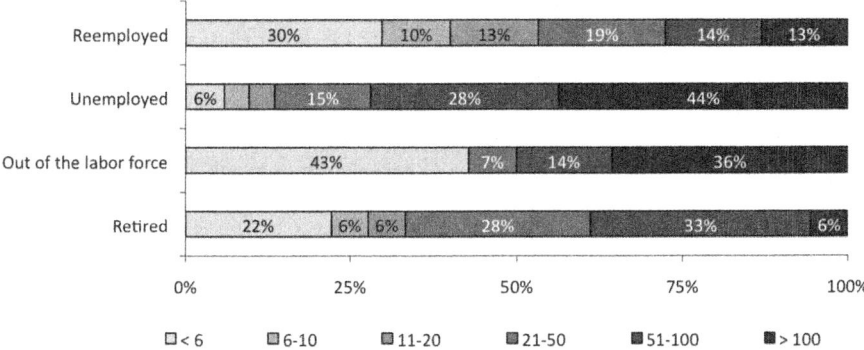

**Fig. 5.3** Number of applications by labor market status. N=499. Reading example: 30 % of the reemployed respondents indicated that they applied less than six times to a job before they were accepted. 10 % of the reemployed indicated that they applied 6–10 times

finding is that workers who applied for unemployment benefits are obliged to actively search for jobs. Moreover, it indicates that most of the unemployed workers were not voluntarily without employment.

## 5.2 Other Strategies of Job Search: Commuting, Training, Temporary Jobs

One strategy to increase the number of potential jobs available is geographical mobility, either in the form of moving house or commuting longer distances. With respect to the first strategy, our analysis shows that only 4 % of the workers in our sample relocated. This result may, however, be biased since those who had moved house more than 1 year before we conducted the survey did not receive our questionnaire.[2] But since only about 10 % of the addresses were invalid, relocation seems to have little importance as job search strategy.

By contrast, a large number of workers accepted a job in a more distant location than their pre-displacement job. Among the reemployed workers, 50 % had a longer journey to their new workplace than before they lost their job. More precisely, 23 % traveled more than 30 min longer per day and 27 % traveled between 5 and 30 min longer. 22 % commuted daily for about the same time as before displacement. Finally, 18 % traveled between 5 and 30 min less per day and 9 % traveled more than 30 min less. Data for the US suggests that commuting is one of the activities that individuals most strongly dislike (Kahneman et al. 2004: 432). Accordingly, many workers seemed willing to accept the drawback of longer traveling distances in order to be able to return to a job.

---

[2] The Swiss post office forwards the mail of people who have relocated to their new address for one year.

The change in commuting time seems to be related to workers' education. 32 % of the workers with a tertiary degree accepted a job further away from home than their former job, while this was the case for only 19 % of the reemployed with upper secondary education or less. With respect to the question whether commuting longer distances pays off in terms of wage gains, a descriptive analysis reveals that workers who commute longer distances experience on average a wage loss of 4 % while workers who commute about the same distance only experience a loss of 1 %. Workers who commute shorter distances also earn on average 4 % less in the new job as compared to the former job. An OLS regression does not reveal a significant correlation between change in commuting distance and change in wages. We thus do not find any evidence in our data that commuting is compensated for by wage gains.

Workers may enhance their labor market prospects if they complete a training course. Among the participants of our survey, 23 % attended training while searching for a job and for 57 % of them the training lasted longer than 1 month. In 41 % of the cases the workers learned new skills, 38 % attended a training course to update their skills and 18 % did some vocational retraining. Our analysis reveals a link between longer unemployment durations and having completed a training course – possibly a consequence of active labor market policies implemented by the public job placement agencies (RAV/ORP). This suggests that workers experiencing longer phases of unemployment decide or are obliged to update their skills or learn another occupation in order to enhance their labor market prospects. Furthermore we find that workers who completed a training course did not have significantly better chances of being be reemployed than workers who did not (77 % as compared to 75 %). Workers who attended a training course also did not have higher earnings or a better job match in their new job than other workers. These findings may be the result of a selection effect: we do not know if the workers who attended a training course improved their labor market outcome as compared to a counterfactual situation.

The transition from the pre-displacement position to a stable job may not be direct; workers may be displaced again or accept temporary jobs. With respect to temporary employment there is a large debate as to whether it functions as a stepping stone into regular employment by serving as screening for employers and as a means to gain work experience for employees. While some studies found evidence for this mechanism for some countries (e.g. Booth et al. 2002 for the UK; Gebel 2013 for Germany and the UK), the results for other countries are more ambiguous (e.g. De Graaf-Zijl et al. 2011 for the Netherlands; Gebel 2013 for Switzerland).

Our analysis shows that – taking all workers together – 18 % (n = 106) indicated that they were employed in a temporary job. 69 % (n = 73) of them were reemployed and 31 % (n = 33) were either unemployed, retired or out of the labor force when we surveyed them. It would be interesting to examine whether having been employed in a temporary job is related to reemployment in a higher quality job. However, as Gebel (2013) has pointed out it is highly probable that there is a selection effect leading less employable workers into temporary jobs. Indeed, we find that workers who *have not* been in temporary employment are significantly better off than those who *have* been in temporary employment in terms of unemployment duration (controlling for age, sex and education). Nonetheless, we cannot exclude that for the workers who were employed in a temporary job this position may have improved their employability and subsequently may have served them as a means to leave unemployment.

Earlier studies have shown that it is not unusual that new employment relations are dissolved quickly – simply because many of them turn out to be bad matches (Farber 1998). Repeated job separations have proved to be painful if they are involuntary because they are accompanied by great uncertainty about the workers' career (Stevens 1997: 176). 66 % of the reemployed workers in our sample did not lose their new job. In contrast, 4 % were dismissed again from their new job, 12 % quit their post-displacement job of their own will and – as we have seen earlier – the remaining 18 % accepted a job with a temporary contract. Among the small number of workers (4 % or n=26) who found a job but were dismissed again, two-thirds were reemployed at the moment of the survey. The other third, however, were still unemployed. For the workers who quit their post-displacement job of their own will, the pattern is different: only 10 % of them were unemployed or out of the labor force at the moment of the survey; the other 90 % were reemployed. This suggests that those quitting voluntarily left their first post-displacement job for a better job. If we look at the socio-demographic characteristics of workers with multiple job separations, we find that younger workers are substantially more likely to voluntarily quit their new job than older workers (17 % for workers aged under 40 as compared to 3 % for workers aged over 55). With respect to involuntary repeated job loss there are no differences between older and younger workers.

## 5.3 Unemployment Duration

In Switzerland, about half of all the job seekers who receive unemployment benefits from the public unemployment insurance are reemployed within 6 months (OECD Statistics).[3] At the same time about 20 % of the unemployed do not find a job within 1 year and are thus defined as long-term unemployed (Babey 2011, 2012).[4] About 15 % of the job seekers reach the end of the eligibility for unemployment benefits, which occurs for a typical worker after 18 months of receiving unemployment benefits (SECO 2010, 2011).[5]

---

[3] Over the period of our survey the figures were 52 % (2009), 44 % (2010) and 42 % (2011).
[4] More precisely, 13 % in 2009, 21 % in 2010 and 20 % in 2011.
[5] Over the period of our survey the figures were 15 % (2009) and 18 % (2010). For the year 2011 there is no information available because the revision of the unemployment insurance in this year led to a particularly high number of job seekers who reached the end of eligibility for unemployment insurance. Source: SECO (2010, 2011).

The analysis of the duration of job search of the workers in our sample reveals similar results. The variable "unemployment duration" is a construct of survey and register data. In the survey, we asked workers how long they searched for a job. This question is somewhat ambiguous since workers may have started job search before they actually lost their job or only some weeks after. In the register data we may be confronted with similar ambiguities: workers may first have tried to find a job without signing up for unemployment benefits. Thus, this variable is not totally unambiguous. Our analysis only includes workers who either searched for a job or who described themselves as unemployed at the moment of the survey. In contrast, workers who directly transited into retirement or dropped out of the labor force are not considered.

Figure 5.4 shows that 36 % of the workers were reemployed within 2 months and 47 % within 4 months. Thus almost half of all the workers in our sample managed to return quickly to the labor force. At the same time 12 % of the workers were unemployed for over 12 months and thus long-term unemployed. 20 % of the workers were still unemployed when we surveyed them. From these still or again unemployed workers, 88 % were unemployed for more than 1 year and 19 % for more than 2 years. Most critical is probably the situation of 3 % of the respondents (representing 21 % of the unemployed workers) who arrived at the end of their eligibility for unemployment benefits (not shown in Fig. 5.4).

Regarding the workers' unemployment duration, a Finnish study on plant closure in manufacturing shows that 44 % of the workers were reemployed after 3 months, and 57 % after 11 months (Jolkkonen et al. 2012: 87). Another Swiss study of job loss in the manufacturing sector reports that 68 % of the workforce was reemployed within 3 months but 2 years after displacement still 20 % of the workers were searching for a job (Wyss 2009: 28, 40). In our sample 36 % of the workers were reemployed after 2 months and 47 % after 4 months, but after 12 months only 69 % of the job seekers were back in a job. Common to all the results is the pattern of

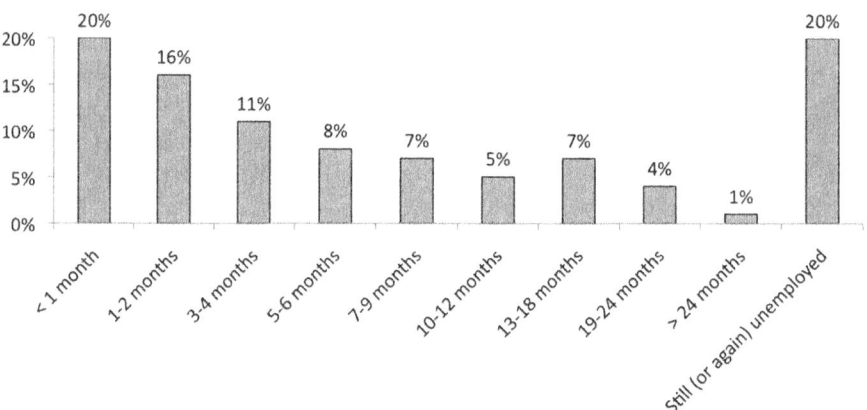

**Fig. 5.4** Unemployment duration. N=755. The analysis only includes workers who were either reemployed or unemployed when we surveyed them

## 5.3 Unemployment Duration

rapid reemployment of large proportions of displaced workers within the first few months which gives then way to a slowing down rate of return to work.

In our survey we asked workers whether the duration of job search corresponded to their expectations. While 55% of the workers indicated that the job search took less time than they estimated, for 33% the duration was longer than anticipated. Only for 13% of the respondents did the duration correspond to their expectations. We tested whether the individual factors age, sex, education, occupation and locus of control[6] predicted the correspondence between unemployment duration and expectation, but found no evidence for an association.

Earlier studies have consistently shown that with increasing unemployment duration, workers' likelihood of exiting unemployment decreases (e.g. Steiner 2001: 103 and Gebel 2009: 677 for West Germany or van den Berg et and van Ours 1996 for the US). Regarding the explanation of this phenomenon there is, however, a debate in the literature (Machin and Manning 1999: 12): according to some studies, unobserved heterogeneity explains this outcome, whereby the most employable workers leave unemployment quickly while the least employable remain in the group of the unemployed. Other authors have argued that there is true duration dependence, meaning either that long spells of unemployment reduce reemployment prospects because the workers lose their knowhow, motivation and self-confidence or that employers perceive long unemployment spells as a negative signal of workers' abilities (Pissarides 1992; Flückiger 2002: 15; Eriksson and Rooth 2014: 1029; Kroft et al. 2013: 1128).

It is likely that the same factors that are associated with workers' reemployment prospects – as discussed in Chap. 3 – are relevant for rapid reemployment. A descriptive analysis (not shown) reveals that there are substantial differences in the duration of job search by age, district unemployment rate and plant. In a next step we therefore first analyze the workers' outflow of unemployment by age before we look into a larger range of factors associated with exit from unemployment. The workers' outflow from unemployment by age is demonstrated by means of a Kaplan-Meier survival analysis. The analysis is based on the same subsample as Fig. 5.4 above. The result – which simply shows how the proportion of job seekers decreases over time – is illustrated in Fig. 5.5. The different lines represent six different age groups.

For the youngest age group of the under-30s the curve is steep: within less than 1 month, already 40% had left the group of the job seekers because they had found a job or quit the labor market for other reasons. One to two months after job loss, another 30% of the youngest age group had exited the group of the job seekers. About 6 months after displacement less than 25% of the youngest workers were still searching for a job. Then, the curve flattens and after more than 24 months only about 10% of the workers below the age of 30 remained unemployed. In strong contrast, the survival curve of the oldest worker cohort (aged 60 and over) is flat. 5–6 months after displacement only about 15% of those older workers who were

---

[6]The concept of locus of control describes people's belief about how much they can control events that affect them (Goldsmith et al. 1996: 337).

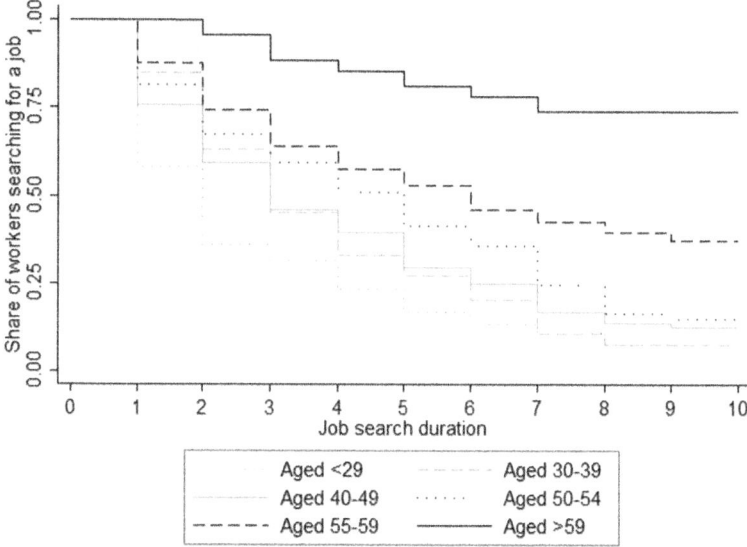

**Fig. 5.5** Survival curve for job seekers according to age (Kaplan-Meier survival estimate). N=747. Note: Job search duration 1=less than 1 month, 2=1–2 months, 3=3–4 months, 4=5–6 months, 5=6–9 months, 6=10–12 months, 7=13–18 months, 8=18–24 months, 9=more than 24 months, 10=still unemployed. The x-axis represents the unemployment duration, 1 standing for an unemployment duration of less than 1 month, 2 for an unemployment duration of 1–2 months and so forth. The y-axis represents the proportion of workers searching for a job, 1.00 meaning 100%, 0.75 for 75% and so forth. Reading example: Among the displaced workers over 60 years, no one went from unemployment to employment within less than 1 month. 1–2 months after job loss, about 4% of the entire group of workers over 60 had found a job and after 3–4 months about 6% of them. 5–6 months after job loss another 2% of the entire group of workers over 60 had found a job and after 6–9 months another 2%. 10–12 months after job loss about 2% of the entire group of workers over 60 had found a job and after 13–18 months another 3%. After 18 months, no more workers of this age group managed to transit from unemployment to employment and the survival curve stabilizes at 75%, meaning that 25% of the workers of this age group had found a job while the remaining 75% has not

searching for a job were successful, and at the moment of the survey still about 75% of them were searching for a job. This oldest age group clearly is an outlier, which is unsurprising given that the workers in this group have less than 5 years until they become retired and employers may therefore be reluctant to hire them. However, we also observe long unemployment durations for the second oldest age group of the 55 to 59 year olds. It takes 9–12 months of job search for 50% of them to have found new employment. The other age cohorts lie in between the two extremes of the youngest and the two oldest age groups. It is noteworthy that the curves are aligned in a strictly linear pattern with respect to age.

In a next step we examine the effect of a larger array of factors on unemployment duration. We again run logistic regression analyses for being reemployed within two and within 12 months, respectively, controlling for sex, civil status, country of residence, district unemployment rate, plant, education, occupation, and nationality.[7] The results are presented in Figs. 5.6 and 5.7.

We find strong differences across age groups for reemployment both within two and within 12 months. Workers aged over 30 are substantially less likely to be reemployed in a short time than younger workers. More precisely, workers aged 30–39 are 20 percentage points less likely to be reemployed within 2 months and 10 percentage points less likely to be reemployed within 12 months than workers below the age of 30. Workers aged 40–49 are 12 percentage points less likely to be reemployed within 12 months than the youngest age group. For workers over the age of 50 the reemployment prospects within two and 12 months are even lower. As an example, workers between 55 and 59 are 39 and 37 percentage points less likely to be reemployed within two and 12 months. The result that older workers are much more at risk of long unemployment durations confirms earlier findings for Switzerland (Wyss 2009: 40, 2010: 31) and the US (Kruse 1988: 411).

The nonlinear outcome for the effect of district unemployment rate on reemployment within 2 months with higher rates of reemployment in areas with higher unemployment is counterintuitive and difficult to interpret. Probably this effect comes about because of strong collinearity between plant and district unemployment rate: while the unemployment rate in the district of Plant 1 (Geneva) was never below 6%, the unemployment rate in the district of Plant 4 (Bern) was never above 4%. Our result for the likelihood of reemployment within 12 months is more plausible, being 7 percentage points lower for workers who were displaced in a macroeconomic context of over 6.6–7.2% of unemployment as compared to workers displaced in a context of 1.6–2.5% of unemployment.

We observe that rapid reemployment varies massively across plants. Workers from Plants 2, 3, 4 and 5 located in the canton of Bern and in North-Western Switzerland are 20–42 percentage points more likely to be reemployed within two or within 12 months than workers from Plant 1 located in Geneva. This suggests that unobservable factors specific to the plants trigger these differences.

Our analysis reveals a positive effect of education on reemployment within 2 months. Workers with tertiary education are 12 percentage points more likely to be reemployed within this time than workers with less than upper secondary education. A similar result has been found by Wyss (2009, 2010) for Switzerland and by Kruse (1988) for the US, who showed that low-qualified workers are more likely to experience long spells of unemployment than high-qualified workers.

With respect to occupation, we observe that machine operators and workers in elementary occupations are 19 and 20 percentage points less likely to be reemployed within 2 months respectively, and 21 and 29 percentage points less likely to

---

[7] We tested other models where we included tenure, pre-displacement wage, job search channel for new job and locus of control. But since these variables did not provide significant effects we did not include them in the model presented. The finding that personality traits do not have a significant effect on the transition from unemployment to employment is in line with some of the results from a German longitudinal study on the transition from school to vocational training (Protsch and Dieckhoff 2011: 83–4).

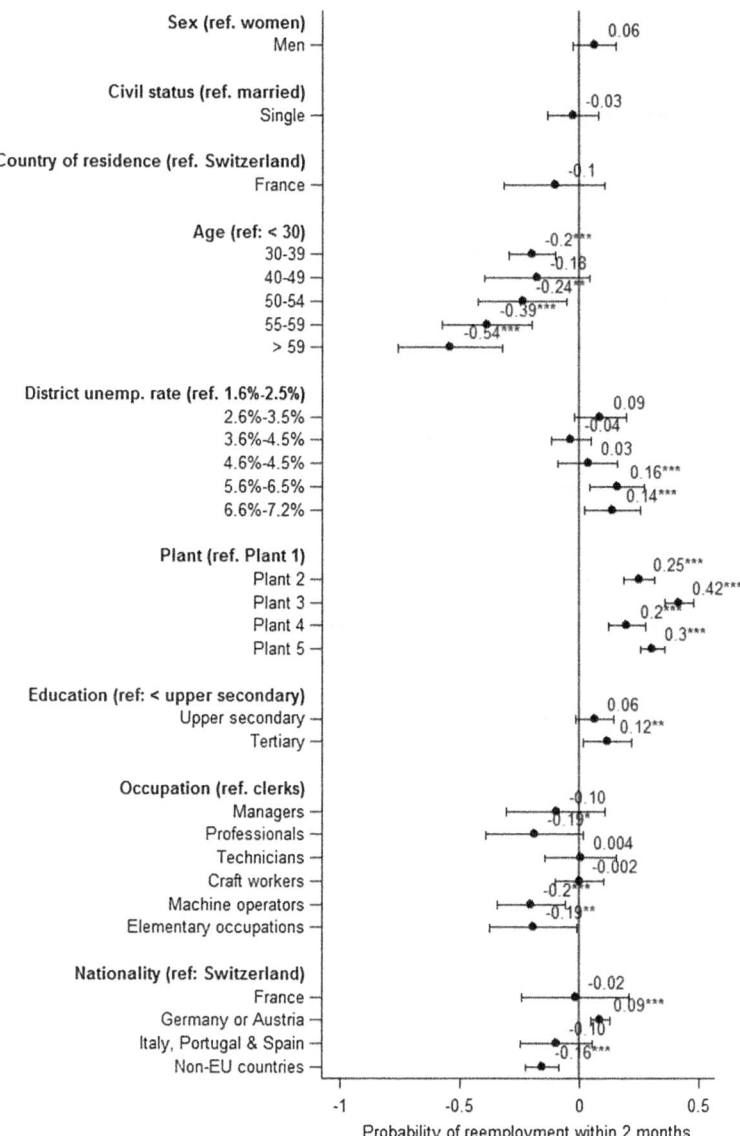

**Fig. 5.6** Average Marginal Effects (AME) for a binomial logistic regression for being reemployed within 2 months. N=567. Note: Significance levels: * $p<0.1$, ** $p<0.05$, *** $p<0.01$. Standard errors are clustered at the plant level. Pseudo $R^2=0.22$. Reading example: As compared to women, men were 6 percentage points more likely to be reemployed within 2 months

## 5.3 Unemployment Duration

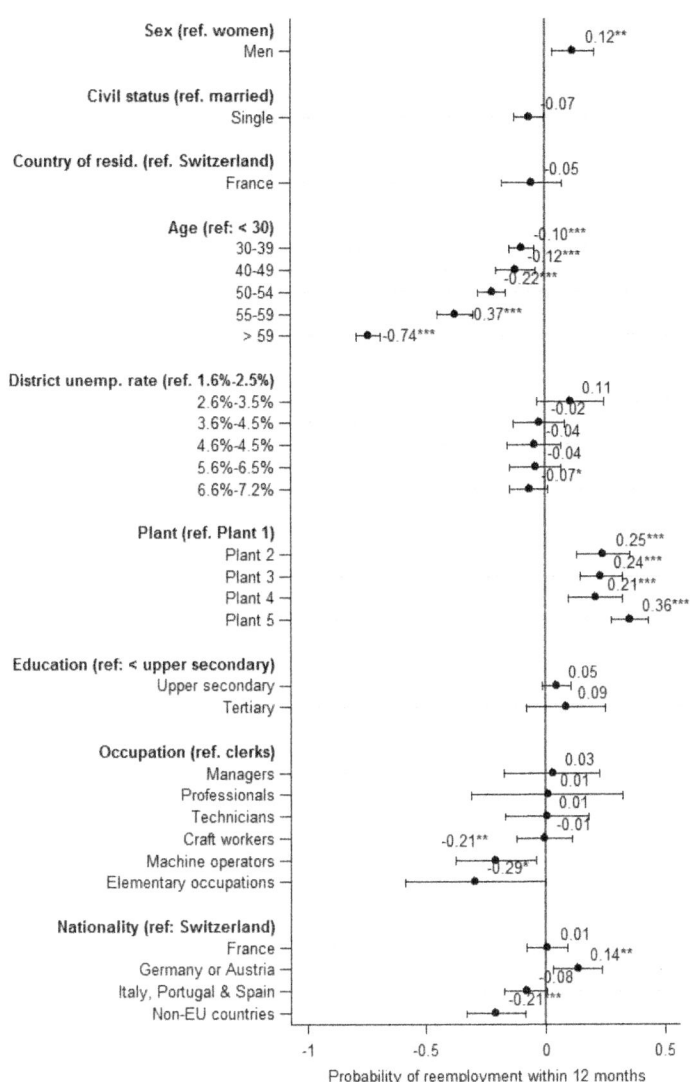

**Fig. 5.7** Average Marginal Effects (AME) for a binomial logistic regression for being reemployed within 12 months. N = 567. Note: Significance levels: * $p<0.1$, ** $p<0.05$, *** $p<0.01$. Standard errors are clustered at the plant level. Pseudo $R^2 = 0.32$. Reading example: As compared to women, men were 12 percentage points more likely to be reemployed within 12 months

be reemployed within 12 months as compared to clerks. This result is interesting in the light of our finding from Chap. 3, which only provides weak evidence for lower reemployment prospects for blue-collar workers as compared to white-collar workers. However, when it comes to unemployment duration, low-qualified blue-collar workers are confronted with considerable disadvantages. This finding corresponds to earlier results by Kruse (1988), who reports for the US that sales workers have shorter spells of unemployment than blue-collar workers. Our analysis also shows that professionals have a 19 percentage points lower likelihood of being reemployed within 2 months as compared to clerks, which possibly shows that the search and recruitment process for highly qualified jobs takes longer.

With respect to nationality, we find that workers with German or Austrian nationality have a 9 and 14 percentage points higher probability of being reemployed within two and 12 months respectively, as compared to Swiss workers. At the same time, workers with a citizenship from outside the European Union have a 16 or 21 percentage points lower likelihood of being reemployed within two and 12 months than those with Swiss citizenship.

Finally, while civil status has no effect, men are 12 percentage points more likely to find a job within 12 months than women. This result may be due to the fact that among the married workers, men tend to be the main breadwinner and subsequently more often go back to employment within 1 year. Indeed, some earlier studies have found that married workers have shorter spells of unemployment because of higher financial responsibilities (Kruse 1988: 411; Teachman et al. 1994). Although the effect of being married in Figs. 5.6 and 5.7 goes in the expected direction, we do not find a significant result with respect to the workers' marital status.[8]

## 5.4 Conclusion

Our analysis shows that workers use a variety of job search strategies to find a new job. While commuting longer distances is an option that many workers accepted, only a few relocated. Over a third of all new positions were found through social contacts, mainly through former colleagues. However, our hypothesis H3 that jobs found through individuals' social network are better in terms of quality is not confirmed: Workers who found a job through their social network experienced higher wage cuts than workers who used other channels. Also with respect to other aspects of job quality such as contract type, risk of job loss or skill mismatch, using informal job search channels does not seem to be an advantage.

Most displaced workers either tended to return very quickly to the labor force or remained long-term unemployed. We found that a third of the workers were reemployed within 2 months and almost half of them within 4 months. At the same time 12 % of the workers were unemployed for over a year and 20 % were still unem-

---

[8] We additionally estimated an interaction effect between sex and civil status. This effect was however not significant.

ployed when we surveyed them. Unemployment duration is principally driven by workers' age. From the age of 55, unemployment durations were substantially longer and from the age of 60 even longer as compared with younger workers. Moreover, blue-collars, workers from non-EU countries and workers in Plant 1 (Geneva) encountered particularly strong difficulties in returning to employment within a short time.

The duration of unemployment is not only important because the job search phase is often difficult and accompanied by financial insecurity, but also because it seems to have an effect on the reemployment conditions. This may be due to depreciation of workers' skills during long phases of unemployment or due to the stigma employers attach to spells of unemployment. In this context it is important to link the duration of unemployment to the quality of the job in which workers are reemployed, a question which we pursue – among others – in the next chapters. From a policy perspective it seems to be crucial to manage to bring workers back to employment quickly, preventing the negative impact of long unemployment spells. Providing workers with advice for job search, motivating them to apply intensely and promoting their participation in active labor market policies have proven to be the most effective ways to address this challenge.

**Open Access** This chapter is distributed under the terms of the Creative Commons Attribution 4.0 International License (http://creativecommons.org/licenses/by/4.0/), which permits use, duplication, adaptation, distribution and reproduction in any medium or format, as long as you give appropriate credit to the original author(s) and the source, a link is provided to the Creative Commons license and any changes made are indicated.
The images or other third party material in this chapter are included in the work's Creative Commons license, unless indicated otherwise in the credit line; if such material is not included in the work's Creative Commons license and the respective action is not permitted by statutory regulation, users will need to obtain permission from the license holder to duplicate, adapt or reproduce the material.

# References

Babey, D. (2011). Arbeitslosenversicherung im Jahr 2010. *Die Volkswirtschaft, 11*, 44–46.
Babey, D. (2012). Arbeitslosenversicherung im Jahr 2011. *Die Volkswirtschaft, 10*, 52–54.
Bonoli, G., Lalive, R., Oesch, D., Turtschi, N., von Ow, A., Arni, P., & Parotta, P. (2013). *L'impact des réseaux sociaux sur le retour à l'emploi des chômeurs.* Publication du SECO, Politique du marché du travail no. 37.
Booth, A. L., Francesconi, M., & Frank, J. (2002). Temporary jobs: Stepping stones or dead ends? *The Economic Journal, 112*(June), 189–213.
Burgess, P. L., & Low, S. A. (1998). How do unemployment insurance and recall expectations affect on-the-job search among workers who receive advance notice of layoff. *Industrial and Labor Relations Review, 51*(2), 241–252.
De Graaf-Zijl, M., Van den Berg, G. J., & Heyma, A. (2011). Stepping stones for the unemployed: The effect of temporary jobs on the duration until (regular) work. *Journal of Population Economics, 24*(1), 107–139.
Eriksson, S., & Rooth, D. (2014). Do employers use unemployment as a sorting criterion when hiring? Evidence from a field experiment. *American Economic Review, 104*(3), 1014–1039.

Farber, H. S. (1998). *Mobility and stability: The dynamics of job change in labor markets* (Working paper no. 400). Princeton: Industrial Relations Section, Princeton University.

Flückiger, Y. (2002). Le chômage en Suisse: Causes, évolution et efficacité des mesures actives. *Aspects de La Sécurité Sociale, 4*, 11–21.

Gallie, D., & Paugam, S. (2000). The experience of unemployment in Europe: The debate. In D. Gallie & S. Paugam (Eds.), *Welfare regimes and the experience of unemployment in Europe* (pp. 1–22). Oxford: Oxford University Press.

Gebel, M. (2009). Fixed-term contracts at labour market entry in West Germany: Implications for job search and first job quality. *European Sociological Review, 25*(6), 661–675.

Gebel, M. (2013). *Is a temporary job better than unemployment? A cross-country comparison based on British, German, and Swiss Panel Data* (SOEP papers on multidisciplinary panel data research no. 543). Berlin: DIW.

Goldsmith, A. H., Veum, J., & Darity, W. (1996). The psychological impact of unemployment and joblessness. *The Journal of Socio-Economics, 25*(3), 333–358.

Granovetter, M. S. (1973). The strength of weak ties. *American Journal of Sociology, 78*(6), 1360–1380.

Granovetter, M. S. (1995 [1974]). *Getting a job. A study of contacts and careers*. Chicago: University Press.

Jolkkonen, A., Koistinen, P., & Kurvinen, A. (2012). Reemployment of displaced workers – The case of a plant closing on a remote region in Finland. *Nordic Journal of Working Life Studies, 2*(1), 81–100.

Kahneman, D., Krueger, A. B., Schkade, D., & Schwarz, N. (2004). Toward national well-being accounts. *The American Economic Review, 94*(2), 429–434.

Kalleberg, A. L. (2009). Precarious work, insecure workers: Employment relations in transition. *American Sociological Review, 74*(1), 1–22.

Kaufmann, V., Bergman, M., & Joye, D. (2004). Motility: Mobility as capital. *International Journal of Urban and Regional Research, 28*, 745–756.

Kroft, K., Lange, F., & Notowidigdo, M. J. (2013). Duration dependence and labor market conditions: Evidence from a field experiment. *The Quarterly Journal of Economics, 128*(3), 1123–1167.

Kruse, D. L. (1988). International trade and the labor market experience of displaced workers. *Industrial and Labor Relations Review, 41*(3), 402.

Machin, S., & Manning, A. (1999). The causes and consequences of long-term unemployment in Europe. In O. Ashenfelter & D. Card (Eds.), *Handbook of labor economics* (1st ed., Vol. 3, pp. 3085–3139). Amsterdam/New York: Elsevier.

Marsden, P. V., & Gorman, E. H. (2001). Social networks, job changes, and recruitment. In I. Berg & A. L. Kalleberg (Eds.), *Sourcebook of labor market: Evolving structures and processes* (pp. 467–502). New York: Kluwer Academic/Plenum Publishers.

Pissarides, C. A. (1992). Loss of skill during unemployment and the persistence of employment shocks. *The Quarterly Journal of Economics, 107*(4), 1371–1391.

Protsch, P., & Dieckhoff, M. (2011). What matters in the transition from school to vocational training in Germany: Educational credentials, cognitive abilities or personality? *European Societies, 13*(1), 69–91.

SECO. (2010, June 8). *Öffentliche Arbeitsvermittlung trotzt der Wirtschaftslage*. Media statement.

SECO. (2011, June 8). *Besser aus der Krise dank Kurzarbeit*. Media statement.

Steiner, V. (2001). Unemployment persistence in the West German labour market: Negative duration dependence or sorting? *Oxford Bulletin of Economics and Statistics, 63*(1), 91–114.

Stevens, A. H. (1997). Persistent effects of job displacement: The importance of multiple job losses. *Journal of Labor Economics, 15*(1), 165–188.

Teachman, J. D., Call, V. R., & Carver, K. P. (1994). Marital status and the duration of joblessness among white men. *Journal of Marriage and the Family, 56*(2), 415–428.

Van den Berg, G. J., & van Ours, J. C. (1996). Unemployment dynamics and duration dependence. *Journal of Labor Economics, 14*(1), 100–125.

Wyss, S. (2009). *Stellenverlust und Lohneinbusse durch die Globalisierung ?* University of Basel, Wirtschaftswissenschaftliches Zentrum der Universität Basel Working Paper No. 05/09

Wyss, S. (2010). *Erhöht die Importkonkurrenz das Arbeitslosigkeitsrisiko der Niedrigqualifizierten?* University of Basel, Wirtschaftswissenschaftliches Zentrum der Universität Basel Working Paper No. 01/10

# Chapter 6
# Sectors and Occupations of the New Jobs

In modern economies, deindustrialization shifts employment out of the manufacturing sector. A prominent argument expects that the decline of job opportunities in manufacturing forces displaced industrial workers to switch to the service sector (Cha and Morgan 2010: 1137). Since the skill profiles of manufacturing workers are likely not to correspond to the skill requirements of similarly qualified and paid jobs in the services, displaced industrial workers may experience an occupational downgrading and in the worst cases be reemployed in low-end service jobs (Iversen and Cusack 2000: 326–7; Bonoli 2007: 498).

It has, however, been shown for OECD countries that most job reallocation happens *within* and not *across* sectors (OECD 2009: 119–120). It is thus possible that the manufacturing sector is able to absorb workers displaced from this sector – and that the workers in our study may find new jobs in their pre-displacement sector. Such a scenario is particularly likely for Switzerland where the pace of deindustrialization over the period of our study was slow. In relative terms, manufacturing accounted for 19.3 % of Swiss employment in 2008 – before the effects of the subprime crisis of the US were felt in Switzerland – and for 18.2 % in 2012 – when the peak of the crisis was over.

The reemployment prospects in the same sector also seem good in Switzerland because the Swiss vocational education system is highly standardized within each sector. The skills acquired in vocational training are thus easily transferable to other firms within the same sector. Accordingly, we expect occupational transitions within the same sector to be smooth (hypothesis H4, see Sect. 1.4). If workers nevertheless change sector, we hypothesize that push rather than pull mechanisms are at work (hypothesis H5). We expect sectoral changes to be triggered by the experience of long-term unemployment rather than by transferable skills.

Even if the workers displaced from the five plants that we examine managed to return to the manufacturing sector, they may have been compelled to adjust to the structural development by changing occupation – a scenario that is likely in a context of rapid automation and technological change in the manufacturing sector and a subsequently increasing demand for high-skilled and decreasing demand for low-skilled labor (Oesch 2013: 72). We examine this issue by first identifying the sectors and occupations in which workers were reemployed and then analyzing which factors potentially favor or hinder sectoral and occupational change.

## 6.1 Sectors

Workers' decision to apply for jobs in other sectors than their pre-displacement sector is subject to push and pull mechanisms. On the side of the push factors, difficulties in finding a job in the pre-displacement sector and a long spell of unemployment force workers to extend their job search to other sectors (Greenaway et al. 2000: 68; Gangl 2003: 206).

On the side of the pull factors, higher levels of education may make it easier to change into other sectors. In particular, general skills seem better portable to other sectors, and credentials act as a signal to future employers of the workers' ability to learn (Estevez-Abe 2005: 188; Fallick 1993: 317). In line with this idea, white-collar occupations – such as managers or clerks – may be more prone to sectoral change because the skills required in these occupations are transferable to other sectors (Gibbons et al. 2005: 704). Findings from a US study that compares wage losses of workers who switch or stay in their pre-displacement sector suggest that high tenure prohibits workers from switching (Neal 1995: 664). The explanation is that the returns on sector-specific skills are lower in other sectors than in the pre-displacement sector.

Women may be more likely to switch to the service sector than men for two reasons: first, there is an increasing demand in the service sector for social skills – skills which women tend to use at work more often than men – such as dealing with people or counseling and advising (Nickell 2001: 621). Second, jobs in the public sector tend to be more easily compatible with family life than jobs in the private sector, which often require geographical or time-related flexibility (Hakim 2006: 282). Overall we thus expect that women, and highly educated, short-tenured and white-collar workers are more likely to be reemployed in the service sector. At the same time, workers who experienced a long spell of unemployment may switch to another sector than their pre-displacement sector.

## 6.2 Sectors in Which Workers Were Reemployed

We start with a descriptive analysis of the workers' reemployment sectors. We measure the sector of employment based on the Swiss General Classification of Economic Activities (NOGA) on a 2-digit level which leaves us with 67 different reemployment sectors. Before displacement, the workers were employed, by definition, in the five manufacturing sectors of their plants which were the production of (i) machines, (ii) metal, (iii) plastic parts, (iv) chemicals, and (v) printing. On

## 6.2 Sectors in Which Workers Were Reemployed

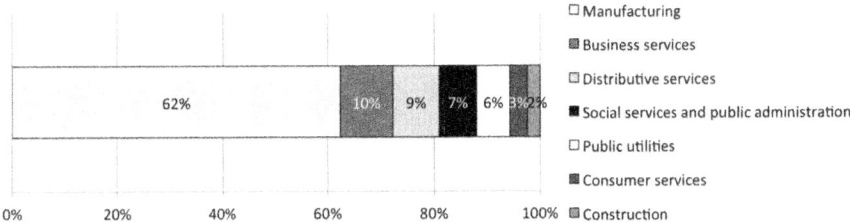

**Fig. 6.1** Economic sector (NOGA) of reemployed workers. N = 549

reemployment, workers most frequently went into manufacturing of machinery and equipment – where 11 % of the reemployed workers were hired –, printing and reproduction of recorded media (10 %), manufacturing of watches, computers, electronic and optical products (8 %), manufacturing of fabricated metal products (8 %), and manufacturing of food products (5 %).

In order to simplify the analysis, we aggregate these 67 sectors into seven groups, distinguishing between (i) manufacturing, (ii) construction, (iii) public utilities, (iv) distributive services, (v) business services, (vi) consumer services, and (vii) social services and public administration.[1] Figure 6.1 presents the proportion of workers in the respective sectors. The key result is that nearly two-thirds (62 %) of the reemployed workers went back into manufacturing. 10 % were reemployed in business services, 9 % in distributive services, 7 % in social services and public administration, 6 % in public utilities, 3 % in consumer services and 2 % in construction. If we pool the three categories manufacturing, construction and public utilities, we find that 70 % of the workers stayed in the secondary sector and 30 % switched to the tertiary sector.

The proportion of workers reemployed in the manufacturing sector in our study exactly corresponds to a recent study on displaced manufacturing workers in Finland (Jolkkonen et al. 2012: 88). But while our result has been produced in a context of economic crisis with stagnation of the Swiss manufacturing sector, the Finnish study was conducted in a context of economic growth.

Although not all workers managed to return to the manufacturing sector, 70 % reemployment in the secondary sector seems to be a high proportion – especially if we consider that manufacturing accounts for less than a quarter of employment in Switzerland. This result thus indicates that job loss in the Swiss manufacturing sector does not necessarily force workers into low-qualified service jobs – so-called McJobs – but that they have robust prospects of returning to jobs in their pre-displacement sector.

---

[1] More precisely, these categories contain the following sectors: (i) Manufacturing, mining, agriculture; (ii) construction and civil engineering; (iii) energy, gas, water, sewerage, waste collection; (iv) retail trade, transport and postal services; (v) financial services, consultancy, legal and accounting activities; (vi) restaurants, hotels, recreational activities; (vii) social services and public administration.

## 6.3 Determinants of Sectoral Change

Do workers reemployed in manufacturing differ from those reemployed in services with respect to socio-demographic characteristics? We address this question by estimating a binomial probit model for being reemployed in services as compared to manufacturing using sex, education, tenure, occupation, duration of unemployment, age and plant as covariates.

Since not all displaced workers found a job, the reemployed workers are a selective group and the analysis of their reemployment sector may be biased. We test for this possibility by using Heckman selection correction analysis presented in Table A.2 in the Annex.[2] The analysis suggests that selection into employment is not a major problem for our analysis of the reemployment sector (i.e. we obtain similar findings without the selection correction).

For this reason we present in Fig. 6.2 below a model without selection correction and indicate the average marginal effects. We find that men are 11 percentage points less likely to be reemployed in the service sector than women. This supports findings from the previous literature that suggest that women possess more skills that are transferable to the service sector or have a preference for jobs that offer flexible working hours. We do not find a significantly higher probability of being reemployed in the service sector for workers with higher levels of education. This result contradicts the view that more highly educated workers are more likely to change sector because credentials help employers in other sectors to evaluate the candidates' skills. But then it is possible that the information we have about the workers' education does not provide us with a complete picture of the workers' credentials. Our hypothesis H4, which predicts that workers with vocational training (measured here by means of the category of upper secondary education) are more likely to remain in their pre-displacement sector than workers with tertiary or less than upper secondary education, does not seem to be confirmed.

With respect to tenure we find that workers with an intermediate tenure of 6–10 years are 6 percentage points *more* likely than short-tenured workers to be reemployed in the services. This worker subgroup is possibly more likely to be in higher hierarchical positions and thus can more easily switch to the service sector. Workers with very high tenures of over 20 years, by contrast, are 7 percentage points *less* likely to change sector if they are reemployed. Our hypothesis which stated that the longer the workers' tenure, the lower their probability of changing sector thus receives ambiguous support. Regarding workers' occupation we find no difference between white- and blue-collar workers. This contradicts the view that white-collar

---

[2] More precisely, we estimate a selection equation on the probability of reemployment and a regression equation on the sector of reemployment (conditional on reemployment), using the STAT command heckprob. In order to do so we use an instrumental variable that affects reemployment, but not the sector of reemployment. We use age as an instrument since it is strongly correlated with the probability of reemployment, but seems to have no effect on the sector of reemployment. The analysis reveals that there is a correlation between the outcome equation and the selection equation (rho=0.26) and accordingly the Wald test is not significant.

6.3  Determinants of Sectoral Change

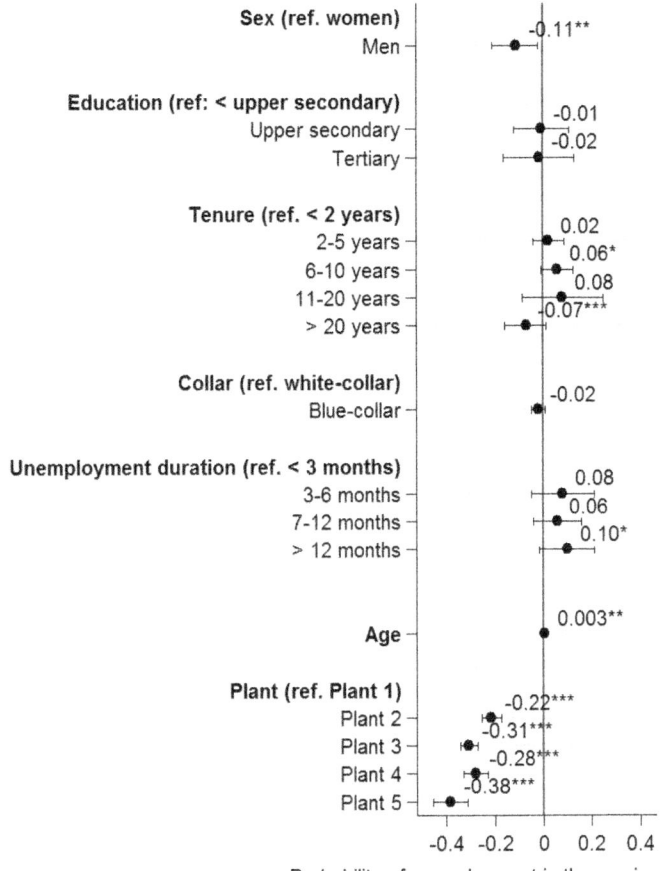

**Fig. 6.2** Average Marginal Effects (AME) of a probit regression for being reemployed in the service sector as compared with the manufacturing sector. N=452. Note: Significance levels: * p<0.1, ** p<0.05, *** p<0.01. Standard errors are clustered at the plant level. Reading example: As compared to women, men are 11 percentage points less likely to switch from the manufacturing to the service sector

workers, who usually have more general skills, have better reemployment prospects in the service sector (White 2010: 1865; Iversen and Cusack 2000: 326). For unemployment duration we find that workers who search for a job for more than 12 months are 10 percentage points more likely to accept a service job as compared to workers who found their new job within 2 months. This result corresponds to our expectation formulated in hypothesis H5 that long term unemployed workers are pushed out of the manufacturing sector, perhaps into *low-end* service jobs.

Finally, our analysis reveals significant effects for age and plant. With each year in age, the probability of switching to the service sector increases by 3 percentage points. Our analysis of differences between plants uses Plant 1 (Geneva) as reference category. We find that workers in all companies are much less likely to be reemployed in the tertiary sector than workers in Plant 1. A possible explanation for this finding may be that the plant in Geneva was located in a large urban labor market dominated by services – a labor market that is twice as large as that in Bern.

We briefly compare the workers' change in wages between the pre- and post-displacement job by unemployment duration to test whether workers with long spells of unemployment ended up in low-paid jobs. Focusing on workers who were reemployed in the services, our descriptive analysis confirms the expectation. In fact, workers who were unemployed for over a year experienced an average drop in wages of 12 percentage points. Workers with spells of unemployment of 7–12 months had an average wage decrease of 4 percentage points and workers with a period of 3–6 months a decrease of 6 percentage points. Only the workers with the shortest unemployment durations of less than 3 months experienced a tiny wage increase of 0.3 percentage points. These results point to an association between long spells of unemployment and occupational downgrading in the case of reemployment in the service sector.

The analysis presented in Fig. 6.2 may not provide a good treatment of sectoral change since we consider services and manufacturing each as a unitary bloc. We therefore construct another measure for sectoral change where we define a sector on the 2-digit NOGA level and run a probit regression with the same specifications as in Fig. 6.2. Workers who were reemployed in the same 2-digit NOGA sector are considered as "stayers" and those who were reemployed in another sector as "switchers". The results are presented in Fig. 6.3.

Interestingly, in Fig. 6.3 we find a highly significant effect for the workers' collar. In fact, blue-collar workers are 10 percentage points less likely to change sector than white-collar workers. This suggests that managers, professionals, technicians and clerks (ISCO 1-digit groups 1, 2, 3 and 4) – whom we define as white-collar workers – are more likely to be reemployed in another sector than blue-collar workers defined as craft workers, machine operators, and workers in elementary occupations (ISCO 1-digit groups 7, 8 and 9).[3] Finally, with respect to unemployment duration we find similar results to those in Fig. 6.2 with a large positive effect for long-term unemployment as compared to very short spells of unemployment. The previous finding that long unemployment durations force workers to leave their pre-displacement sector thus also seems to be valid for 2-digit sector changes and our hypothesis H5 is further corroborated.

The finding that is consistent across both analyses is that longer unemployment durations more frequently lead to sectoral change. Gangl (2003: 205) found a similar link between sectoral mobility and unemployment duration for Germany and the

---

[3] We also tested a model where we entered the ISCO 1-digit group as a categorical variable but the coefficients were not significant. Only if we pool the occupational groups into the categories of blue- and white-collar occupations do we find a statistically significant effect.

6.4 Determinants of Switching into Different Subsector in the Services

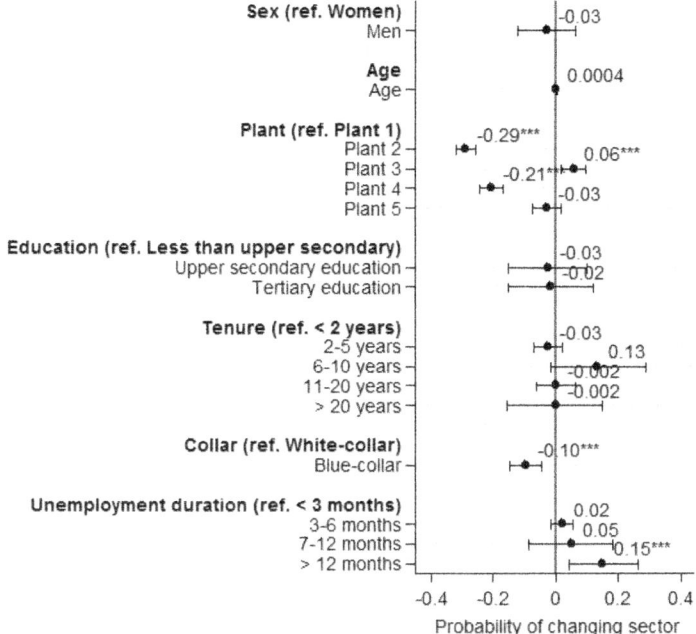

**Fig. 6.3** Average Marginal Effects (AME) of a probit regression for being reemployed in a different sector (NOGA 2-digit level) than the pre-displacement sector. N=452. Note: The dependent variable is binomial and differentiates between two outcomes: reemployed in (i) the pre-displacement sector or (ii) a different sector (on the 2-digit NOGA level). Significance levels: ** $p<0.05$, *** $p<0.01$. Standard errors are clustered at the plant level. Reading example: As compared to women, men are 3 percentage points less likely to be reemployed in another sector

US. Based on German longitudinal data he found the risk of changing sector to be twice as great for workers with an unemployment duration of over a year as for workers with a duration of 1 month. For the US the effect is smaller: workers with unemployment durations of more than 1 month are about 30 % more likely to change sector than workers with a very short spell of unemployment. Greenaway et al. (2000: 69), who analyzed data from the UK and the US, found for both countries that workers who change sector experience on average slightly longer spells of unemployment than those who are reemployed in the pre-displacement sector.

## 6.4 Determinants of Switching into Different Subsector in the Services

Our analysis of sectoral change may be imprecise since we define the service sector as a unitary bloc. However, the service sector includes various different industries in terms of skill requirements and wage levels (OECD 2000: 95). We therefore divide the service sector into three sub-sectors: (i) distributive and consumer services (e.g. transport, retail trade and restaurants), (ii) business services (e.g. finance, IT and real estate), and (iii) social and public services (e.g. health care, education and public administration). We compute a multinomial logistic model on being reemployed in one of these three sub-sectors in comparison with being reemployed in the manufacturing sector, using the same independent and control variables as in Fig. 6.3. However, for this analysis it proves fruitful to distinguish two types of tertiary education: tertiary vocational and tertiary general degrees.

The results of the analysis are presented in Table 6.1. Our analysis suggests that being a man and having tenure of over 11 years decrease the probability of reemployment in *distributive and consumer services* in comparison to returning to manufacturing. At the same time, having searched for a job for more than 3 months increases the chances of switching to this sector.

With respect to the probability of going into *business services* as compared to remaining in the manufacturing sector we find a significant effect for age, plant and the duration of unemployment. For workers of higher ages and those who searched for a new job for between 3 and 12 months there is a higher chance of switching to this sector. Workers from Plant 5 have a lower chance of switching sectors than workers from other plants.

Finally, we find that blue-collar workers are 10 percentage points less likely than white-collar employees, and workers with 2–5 years of tenure 9 percentage points less likely than workers with less than 2 years of tenure, to shift to *social and public services*. While the finding regarding the blue-collar workers seems plausible, the reasons for the effect of tenure are less evident. Perhaps there is spuriousness as a consequence of the small number of observations for each sector (e.g. $n=72$ for social and public services).

In order to provide a clearer picture of how the workers' sex and duration of unemployment affect the probability of sectoral change, we present in Fig. 6.4 the predicted probabilities of being reemployed in a given subsector for a white-collar worker with upper secondary education and 2–5 years of tenure (based on the model in Table 6.1).

The figure shows that among workers who are reemployed in *manufacturing* or the *distributive and consumer service sector* there is a divergent pattern with respect to gender. In fact, men are 15–20 percentage points more likely to return to *manufacturing* while women are overrepresented in *distributive and consumer services*. These differences are however less pronounced with respect to reemployment in *business services* or *social and public services*.

Unemployment duration of less than 3 months seems to enhance the likelihood of being reemployed in the manufacturing sector by about 10 percentage points. In contrast, workers with an unemployment duration of 3–6 months switched to a service sector more frequently than workers with shorter or longer spells. The pattern confirms the idea that workers first tried to find a job in their pre-displacement sector. If they were not successful, they started to apply for jobs in other sectors after about 2 months of job search.

## 6.4 Determinants of Switching into Different Subsector in the Services

**Table 6.1** Average Marginal Effects (AME) for a multinomial logistic regression on being reemployed in a service subsector relative to being reemployed in manufacturing

|  | Distributive and consumer services AME (SE) | | Business services AME (SE) | | Social and public services AME (SE) | |
|---|---|---|---|---|---|---|
| Age | 0.0004 | (0.00) | 0.001** | (0.00) | −0.0005 | (0.00) |
| Plant (ref. Plant 1 (Geneva)) | | | | | | |
| Plant 2 (Biel) | −0.07 | (0.05) | −0.03 | (0.06) | −0.04 | (0.03) |
| Plant 3 (NWS 1) | −0.09 | (0.06) | −0.11 | (0.08) | 0.09* | (0.05) |
| Plant 4 (Bern) | −0.08 | (0.09) | −0.11 | (0.10) | 0.06 | (0.07) |
| Plant 5 (NWS 2) | −0.07 | (0.04) | −0.18*** | (0.06) | −0.02 | (0.03) |
| Sex (ref. women) | | | | | | |
| Men | −0.07** | (0.04) | −0.03 | (0.04) | −0.02 | (0.08) |
| Education (ref. less than upper secondary education) | | | | | | |
| Upper secondary | −0.00 | (0.05) | −0.02 | (0.04) | −0.05 | (0.06) |
| Vocational tertiary | −0.06 | (0.06) | 0.02 | (0.05) | −0.03 | (0.07) |
| General tertiary | −0.03 | (0.06) | 0.02 | (0.05) | 0.04 | (0.05) |
| Tenure (ref. < 2 years) | | | | | | |
| 2–5 years | 0.02 | (0.06) | 0.06 | (0.04) | −0.09** | (0.04) |
| 6–10 years | 0.04 | (0.04) | 0.03 | (0.04) | −0.01 | (0.03) |
| 11–20 years | −0.04** | (0.02) | 0.02 | (0.05) | 0.04 | (0.03) |
| Occupation (ref. white-collar) | | | | | | |
| Blue-collar | 0.02 | (0.04) | 0.00 | (0.02) | −0.10*** | (0.03) |
| Unemployment duration (ref. < 3 months) | | | | | | |
| 3–6 months | 0.06* | (0.03) | 0.05* | (0.03) | −0.03 | (0.04) |
| 7–12 months | 0.04 | (0.05) | 0.02 | (0.03) | 0.01 | (0.04) |
| >12 months | 0.05 | (0.03) | −0.02 | (0.07) | 0.04 | (0.10) |
| Pseudo $R^2$ | 0.08 | | | | | |
| N | 443 | | | | | |

Note: The model includes controls for the unemployment rate of the district in the month of displacement. The dependent variable is multinomial and distinguishes four outcomes: reemployment in (i) manufacturing (reference category), (ii) distributive and consumer services, (iii) business services, (iv) social and public services

Standard errors are clustered at the plant level. Significance levels: * $p<0.1$, ** $p<0.05$, *** $p<0.01$

Reading example: As compared to women, men are 7 percentage points less likely to be reemployed in distributive and consumer services

Finally, we give a short account of the type of employer with which the workers are reemployed: Three quarter of the workers (75%) have a private, 23% a public employer and 2% work for an association or an NGO. Among the workers reemployed by a *private* employer, 78% work in the secondary and 22% in the tertiary sector. Among workers who found a job with a *public* employer, 47% indicate working in the manufacturing sector and 53% in services.

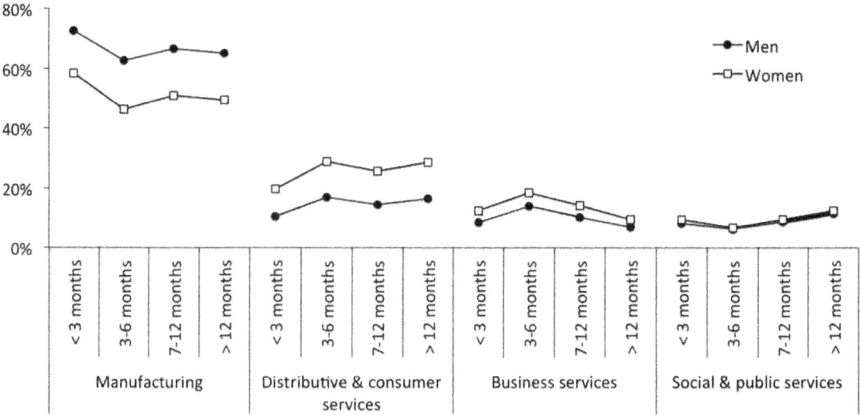

**Fig. 6.4** Predicted probabilities of being reemployed in a given sector by sex and unemployment duration. N=443. Note: Strictly speaking the dots in the figure should not be connected by lines as we use a categorical independent variable. However, the lines are helpful to facilitate the interpretation of the results

## 6.5 Occupations of Reemployment

As for the reemployment sector, push and pull mechanisms may be at work behind potential changes of the workers' occupation upon reemployment after displacement. Previous research on horizontal occupational mobility suggests that an older age, being a women and having a higher income reduce the likelihood of occupational change (Longhi and Brynin [2010: 660] for the UK and Germany; Parrado et al. [2007: 446] for the US; Velling and Bender [1994: 224] for Germany). Although these studies do not focus on displaced workers, they give us an idea of potential factors that are linked to occupational changes after plant closure.

We start our analysis of occupational change by comparing the proportion of workers employed in each category of the 1-digit groups of the International Standard Classification of Occupations (ISCO) before and after displacement. We include in the analysis only those workers who were reemployed at the moment of our survey and both information about pre- and post-displacement occupations are provided only for reemployed workers.[4]

Figure 6.5 shows how workers were distributed across eight occupational categories before and after displacement. There has been a decline in typical production occupations: the proportion of technicians decreased from 20 to 18 %, the proportion of craft workers from 26 to 23 % and the proportion of machine operators from

---

[4]This approach may induce biased results since reemployment is not random. As we have seen in the previous section, long-term unemployed workers tend to change sector in order to avoid labor market exit. Accordingly, since we do not know the reemployment occupation of the workers who were still unemployed when we surveyed them, we probably underestimate the scope of occupational change.

6.5 Occupations of Reemployment

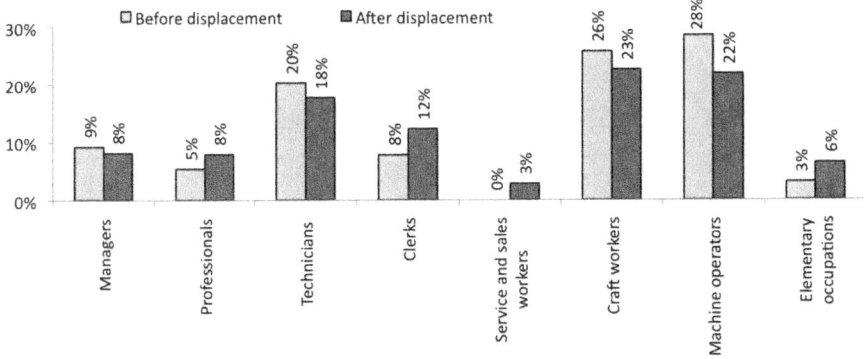

**Fig. 6.5** Distribution of reemployed workers across occupations before and after displacement (at the ISCO 1-digit level). N=576

28 to 22%. In contrast, white-collar occupations are more strongly represented: the proportion of professionals increased from 5 to 8%, the proportion of clerks from 8 to 12% and the proportion of sales workers from 0 to 3%. At the same time, upon reemployment more workers were reemployed in elementary occupations (increase from 3 to 7%) which points to the experience of an occupational downgrading for some workers. The proportion of managers remained roughly constant, decreasing slightly from 9 to 8%.

How can we interpret this result in the light of earlier findings? On the one hand, the decrease in the proportion of workers reemployed in typical production occupations such as craft workers and machine operators corresponds to the observation that these types of jobs are declining in Switzerland (Oesch and Rodriguez Menes 2011: 527). Thus, if fewer jobs in these occupations are available on the labor market, displaced workers are less likely to be reemployed in these occupations. Accordingly, plant closure in manufacturing seems to mediate the structural adjustment from an economy based on manufacturing to a service economy.

On the other hand, the proportion of workers reemployed in occupations typical of industrial production is still large. If we pool craft workers, machine operators and workers in elementary occupations, we find that 51% of the workers in our sample were still employed in typical production occupations. This suggests that manufacturing occupations are not vanishing, but that there is a sizable creation of new production jobs (OECD 2009: 124).

Figure 6.5 shows aggregate change in the occupational structure of the displaced workers, but does not account for individual change. In a next step we therefore investigate the occupational transitions on an individual level. A descriptive analysis reveals that on average 52% of the reemployed workers remain in the same ISCO 1-digit occupational category after reemployment.[5]

---

[5] We do not indicate occupational changes on the 2-digit level since the data is subject to measurement error as the coding of the occupations was not always unambiguous.

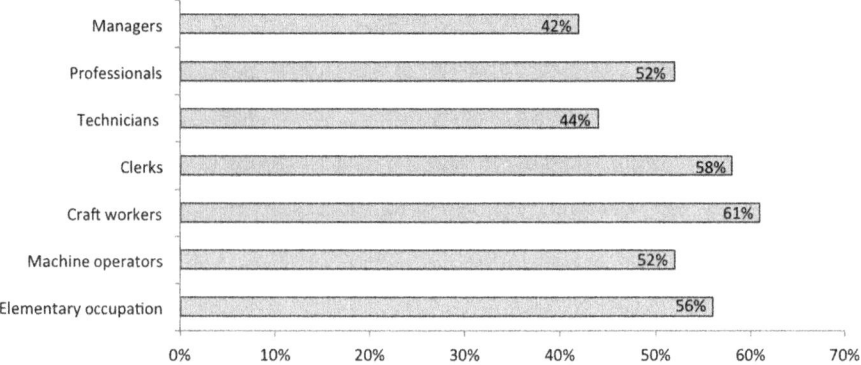

**Fig. 6.6** Proportion of workers reemployed in their pre-displacement occupation by ISCO 1-digit occupational category. N = 576

Figure 6.6 illustrates for each occupation the proportion of workers who have been reemployed in the same occupation. At one end of the spectrum, managers and technicians are the least likely to be reemployed in their pre-displacement occupation (42 % and 44 % respectively). They seem to be the most horizontally mobile. A possible explanation is their usually higher level of education and more general tasks which may allow them to switch occupation more easily than workers in other occupations. At the other end of the spectrum we find that craft workers and clerks are the most likely to be reemployed in the same occupation (61 % and 58 % respectively). This suggests that they have a large proportion of occupation-specific skills which are difficult to transfer to other occupations. An intermediate mobility is observed for professionals, machine operators and workers in elementary occupations (52 %, 52 % and 56 % respectively).

We now turn to the 48 % of reemployed workers who *changed* occupation and conduct a descriptive analysis of the occupational destinations for each pre-displacement ISCO 1-digit occupational group. Figure 6.7 shows that for workers who were active as *managers* before displacement, the most frequent destinations after manager were technicians (25 %) and professionals (17 %). Among *professionals*, 29 % were reemployed as technicians and 13 % as managers. 15 % of the *technicians* worked as clerks and 14 % as professionals. 18 % of the workers who were active as *clerks* before displacement were reemployed as technicians and 9 % as machine operators. *Craft workers* most often became machine operators (16 %) or technicians (7 %). *Machine operators* were reemployed mainly as craft workers (13 %) and in elementary occupations (10 %). Finally, among the workers in *elementary occupations*, 22 % were reemployed as machine operators and 11 % as service workers.

These results indicate three conclusions. First, some occupations seem to enable workers to switch into a large number of other occupations while others only lead to a small number of occupations. Workers employed before displacement as professionals or in elementary occupations ended up in three different occupations after

6.5 Occupations of Reemployment

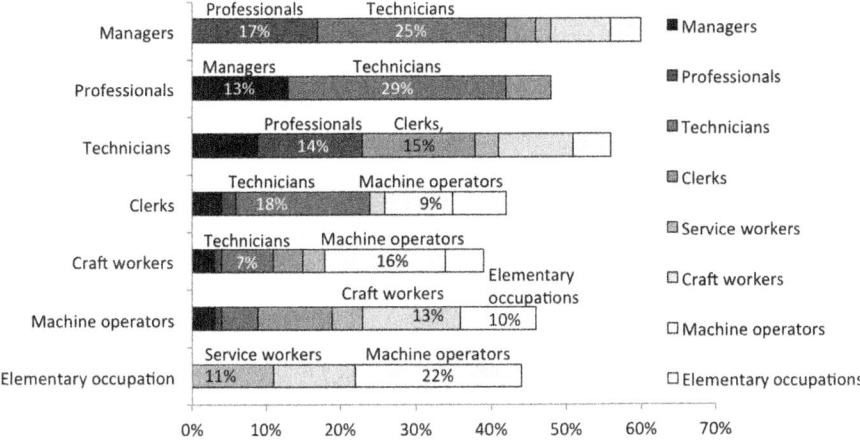

**Fig. 6.7** Occupational destinations of the workers who change occupation. N=576. Note: The percentages indicated in the figure add up to 100% if we include workers who stayed in their occupational group. Reading example: Among managers, 17% were reemployed as professionals, 25% as technicians, a smaller percentage as clerks, service workers, craft workers and machine operators. No one has been reemployed in elementary occupations. The remaining share of managers has been reemployed as managers – 42% as Fig. 6.6 tells us

displacement while workers in the other occupations were reemployed in twice as many different occupations. This finding may indicate on the one hand that unqualified workers in elementary occupations do not have many options in terms of occupational choice. On the other hand, because of their specialization, professionals may have relatively little flexibility – or, above all, incentives – to change occupation upon reemployment.

Second, the occupations of managers, professionals and technicians seem to be permeable, and switching between these three categories thus relatively easy. This may be due to the fact that these occupations often require a tertiary educational degree. Changing into these occupations without credentials is thus less likely. Third, the only occupational group where a considerable proportion of workers has changed into service jobs is elementary occupations. Workers in elementary occupations – who usually are low-skilled – thus seem to be the ones at risk of ending up in McJobs, low-end jobs in restaurants or retail trade.

A change of occupation may be accompanied by a change in the employment relationship and job quality and thus by occupational up- or downgrading. Changing occupation may allow workers to progress and pursue new challenges. But it may also mean that they are overqualified for their new position or that they have to acquire new skills and learn new tasks which may be strenuous.

One question in our questionnaire examined whether reemployed workers consider themselves, in their new job, to be in a higher, equal or lower social position than the position they had before their displacement. We find that 29% of the workers who *changed* occupation experienced downward mobility, 21% upward mobility and 50% no mobility (see Fig. 6.8). Among workers who did *not* change their

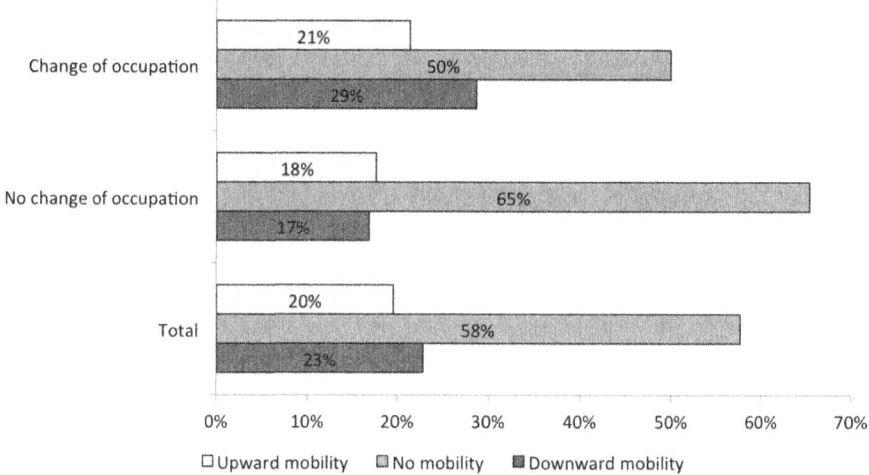

**Fig. 6.8** Change in social status between the pre- and post-displacement job by occupational change on the ISCO 1-digit level. N=487. Note: Change in social status was assessed by asking workers "Compared to your job before displacement, does your new job represent: (i) upward mobility, (ii) a similar social position, or (iii) downward mobility?" Reading example: Amon those workers who changed occupation, 21 % have experienced upward mobility, 50 % no mobility and 29 % downward mobility

occupation, only 17 % experience downward mobility, 18 % upward mobility and 65 % no mobility. On average (see total), 58 % of the workers experience no mobility while 23 % experienced downward and 20 % upward mobility. This implies that, overall, a majority of the workers experienced no mobility, independent of whether they changed occupation. In addition, this finding suggests that changing occupational increases workers' risk of experiencing downward mobility.

## 6.6 Determinants of Occupational Change

Finally, we scrutinize the factors that are associated with the workers' change of occupation. The literature suggests that a younger age, being a man and a low income are associated with a higher propensity to change occupation (Longhi and Brynin 2010; Parrado et al. 2007; Velling and Bender 1994). In order to identify the determinants of occupational change, we compute a logistic regression for the probability of changing occupation on the ISCO 1-digit level and indicate the average marginal effect (see Fig. 6.9). We run a model with the covariates plant, tenure, education, ISCO 1-digit level pre-displacement occupation, sex, age and pre-displacement wage.

We find large and significant differences in the propensity to change occupation according to plant, education and pre-displacement occupation. Workers from Plant

## 6.6 Determinants of Occupational Change

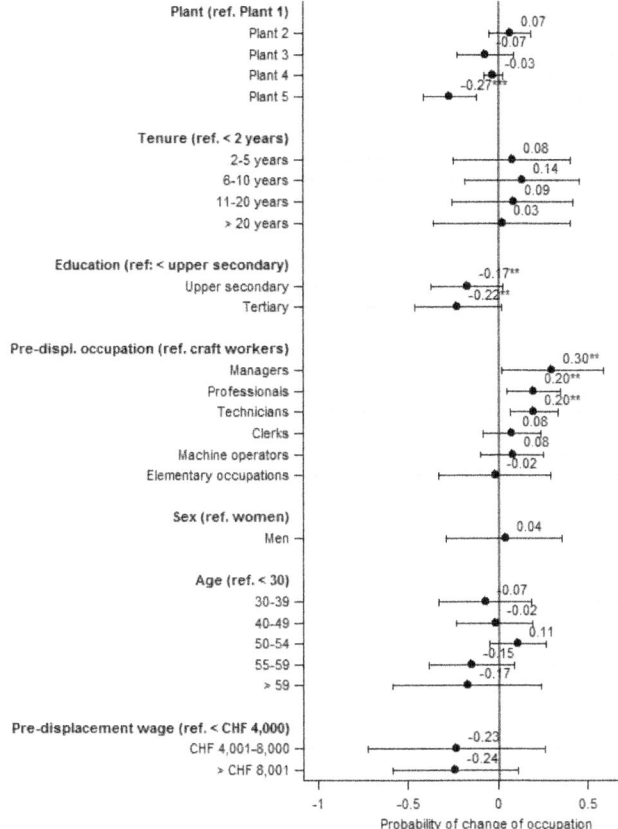

**Fig. 6.9** Average marginal effects (AME) for a logistic regression for change of occupation on an ISCO 1-digit level. N = 366. Note: The dependent variable is binomial and differentiates between two outcomes: reemployed in the (i) same occupation or in (ii) a different occupation, measured on the ISCO 1-digit level. Significance levels: * $p<0.1$, ** $p<0.05$, *** $p<0.01$. Standard errors are clustered at the plant level. Reading example: As compared to workers from Plant 1, workers from Plant 2 were 7 percentage points more likely, those from Plant 3 7 percentage points less likely, those from Plant 4 3 percentage points less likely and those from Plant 5 27 percentage points less likely to change occupation

5 in North-Western Switzerland (NWS 2) were 26–30 percentage points – depending on the model – less likely to change occupation than workers in the plant located in Geneva. In the analysis of the determinants of *sectoral* change in Fig. 6.2 above we found that workers from Plant 5 had the lowest probability of all workers of switching sector. We therefore assume that workers in Plant 5 were particularly often able to be reemployed in jobs that are similar to their pre-displacement jobs – with respect to both sector and occupation.

Interestingly, workers with upper secondary or tertiary education were 17–22 percentage points less likely to be reemployed in another occupation than workers with less than upper secondary education. This suggests that higher levels of education offer better chances of being reemployed in the pre-displacement occupation while lower levels of education push workers out of their occupations. In the analysis of the effect of the workers' pre-displacement occupation we use craft workers as reference category because the descriptive analysis in Fig. 6.6 above indicates that they are particularly unlikely to change occupation. The regression analysis provides us with the result that managers, professionals and technicians are 20–30 percentage points more likely to change occupation than craft workers.

## 6.7 Conclusion

A central result of this chapter is that over two-thirds of the reemployed workers returned to a job in the manufacturing sector. This finding suggests that plant closure in manufacturing does not force the majority of displaced workers to accept low-end jobs in the service sector. However, our hypothesis H4 that workers with vocational – or upper secondary – training are more likely to be reemployed within the same sector than workers with other types of education has not been confirmed. We find that women and workers with long unemployment durations are significantly more likely to be reemployed in the service sector than men and workers with short spells of unemployment. This is consistent with earlier findings that typical female skills pull women into the services. In addition, our hypothesis H5 regarding long-term unemployment seems to be supported as we find that long unemployment durations push workers out of their pre-displacement sector into low-paid service jobs in consumer and distributive services or the social services and public administration (see Oesch and Baumann 2015: 115).

In addition, more than half of all reemployed workers found a new job in an *occupation* that is typical for manufacturing such as craft worker, machine operator or technician. The most important determinants for being reemployed in the pre-displacement occupation are higher levels of education and being a craft worker. Our analysis seems to suggest that workers with lower levels of education are pushed out of their former occupation and that managers, professionals and technicians have the opportunity to change occupation. Displaced workers who did change to a job in the service sector most often went into business or distributive services. Not surprisingly, we thus observe a shift in the distribution of occupations upon reemployment towards occupations such as clerks, sales and service workers and professionals.

From the perspective of the economy as a whole it seems far from beneficial if workers are trained on a particular job but then work in another. Of course knowledge about other occupations or sectors may be an advantage in many jobs, but if workers end up in an employment that is completely different from what they were trained for, their skills are likely to be lost. For this reason it would be beneficial for both employers and employees to invest in transferable skills, for example through continuous training. These skills would allow displaced workers to switch more easily to other sectors and occupation and these skills would not be lost.

The discussion about workers' reemployment sectors and occupations is closely linked to the quality of the new jobs. Sectoral and occupational changes can be associated with occupational up- or downgrading and changes in wages. Workers who change sector or occupation – or both – may lose out in financial terms since they lose the returns on sector- or occupation-specific skills that they received before displacement. We therefore examine in the two next chapters the quality of workers' new employment. We begin with an analysis of wages and continue with job quality and job satisfaction.

**Open Access** This chapter is distributed under the terms of the Creative Commons Attribution 4.0 International License (http://creativecommons.org/licenses/by/4.0/), which permits use, duplication, adaptation, distribution and reproduction in any medium or format, as long as you give appropriate credit to the original author(s) and the source, a link is provided to the Creative Commons license and any changes made are indicated.

The images or other third party material in this chapter are included in the work's Creative Commons license, unless indicated otherwise in the credit line; if such material is not included in the work's Creative Commons license and the respective action is not permitted by statutory regulation, users will need to obtain permission from the license holder to duplicate, adapt or reproduce the material.

# References

Bonoli, G. (2007). Time matters: Postindustrialization, new social risks, and welfare state adaptation in advanced industrial democracies. *Comparative Political Studies, 40*(5), 495–520.
Cha, Y., & Morgan, S. L. (2010). Structural earnings losses and between-industry mobility of displaced workers, 2003–2008. *Social Science Research, 39*(6), 1137–1152.
Estevez-Abe, M. (2005). Gender bias in skills and social policies: The varieties of capitalism perspective on sex segregation. *Social Politics: International Studies in Gender, State & Society, 12*(2), 180–215.
Fallick, B. C. (1993). The industrial mobility of displaced workers. *Journal of Labor Economics, 11*(2), 302–323.
Gangl, M. (2003). Labor market structure and re-employment rates: Unemployment dynamics in West Germany and the United States. *Research in Social Stratification and Mobility, 20*(03), 185–224.
Gibbons, R., Katz, L. F., Lemieux, T., & Parent, D. (2005). Comparative advantage, learning, and sectoral wage determination. *Journal of Labor Economics, 23*(4), 681–724.
Greenaway, D., Upward, R., & Wright, P. (2000). Sectoral transformation and labour-market flows. *Oxford Review of Economic Policy, 16*(3), 57–75.
Hakim, C. (2006). Women, careers, and work-life preferences. *British Journal of Guidance & Counselling, 34*(3), 279–294.
Iversen, T., & Cusack, T. R. (2000). The causes of welfare state expansion: Deindustrialization or globalization? *World Politics, 52*(3), 313–349.
Jolkkonen, A., Koistinen, P., & Kurvinen, A. (2012). Reemployment of displaced workers – The case of a plant closing on a remote region in Finland. *Nordic Journal of Working Life Studies, 2*(1), 81–100.

Longhi, S., & Brynin, M. (2010). Occupational change in Britain and Germany. *Labour Economics, 17*(4), 655–666.

Neal, D. (1995). Industry-specific human capital: Evidence from displaced workers. *Journal of Labor Economics, 13*(4), 653–677.

Nickell, S. (2001). Introduction. *Oxford Bulletin of Economics and Statistics, 63*(Special Issue), 617–628.

OECD. (2000). Employment in the service economy: A reassessment. In *OECD employment outlook* (pp. 129–166). Paris: OECD Publishing.

OECD. (2009). Employment outlook: How do industry, firm and worker characteristics shape job and worker flows? In *OECD employment outlook* (pp. 117–163). Paris: OECD.

Oesch, D. (2013). *Occupational change in Europe. How technology and education transform the job structure*. Oxford: Oxford University Press.

Oesch, D., & Baumann, I. (2015). Smooth transition or permanent exit? Evidence on job prospects of displaced industrial workers. *Socio-Economic Review, 13*(1), 101–123.

Oesch, D., & Rodriguez Menes, J. (2011). Upgrading or polarization? Occupational change in Britain, Germany, Spain and Switzerland, 1990–2008. *Socio-Economic Review, 9*(3), 503–531.

Parrado, E., Caner, A., & Wolff, E. N. (2007). Occupational and industrial mobility in the United States. *Labour Economics, 14*(3), 435–455.

Velling, J., & Bender, S. (1994). Berufliche Mobilität zur Anpassung struktureller Diskrepanzen am Arbeitsmarkt. *Mitteilungen aus der Arbeitsmarkt- und Berufsforschung, 3*, 212–231.

White, R. (2010). Long-run wage and earnings losses of displaced workers. *Applied Economics, 42*(14), 1845–1856.

# Chapter 7
# Wages

The two preceding chapters suggest that displaced manufacturing workers in Switzerland have comparatively good reemployment chances – with the exception of the older workers. However, finding a job *per se* does not guarantee that displaced workers will experience a successful occupational transition after plant closure and that they can continue their careers without major ruptures. Indeed, workers may have accepted major wage losses.

The human capital theory introduced by Gary Becker (1962) suggests that wages represent returns on workers' productivity. According to this logic, wage change following job change is an expression of how the new employer values the workers' skills as compared with the former employer. Wage losses can be the consequence of low transferability of the workers' skills to a new employer. Accordingly, workers who have skills that are very specific to the former employer or sector[1] may experience larger wage losses upon reemployment than workers who mainly possess general skills that are transferable to any company or sector (Neal 1995: 656). The share of specific skills as compared with that of general skills is higher for workers who have completed on-the-job training or worked in the same company for many years. We therefore expect that the high-tenured, the low-qualified and workers who changed sector or occupation are most strongly affected by wage losses (hypothesis H6, see Sect. 1.4).

An alternative explanation has been provided by the signaling theory, which suggests that episodes of unemployment are signals of job candidates' low productivity to potential employers (Spence 1973). Accordingly, employers are likely to offer job seekers wages which are below their pre-displacement wage. Finally, wage losses can be a result of skill depreciation in a long phase of unemployment (Arulampalam 2001: F603; Flückiger 2002: 15). Based on these arguments, in the

---

[1] Such specific skills may be the knowledge required to use machines or software that are only used in a particular sector or contacts with the clients and markets of a particular firm. This knowledge may be important in the workers' pre-displacement firm, but if the worker changes job his or her skills and contacts may be of little use to the new employer.

second part of hypothesis H6 we expect that workers who were unemployed for a long period experience substantial wage losses.

In this chapter we start by examining the wage distribution before and after displacement. We present our results of average wage changes for displaced workers and in comparison with the control group of non-displaced workers in the Swiss Household Panel. We then analyze the factors that are linked to wage losses.

## 7.1 Wage Distribution Before and After Displacement

We start with the presentation of the distribution of workers' wages. In Table 7.1 we show the distribution before and after displacement. This analysis is mainly based on a question asked in the survey on workers' precise gross monthly pre- and post-displacement wage.[2]

Standardizing wages for 40 h per week and 12 monthly salaries per year,[3] we find that wages under CHF 4000 – which corresponds to 66 % of the Swiss national median wage for all sectors and positions – were less frequent before displacement than after. Before the plants closed down, 6 % of the workers earned CHF 4000 or less for a full-time job of 40 h per week. After the closure, 9 % did – among the

**Table 7.1** Distribution of gross monthly wages before and after displacement in CHF (standardized for 40 h per week and 12 salaries per year)

|  | Before displacement | After displacement |
|---|---|---|
| 5 % | 4000 | 3111 |
| 10 % | 4409 | 3702 |
| 25 % | 5159 | 4190 |
| 50 % (median) | 6000 | 5700 |
| 75 % | 6950 | 6857 |
| 90 % | 8450 | 8457 |
| 95 % | 10,850 | 11,429 |
| Mean | 6220 | 6039 |
| N | *749* | *401* |

Reading example: 5 % of the workers earned CHF 4000 or less before displacement. After displacement, 5 % of the workers earned CHF 3111 or less

Note: Before displacement the median wage was close to the Swiss median of CHF 5979

---

[2] Information about wages is sensitive data and its assessment is often subject to measurement error. As discussed in Chap. 2, a strategy to address this issue was to use register data. An analysis of the measurement error in fact revealed that the data collected with the survey deviates by about 2 % from the register data. However, register data is only available for 365 (30 %) of the 1203 workers in our sample and the information presented in Table 7.1 is thus approximate.

[3] The 13th monthly wage was included in the calculation if workers declared having had one.

subgroup of workers who found a job. At the top end of the wage distribution there was no significant change: before displacement 2.4 % of the workers earned CHF 10,000 or more, after displacement this was the case for 3 % of the workers– which is not significantly different. In parallel, the median wage fell from CHF 6000 to CHF 5700.

Compared to the situation before displacement, the wage distribution has become more unequal: the relation between the wage at the 95th and the 5th percentile (p95/p5) has increased from 2.71 to 3.67, at the 90th and the 10th percentile (p90/p10) from 1.92 to 2.02 and at the 75th and the 25th percentile (p75/p25) from 1.35 to 1.38. The plant closures thus seem to have increased the inequality in workers' wages. This finding may also reflect the fact that the wages of high income earners have generally risen whereas wages at the bottom end of the wage distribution have either stagnated or decreased.

Since only a proportion of the displaced workers have searched for a job and been reemployed, we have almost twice as many observations for the wages before displacement as after displacement. Accordingly, in Table 7.1 we compare two different subsamples and this gives us only limited information about changes in the individual workers' earning situation. We therefore continue with an individual-level analysis of the wage change, focusing on the reemployed workers.

## 7.2 Average Wage Change

We start with the analysis of the *average* wage change. In order to produce results that are comparable with earlier findings in the literature, we examine wage changes in four different ways. First, we compute the changes exclusively for the reemployed workers – measuring the difference between pre- and post-displacement wage and then calculating the average wage change as has been done for example in the study by Bender et al. (2002: 56). Second, we measure wage change for reemployed and unemployed workers together – replacing the unemployed workers' income with zero as has been done in several studies from the US (e.g. Jacobson et al. 1993) or by Balestra and Backes-Gellner (2016) for Switzerland.[4] Third, we analyze wage change only for workers in our sample with two and more or five and more years of tenure, respectively. This allows us to compare our results with American studies based on the Displaced Worker Survey (DWS).

Fourth, we compare our results with workers from the Swiss Household Panel who did not lose their job in 2009.[5] We assess their wage change over time by

---

[4] We carry out this analysis only for the purposes of comparison with other studies. The large majority of Swiss workers do not face an income of zero in the case of unemployment. Instead if they claim unemployment benefits they obtain between 70 and 80 % of their former wage for workers with dependent children or a pre-displacement wage below about 60 % of the median wage).

[5] The workers in our sample were matched to workers in the SHP by means of radius caliper propensity score matching with a radius of 0.001, based on the socio-demographic characteristics sex,

**Table 7.2** Difference in wages before and after displacement for different worker subgroups

|  | Difference before-after | Difference before-after for tenure of 2 years and more | Difference before-after for tenure of 5 years and more |
| --- | --- | --- | --- |
| (1) Reemployed | −4% (n=377) | −4% (n=341) | −5% (n=253) |
| (2) Reemployed and unemployed | −29% (n=468) | | |
| (3) Non-displaced (SHP) | +2% (n=1444) | | |

Note: The wages are inflation-adjusted. Consumer prices in Switzerland rose by 0.7% between 2009 and 2010 and 0.2% between 2010 and 2011 (OECD Statistics). Reading example: The average wage loss of the reemployed displaced workers is 4%. If we take only the reemployed displaced workers with 5 and more years of tenure into account, their average wage loss is 5%

following them through 2011. This approach allows us to make a difference-in-difference analysis that considers how wages would have evolved if the workers had not been displaced. This control group provides us with a counterfactual and thus enables us to make a causal interpretation of our findings about workers' wage losses after redundancy.

As a fifth option, some authors use log post-displacement wages as the dependent variable in order to take account of the fact that the same absolute amount of wage loss is larger in relative terms for workers with low pre-displacement wages than for those with high pre-displacement wages (e.g. Zwick 2012: 15). We do not follow this approach since our dependent variable is wage *difference* between the pre- and post-displacement job rather than the post-displacement wage used by Zwick (2012). However, we use the percentage difference to take this issue into consideration.

The following analysis is based on a combination of survey and register data for the pre-displacement wage and on survey data only for the post-displacement wage since for the latter measure there was no register data available. Table 7.2 shows that the displaced workers who were reemployed at the moment of the survey experienced, on average, an inflation-adjusted wage loss of 4%. The result remains unchanged if we include only workers with pre-displacement tenure of more than 2 years into the analysis. If we calculate the wage difference between the job before and the job after displacement for reemployed workers who were tenured more than 5 years in their former plant, we find slightly larger wage losses of 5%. For the reemployed and unemployed workers together the average wage loss amounts to 29%.

---

education, age and sector. Our calculation is based on workers who were employed in 2009 *and* 2011 – in order to assess their wage *differential* – whereby some of them may have changed job while others have remained in the same job. Only full-time workers who worked at least 35 h a week were included in the analysis. Wages in both the treatment and the control group were standardized for 40 h per week (see Chap. 2).

Over the period of the study the wages of our control group of *non-displaced* workers in the Swiss Household Panel (SHP) increased by 2%. Consequently, if we compare the change in wages of the *displaced* workers with the *non-displaced*, we find that the reemployed displaced workers lost on average 6% of their wages by having been laid off – without counting wages foregone in possible phases of unemployment.[6]

As the control group, constructed based on the Swiss Household Panel, differs from the treatment group in terms of education and sex – as discussed in Chap. 2 – we test the robustness of the control group by using data from the Swiss Federal Office of Statistics on the evolution of real wages (corrected for inflation).[7] We compare the real wage change between 2009 and 2011 of the control group with the wage change of the entire working population of Switzerland over the same period. Between 2009 and 2010, real wages in Switzerland increased by 0.1% and between 2010 and 2011 by 0.7%. Taking the period from 2009 to 2011 together, the increase was 0.8007%. As Table 7.2 above shows, the real wage increase of the control group was 2% over the same period and thus higher than for average Swiss workers. Using our control group, we therefore may overestimate the counterfactual wage increase – the increase of the displaced workers' wages if they had not been displaced. Accordingly, considering the real wage change of the entire Swiss working population, we find that displaced workers experience wage losses of 4.8% – instead of 6% as computed based on the SHP control group.

How do our results compare with earlier findings in the literature? We first look at studies that assess the wage changes for reemployed workers without comparing them with a control group. Abe et al. (2002: 236) examining wage losses of displaced workers in Japan, find that male workers who were displaced in 1995 experienced on average wage losses of 4%. Carrington (1993: 443), who analyzes data from the US Displaced Worker Survey, reports wage losses of 12%. The findings from Japan are close to our own results for Switzerland, while post-displacement wage losses in the US are much larger. A possible explanation for the high wage losses reported by Carrington may be that the Displaced Worker Survey includes only workers with more than 3 years of tenure. However, even if we take workers' tenure into consideration, we find substantially lower wage losses than this US study.

Carneiro and Portugal (2006: 15–6) measure wages losses of displaced workers in Portugal who managed to get back into the labor force and compare them with a non-displaced control group. The authors find that the workers' wages decreased by 4% between the year before and the year after displacement. A German study that follows the same approach reports wage losses of a similar extent: Burda and

---

[6] The findings from our survey regarding the wage differences for different tenure categories cannot be compared to the data from the Swiss Household Panel as in the Panel different tenure categories are used.

[7] Bundesamt für Statistik. T 39 Entwicklung der Nominallöhne, der Konsumentenpreise und der Reallöhne (1939–2014). http://www.bfs.admin.ch/bfs/portal/de/index/themen/03/04/blank/data/02.html

Mertens (2001: 30) find losses of 3%. These results are similar to our own finding of 6%. In contrast, a study that uses this approach based on US data again reveals much larger losses of 12% (Farber 1997: 112).

Finally, some studies assess displaced workers' wage losses by considering reemployed and unemployed workers, setting the unemployed workers' post-displacement wage at zero and comparing the outcome to non-displaced workers. Based on this approach, Jacobson et al. (1993: 697) report 25% wage losses for high-tenured workers in Pennsylvania 6 years after displacement. A study that follows the same analytical procedure but uses data from Connecticut finds losses of 32% (Couch and Placzek 2010: 585). A Swiss study focusing on involuntary job losses in general – which is a much broader category than displaced workers – finds losses of 17% 1 year after job loss and 16% 4 years after job loss (Balestra and Backes-Gellner 2016: 13). The losses are thus comparable to our own survey.

Overall, the wage losses are substantially larger in the US context. What might explain these different outcomes in terms of wage losses in the United States compared to Europe? A first reason is probably that the US Bureau of Lab or Statistics has defined displaced workers as high-tenured adults who, after holding a job for 3 years or more, lost that job (Fallick 1996: 6). This definition has been integrated into the major US surveys such as the Current Population Survey and the Displaced Worker Survey (Devens 1986: 40). Some authors have used less or more restrictive definitions: Fallick (1993: 319) focused on displaced workers whose job tenure was at least 1 year and Jacobson et al. (1993: 689) on workers with more than 5 years of tenure. Such restrictions are not made in most European (or Japanese) studies. Displaced workers analyzed in US studies are thus a more selective group who are much more attached to their firms – because of higher tenure – and therefore may find it more difficult to find as good a job match as they did in their old job. However, as our own analysis suggests, this factor alone does probably not explain the consistently larger wage losses in US than in European (or Japanese) studies.

Another potential explanation for the differences between US and European studies lies in institutional factors such as unemployment benefits. Low replacement rates and short benefit durations – as is the case in the United States – may compel displaced workers to find a job quickly, and force them to reduce their reservation wage more strongly (Gangl 2004: 174; Lentz 2009: 50; Feather 1997).[8] In addition, it has been argued that in the US unionized firms provide workers with rents which are lost upon job loss (Jacobson et al. 1993). Finally, differences in wage losses may also be due to differences in the business cycle. Appelqvist (2007: 26–7) found for Finland earning losses of 9% in a period of recession but zero losses in a situation of economic growth. Similarly, Farber (1997: 101) or Kletzer (2001) find that losses are larger in economic downturns than in boom phases.

---

[8] The OECD has developed measures to compare unemployment benefit entitlements across countries. We consider the net replacement rate in 2012 for an unemployed person having earned before job loss a wage at the national average, being the main breadwinner and having two children. The net replacement rate for the United States was 43%, for Finland 65%, Germany 70% and Switzerland 86%.

7.3 Distribution of Wage Change                                                          133

A problem that likely arises in our way of calculating wage losses is the fact that we assess the workers' pre-displacement wage directly before displacement. As scholars have pointed out, this way of calculating probably underestimates the workers' wage losses as many companies reduced their workers' wages when they started having economic difficulties (Jacobson et al. 1993: 691; Arulampalam 2001: F587; Carneiro and Portugal 2006: 13).

Indeed, for the plant in our sample located in Biel we know that this happened: workers accepted wage cuts 1 year before the closure in order to enhance the plant's chances of continuing to operate. If we compare the median pre-displacement wage of the (matched) workers in our sample with the workers in the Swiss Household Panel we find a lower value for workers in our sample (CHF 6239) than for workers in the SHP (CHF 6667). This supports the argument that displaced workers experienced wage cuts – or periods of wage stagnation – before the plant closure happens.

## 7.3 Distribution of Wage Change

So far, we have analyzed the reemployed workers' average wage change. We now turn to the examination of how the wage changes are distributed among the reemployed workers. We start out with the computation of the wage changes in percentages, based on the precise assessment of workers pre- and post-displacement wage. We then collapse the individuals into seven categories as presented in Fig. 7.1. On the side of the workers who experienced wage losses, we find that 14 % of the workers experienced large wages losses of over 20 %. Twenty percent of the workers experienced intermediate wage losses of between 10 and 20 %. Twenty four percent experienced small wage losses of between 1 and 9 %. Five percent of the workers experienced almost no change in wages, earning 1 % more or less in their new job as compared to their old job. On the side of the workers who experienced wage gains, 20 % experienced small wage gains of between 1 and 9 %. Ten percent

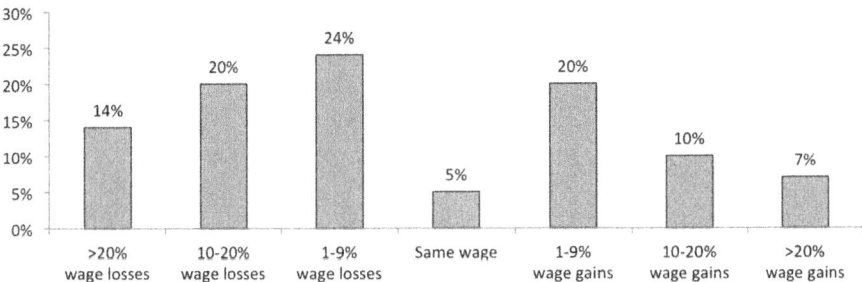

**Fig. 7.1** Distribution of wage difference (based on numerical assessment of workers' wages) of the reemployed workers. N=387. Reading example: 14 % of the reemployed had wage losses of 20 % or more in their new job relative to their pre-displacement job

experienced intermediate wage gains of between 10 and 20%. Seven percent experienced large wage gains of over 20%.

In a nutshell, the proportion of the reemployed workers who experienced wage losses is clearly larger (58%) than the proportion of those who experienced wage gains (37%). If we focus on the substantial wage changes of 10% and more, we find that twice as many workers experienced strong wage losses (34%) as strong wage gains (17%). At the same time, for about a seventh (14%) of all reemployed workers the losses were larger than 20% and thus very substantial.

Workers who were (still or again) unemployed when we surveyed them are not included in this analysis. It is likely that, if these workers managed to find a job after our survey, they experienced, on average, wage losses – as long unemployment durations may act as a signal of low productivity for employers and the workers' skills may depreciate during a long spell of unemployment. Accordingly, we consider the unemployed workers together with those who experienced strong wage losses to be the most negatively affected workers after a plant closure.

The surveys conducted by Weder and Wyss (2010: 38) in Switzerland and by Jolkkonen et al. (2012: 91–92) in Finland find that about a third of the reemployed workers experience a wage increase and about a third a decrease. Thus the comparison shows that workers in our survey experienced larger losses than workers examined in these other studies. While these surveys were conducted in a context of economic growth, ours was carried out in a phase of economic downturn. The higher proportions of workers experiencing wage losses in our study may thus stem from a more adverse labor market situation.[9]

In a next step we analyze the question put to the survey respondents of whether their current wage was much lower, slightly lower, about the same, slightly higher or much higher than their pre-displacement wage. The advantage of this measure is that a larger number of workers were willing to answer this question as compared with the more sensitive question about their wage in a numerical format (n = 495 as compared to n = 387).

Figure 7.2 shows that 22% of the reemployed indicated their post-displacement wage as being much lower and 23% as slightly lower than their pre-displacement wage. 13% of them earned – according to their own assessment – about the same, 31% slightly more and 11% much more than before their plant closed down. If we compare the proportion of workers who experienced wage losses with the proportion of workers who experienced wage increases, 45% earned less than before displacement and 41% earned more. Accordingly, the losses and gains are balanced although the proportion of workers who indicated a strong wage decrease (22%) is clearly larger than the proportion who indicated a strong increase (11%).

Comparing the results from Figs. 7.1 and 7.2 suggests that either the higher number of survey responses changed the composition of the workers and accordingly the distribution of wage change or that those workers experiencing wage losses tended to indicate a better – or positively biased – wage development than they actu-

---

[9] Interestingly, however, our results do not greatly differ from the studies by Weder and Wyss (2010) and Jolkkonen et al. (2012) in terms of the post-displacement reemployment rate.

7.4 Determinants of Wage Change

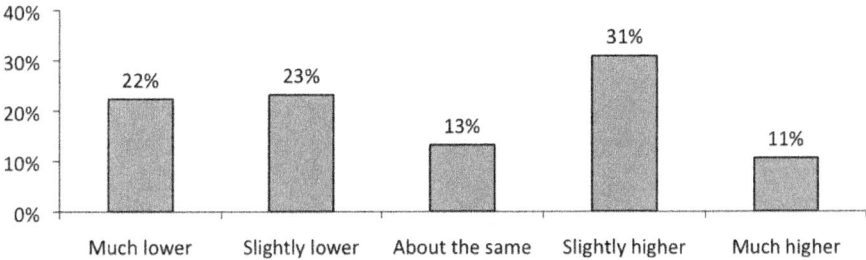

**Fig. 7.2** Distribution of perceived wage change of the reemployed workers. N=495. Note: This figure represents the answer to the survey question: "As compared to your pre-displacement job, your current wage is …" Reading example: 22% of the reemployed indicated earning much lower wages in their new job relative to their pre-displacement job

ally experienced. With respect to the latter option, it is remarkable that the share of workers who indicate a wage increase is similar in Figs. 7.1 and 7.2 (37% vs. 42%). There is however a stronger difference between Figs. 7.1 and 7.2 with respect to wage losses (58% vs. 45%).

This result is surprising in the light of the prospect theory, developed by Tversky and Kahneman (1992), which suggests that the same amount of objectively measured (e.g. financial) losses and gains do not have the same effect on the – subjectively perceived – decrease and increase in utility. In contrast to the conventional utility theory, prospect theory suggests that individuals are negatively biased and experience losses as a stronger burden than gains provide an advantage. If this mechanism were at work in our findings, we would observe that in Fig. 7.2 "much lower" and "slightly lower" wages are overrepresented as compared to Fig. 7.1. This does however not seem to be the case. For this reason, the other option, namely that the fact that individuals who responded to the question represented in Fig. 7.2 more frequently experienced positive changes than respondents to the question represented in Fig. 7.1, seems to be more plausible.

## 7.4 Determinants of Wage Change

Earlier research has shown that different worker subgroups are affected unequally by wage changes. If we analyze wage change in categories by different sociodemographic characteristics, we find the largest differences according to age. Figure 7.3 shows that the large majority of the youngest cohort earn more after displacement: 39% of them answered that, as compared with their pre-displacement job, their post-displacement wage was much higher and 37% of them that it was slightly higher. In contrast, the majority of the two oldest age cohorts earned less after reemployment than before: 36% of the workers aged between 55 and 59 earned much less and 34% earned slightly less than before displacement. With

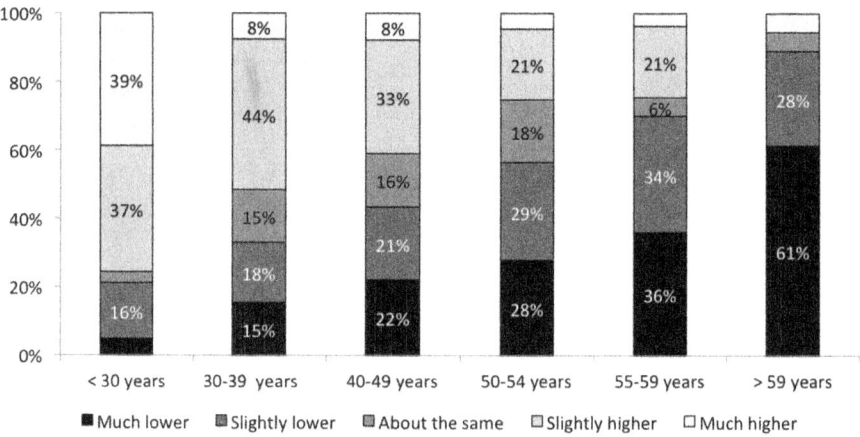

**Fig. 7.3** Distribution of perceived wage difference of the reemployed workers by age. N=489. Note: This figure represents the answer to the survey question: "As compared to your pre-displacement job, your current wage is …". Shares of less than 5 % were not labeled in the figure. Reading example: 61 % of the reemployed over 59 years had in their new job a wage that was much lower than in their pre-displacement job

respect to the workers aged over 60, 61 % earned much less and 28 % slightly less. For the age cohorts in between, the wage change was gradually linked to age: the older the cohort, the larger was the proportion of workers who experience wage losses and the smaller the proportion of workers who experience wage gains. If we use instead the other wage difference variable where we constructed the difference by subtracting the current wage from the former wage, we obtain slightly different results, but the pattern that wage losses increased with age remains the same.

However, this age difference may possibly be explained by the workers' tenure. In fact, the theory suggests that, with longer tenure, workers accumulate more firm-specific skills that do not generate financial returns in a new company (Cha and Morgan 2010: 1145). Moreover, it has been argued that firms reward seniority by paying wages for workers with higher tenure that are higher than their productivity, while younger workers are paid below their productivity (Daniel and Heywood 2007: 49). In the case of a job separation, the seniority and consequently the seniority bonus are lost and the workers thus experience wage losses.

We argued that the change in workers' wages may be linked to their level of education, their pre-displacement tenure, the duration of a potential spell of unemployment and whether they changed occupation. We test these hypotheses by running an OLS regression on inflation-adjusted percentage wage change with these variables, controlling for age, sex, collar, nationality,[10] district unemployment rate and plant.[11]

---

[10] We use here a proxy based on workers' surnames.

[11] In contrast to the last section, we now use the wage difference measure that indicates the percentage wage change for each individual. We use this measure in order to have a linear instead of an ordinal dependent variable.

## 7.4 Determinants of Wage Change

Since not all displaced workers found a new job, the analysis of change in wages is likely to be affected by selection bias. We test for this risk by using a Heckman selection correction analysis, using education as an instrumental variable (results not shown).[12] The results suggest that selection into employment is not a major problem for our analysis of wage change (i.e. we obtain similar findings without the selection correction).

The results are presented in Fig. 7.4. The regression results confirm the descriptive findings from above that age has a negative effect on wage change. Compared to women, men's wage reduction was about 7 percentage points larger. Blue-collar workers experienced 4 percentage points larger losses than white-collar workers. With respect to the nationality proxy we find that workers with surnames from non-EU countries experienced a wage drop that is about 4 percentage points greater than for workers with local surnames. Workers from Plants 3 and 4 experienced wage increases that are 8 percentage points higher than those in the reference category (Plant 1).

We now turn to the independent variables of interest. As expected, long unemployment durations are associated with negative wage changes. Workers with intermediate unemployment duration of 3–12 months experienced a wage loss of 5 percentage points relative to workers who found their new job within 2 months. Workers who were unemployed for more than 12 months lost 11 percentage points in wages as compared to workers who found their job within 2 months. This finding may be due to the negative effect of long unemployment durations on workers' post-displacement wages – because of skill depreciation in long spells of unemployment or a negative signaling effect of such spells. Alternatively, it may also be due to a selection effect: the most dynamic and productive job seekers leave unemployment first, the least dynamic and productive workers last (Machin and Manning 1999: 18).

The next independent variables we consider are change of sector and change of occupation. Changing sector means that workers were reemployed in the services, while changing occupation means that workers were reemployed in a different ISCO 1-digit occupation category than the one in which they worked before displacement. With respect to change of sector we only distinguish between service and manufacturing sector since the literature suggests that this distinction matters most with respect to wage (Jacobson et al. 1993). We do not find a statistically significant effect for change of sector. In contrast, we change of occupation is significant although it is relatively small. The result suggests that workers who are reemployed in a different occupational group experienced a 3 percentage points decrease in wages as compared to those reemployed in their pre-displacement occupation. This result is in line with the literature on skill regimes which suggests that, in highly standardized vocational training systems such as the Swiss system, workers transit smoothly between jobs within the same sector. This outcome results from workers acquiring sector-specific skills rather than solely firm-specific skills during vocational education.

---

[12] There is a correlation between the outcome equation and the selection equation (rho=0.78) and accordingly the Wald test is not significant.

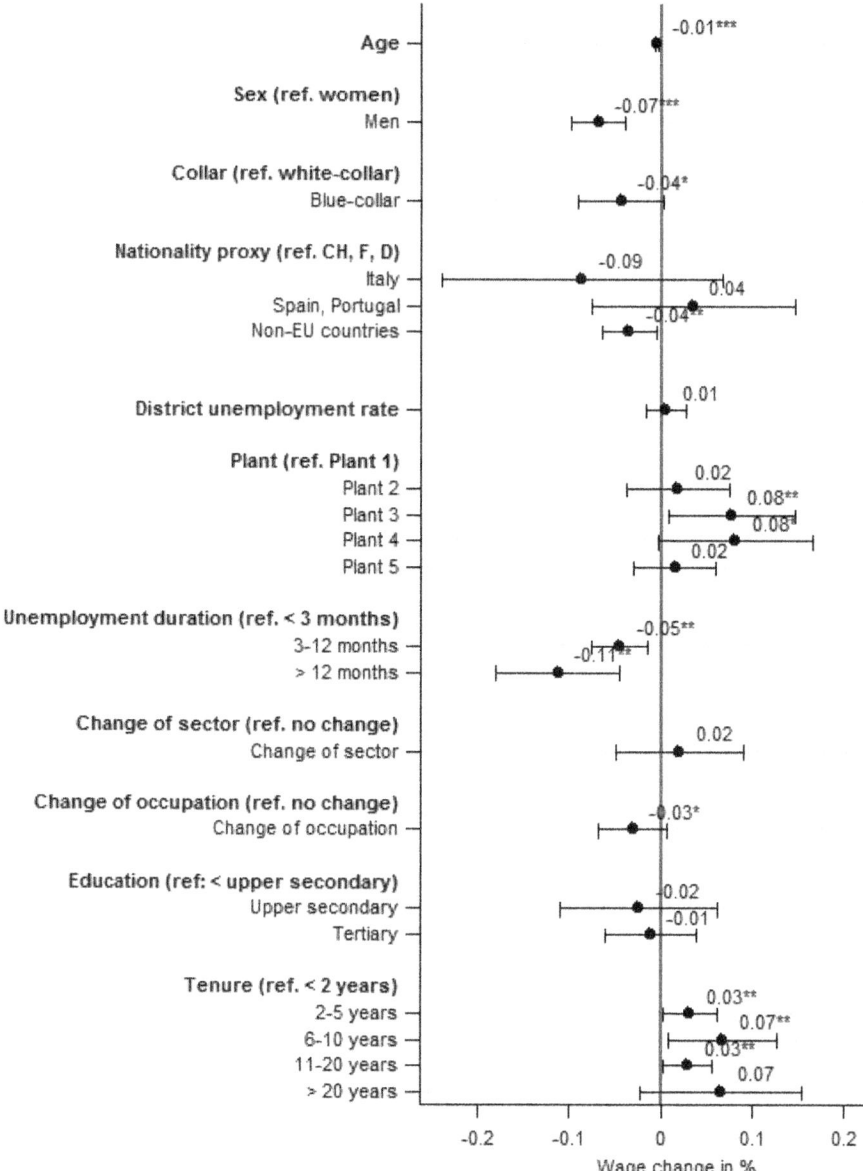

**Fig. 7.4** Coefficients for an OLS regression for wage change (in %) between the job before and after displacement. N=341. Note: We also ran models where we entered plant as a control variable. The results were not affected by this variable. Significance levels: * $p<0.1$, ** $p<0.05$, *** $p<0.01$. Standard errors are clustered at the plant level. Reading example: For each year in age, the wage loss is 1 percentage point

## 7.4 Determinants of Wage Change

With respect to education our findings do not confirm our expectations. The effects are small and statistically non-significant. This suggests that while low levels of education reduce the chances of reemployment, they do not increase the risk of wage loss relative to intermediate or high levels of education.

Finally, tenure reveals significant effects but they run in the opposite direction to our prediction and the link is not linear. In order to test the robustness of this effect, we run a model without the age variable. However, the result is similar with small positive but significant effects for 2–5 years of tenure and 6–10 years of tenure. Consequently, our hypotheses with respect to education and tenure cannot be supported by these findings.

Overall, we find less support for the human capital theory which explains workers' wage losses after job separations as a consequence of lower returns on their skills. With respect to the finding that long spells of unemployment considerably affect workers' wage changes, it is not clear whether this result is due to a skill depreciation effect, a signaling effect or a selection effect. But since the other findings – in particular with regard to education and type of collar – provide little evidence for human capital mechanisms being at work, signaling theory is perhaps a better explanation. The fact that we find a negative wage effect for workers with surnames originating from non-EU countries may also point to this mechanism. With respect to nationality and ethnic background, it has indeed been shown for Switzerland that simply changing the name (and thus implicitly the nationality or migration background) on a job application negatively affects the job seekers' chances of being invited to an interview (Fibbi et al. 2003).

If we compare our results with earlier findings, Carneiro and Portugal (2006: 18) also find that the duration of joblessness has an important effect on earning losses. They report that this factor explains about a third of the losses. But in contrast to our analysis they find that job tenure even explains a larger proportion of the wage losses, namely about 50%. Other authors have pointed out that changes from the manufacturing sector to the service sector are particularly costly. Cha and Morgan (2010: 1144) reveal wage losses of 35% for workers who changed from the secondary to the tertiary sector. These findings are not confirmed by our analysis for Switzerland. An additional descriptive analysis that simply compares the average wage changes for workers reemployed in manufacturing and the services reveals almost no difference between "stayers" and "switchers".

Only our result that change of occupation is a more important determinant than change of sector seems to correspond to earlier findings. Haynes et al. (2002: 250) report that individuals with a sector tenure of 10 years lost around 1% of their wages when switching sector while workers with an occupation tenure of 15 years lost 15% of their wages when changing occupation. While we also find that change of occupation is more relevant than change of sector, the effects for the workers in our sample are much smaller.

## 7.5 Conclusion

The analysis of the reemployed workers' wages has revealed the costs of job loss that workers experience even if they are reemployed. On average, they are confronted with moderate wage losses if we compare their pre- and post-displacement wages. However, the full amount of wage losses can only be assessed if we compare these losses with the counterfactual outcome – the outcome of workers who did not lose their jobs. Comparing the wage losses of the displaced workers with the wage development of non-displaced workers from the Swiss Household Panel, we find that the full losses of displaced workers amount on average to 6%. As discussed in more detail in Chap. 2, the control and the treatment group are alike in terms of age but not in terms of education and sex. The control group contains a larger share of women and of workers with higher levels of education. Our estimation of the counterfactual outcome may therefore overestimate the wage losses since our analysis suggests that men and higher skilled workers experience stronger wage losses after job displacement than women and lower skilled workers. At the same time, since the control and treatment group are alike with respect to the variable that affects wage development most strongly, age – minus one percent for each year of age –, the counterfactual outcome may not be too strongly misspecified.

Our expectations that high-tenured workers, low-qualified workers and workers who were reemployed in another sector or occupation experience the highest wage losses cannot be corroborated. But we find that long unemployment durations are linked to wages losses, which is in line with our hypothesis H6. However, wage changes are most strongly affected by age. Reemployed workers of the oldest cohort, the over 60s, are much more likely to experience wage losses than the other age groups – even after controlling for other socio-demographic factors. On average, younger workers experienced substantial increases in their hourly wages (+8% for those under 30), whereas reemployed older workers had to put up with substantial wage cuts (−14% for those aged 55–59, −17% for those aged 60–65). Older workers thus do not only have bleaker reemployment chances after a plant closure, but they also have to accept substantial wage losses. In contrast, the great majority of younger workers experience successful occupational transitions after plant closure which tend to be accompanied by increased wages.

In this chapter we have shown that there is huge variation in how wages are affected by non-self-inflicted job loss. Although the average wage loss is an important number to estimate because it allows for comparison with studies from other countries, it provides only limited information. From a scientific point of view it is important to understand how different worker subgroups are affected. This allows receiving a better understanding of the mechanisms underlying workers' wage losses. As workers' wage curve tends to steadily increase during the first decades of their careers, it usually slightly declines towards the end of the career. Finding that the older workers in our study are confronted with the highest wages is thus not surprising at first glance. However, the decreases are strong – even if we consider only those who returned to a job –, which seems to give a hint that other mechanisms are at work. The large wage losses of older workers seem to be an indicator for the low interest employers take in hiring them.

The consequences on an individual level are that these workers have to put up with lower wages and lower old-age pension savings. Lower wages may be less of a problem as children, if there are any, are no longer likely to be financially dependent on their parents. In contrast, substantial reductions in old-age pension savings may leave workers with long-lasting hardship and deprive them for instance from making life-changing investments in their health. From a societal point of view losing one's job – in particular at the end of the career – is a trigger of economic inequalities, leaving displaced workers with substantial economic and social disadvantages as compared to non-displaced workers.

**Open Access** This chapter is distributed under the terms of the Creative Commons Attribution 4.0 International License (http://creativecommons.org/licenses/by/4.0/), which permits use, duplication, adaptation, distribution and reproduction in any medium or format, as long as you give appropriate credit to the original author(s) and the source, a link is provided to the Creative Commons license and any changes made are indicated.

The images or other third party material in this chapter are included in the work's Creative Commons license, unless indicated otherwise in the credit line; if such material is not included in the work's Creative Commons license and the respective action is not permitted by statutory regulation, users will need to obtain permission from the license holder to duplicate, adapt or reproduce the material.

# References

Abe, M., Higuchi, Y., Kuhn, P. J., Nakamura, M., & Sweetman, A. (2002). Worker displacement in Japan and Canada. In P. J. Kuhn (Ed.), *Losing work, moving on. International perspective on worker displacement* (pp. 195–300). Kalamazoo: W.E. Upjohn Institute for Employment Research.

Appelqvist, J. (2007). *Wage and earnings losses of displaced workers in Finland*. Government Institute for Economic Research Finland (VATT), Helsinki, Discussion Paper, No. 422.

Arulampalam, W. (2001). Is unemployment really scarring? Effects of unemployment experiences on wages. *The Economic Journal, 111*(475), F585–F606.

Balestra, S., & Backes-Gellner, U. (2016). *When a door closes, a window opens? Long-term labor market effects of involuntary separations* (German Economic Review, (advanced online access) 1–21.

Becker, G. S. (1962). Investment in human capital: A theoretical analysis. *Journal of Political Economy, 70*(5), 9–49.

Bender, S., Dustmann, C., Margolis, D., & Meghir, C. (2002). Worker displacement in France and Germany. In P. J. Kuhn (Ed.), *Losing work, moving on. International perspectives on worker displacement* (pp. 375–470). Kalamazoo: W.E. Upjohn Institute for Employment Research.

Burda, M. C., & Mertens, A. (2001). Estimating wage losses of displaced workers in Germany. *Labour Economics, 8*(1), 15–41.

Carneiro, A., & Portugal, P. (2006). *Earnings losses of displaced workers. Evidence from a matched employer-employee data set* (Estudos e Doumentos de Trabalho working papers No. 14).

Carrington, W. J. (1993). Wage losses for displaced workers: Is it really the firm that matters? *The Journal of Human Resources, 28*(3), 435.

Cha, Y., & Morgan, S. L. (2010). Structural earnings losses and between-industry mobility of displaced workers, 2003–2008. *Social Science Research, 39*(6), 1137–1152.

Couch, K. A., & Placzek, D. W. (2010). Earnings losses of displaced workers revisited. *American Economic Review, 100*(1), 572–589.

Daniel, K., & Heywood, J. S. (2007). The determinants of hiring older workers: UK evidence. *Labour Economics, 14*(1), 35–51.

Devens, R. M. (1986). Displaced workers: One year later. *Monthly Labor Review, 109*, (July), 40–44.

Fallick, B. C. (1993). The industrial mobility of displaced workers. *Journal of Labor Economics, 11*(2), 302–323.

Fallick, B. C. (1996). A review of the recent empirical literature on displaced workers. *Industrial and Labor Relations Review, 50*(1), 5–16.

Farber, H. S. (1997). The changing face of job loss in the United States, 1981–1995. *Brookings Papers on Economic Activity. Microeconomics, 1997*(1997), 55–142.

Feather, N. T. (1997). Economic deprivation and the psychological impact of unemployment. *Australian Psychologist, 32*(1), 37–45.

Fibbi, R., Kaya, B., & Piguet, E. (2003). Le passeport ou le diplôme? *Forum suisse pour l'étude des migrations et de la population, 31.*

Flückiger, Y. (2002). Le chômage en Suisse: Causes, évolution et efficacité des mesures actives. *Aspects de La Sécurité Sociale, 4*, 11–21.

Gangl, M. (2004). Institutions and the structure of labour market matching in the United States and West Germany. *European Sociological Review, 20*(3), 171–187.

Haynes, M., Upward, R., & Wright, P. (2002). Estimating the wage costs of inter- and intra-sectoral adjustment. *Weltwirtschaftliches Archiv, 138*(2), 229–253.

Jacobson, L. S., LaLonde, R. J., & Sullivan, D. G. (1993). Earning losses of displaced workers. *The American Economic Review, 83*(4), 685–709.

Jolkkonen, A., Koistinen, P., & Kurvinen, A. (2012). Reemployment of displaced workers – The case of a plant closing on a remote region in Finland. *Nordic Journal of Working Life Studies, 2*(1), 81–100.

Kletzer, L. G. (2001). *Job loss from imports: Measuring the costs*. Washington, DC: Institute for International Economics.

Lentz, R. (2009). Optimal unemployment insurance in an estimated job search model with savings. *Review of Economic Dynamics, 12*(1), 37–57.

Machin, S., & Manning, A. (1999). The causes and consequences of long-term unemployment in Europe. In O. Ashenfelter & D. Card (Eds.), *Handbook of labor economics* (1st ed., Vol. 3, pp. 3085–3139). Amsterdam/New York: Elsevier.

Neal, D. (1995). Industry-specific human capital: Evidence from displaced workers. *Journal of Labor Economics, 13*(4), 653–677.

Spence, M. (1973). Job market signaling. *The Quarterly Journal of Economics, 87*(3), 355–374.

Tversky, A., & Kahneman, D. (1992). Advances in prospect theory: Cumulative representation of uncertainty. *Journal of Risk and Uncertainty, 5*(5), 297–323.

Weder, R., & Wyss, S. (2010). *Arbeitslosigkeit unter niedrig Qualifizierten: Die Rolle der Globalisierung* (SECO Publikation Arbeitsmarktpolitik No. 29). Bern: SECO.

Zwick, T. (2012). Earning losses after non-employment increase with age. *Düsseldorf, Schmalenbach Business Review, 64*, 2–19.

# Chapter 8
# Job Quality

Wages are only one dimension of the quality of workers' new jobs. Other aspects also matter for the workers' life and career opportunities. It has been argued that work is intimately related to other social, economic and political issues ( Kalleberg 2009: 8). For instance, job insecurity not only increases workers' levels of stress (De Witte 1999), but may also make them risk averse. Parents with unstable jobs thus may invest less in their children's education, which affects the children's long-term opportunities and quality of life (Esping-Andersen 2008: 75).

Previous research suggests that workers who had experienced a spell of unemployment were at risk of being reemployed in jobs of lower quality (Brand 2006: 290; Dieckhoff 2011: 242). One explanation comes from the human capital theory, suggesting that displaced workers' skills may be less useful in their new job than in their former job and workers thus have to accept offers for jobs for which they are overqualified (Becker 1962). Alternatively, reemployment in jobs of lower quality may also come about as a consequence of long spells of unemployment, which lead to skill depreciation, or loss of self-esteem and motivation (Pissarides 1992; Arulampalam 2001).

Our hypothesis with respect to job quality highlights the effects of long-term unemployment, expecting workers with long spells of unemployment to be most vulnerable to being reemployed in jobs of lower quality (hypothesis H7, see Sect. 1.4). Previous studies further indicate that workers with tertiary education and white-collar workers are particularly vulnerable to a decrease in job quality upon reemployment. Our models therefore include education and collar. In addition, we control for age, sex, tenure, district unemployment rate and plant.

This chapter focuses on four dimensions of the quality of the new jobs. We examine the type of contract, job security, skill match, and job authority. Wherever possible, our focus lies on the comparison between the workers' pre- and post-displacement situation. In each section we start with a descriptive analysis and then proceed with an analysis of potential determinants of job quality. Finally, we examine workers' job satisfaction and discuss its strongest determinants.

## 8.1 Contract Type

Figure 8.1 presents the contract type in which workers were reemployed. Upon reemployment, 86% of the workers had a permanent contract, 7% a fixed-term contract, 4% a temporary contract, 1% a call-off contract and 2% other types of contract. This result suggests that the great majority have found a comparatively stable job. This result is similar to other findings from Switzerland reported by (Wyss 2009: 27). She analyses whether workers experienced a change in their contact type, comparing their pre- and post-displacement job, and finds that, depending on the company, between 79 and 100% of the workers were reemployed in the same type of contract. The study does not, however, indicate whether these workers were permanently employed before job loss.

In their literature review on non-standard employment, Hipp et al. (2015: 357) point out that collective bargaining systems that ensure wage flexibility tend to go along with a low prevalence of temporary employment. Accordingly, our finding may be explained by the high level of wage flexibility in Switzerland, which in turn may be a result of the high degree of coordination in collective bargaining. In addition, our finding has to be interpreted in the context of the Swiss labor market, which is characterized by weak employment protection (OECD 2004: 72). Accordingly, a permanent contract guarantees less job security than in most other continental European countries. At the same time, non-permanent contracts may be a better alternative to unemployment. Although fixed-term and temporary jobs usually imply fewer fringe benefits and less opportunity for career development (Green 2008: 151), they can sometimes be a stepping stone towards permanent jobs and protect workers from long-term unemployment (Gerfin et al. 2005: 820).

If we examine the contract type after reemployment by age (not shown), we find that workers aged over 60 had a significantly lower chance of being reemployed in a permanent contract (64% as compared to 82–94% for the younger cohorts). 14% of this oldest age group was reemployed in a fixed-term and 21% in a call-off contract, much more than in the younger age groups. Among the age groups between 16 and 55 the proportion of workers reemployed in the different types of contracts does not vary greatly. This suggests that workers aged over 55 and especially those over 60, who are rapidly approaching the legal retirement age, have a particular – and weak – position in the labor market. Once they lose their job, they not only face high barriers to return to the labor force, but also have to put up with large wage losses and jobs on probation.

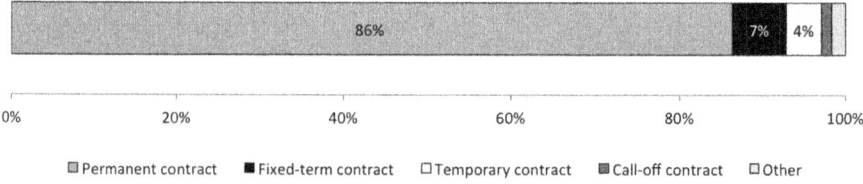

**Fig. 8.1** Contract type of the new job. N=481

## 8.1 Contract Type

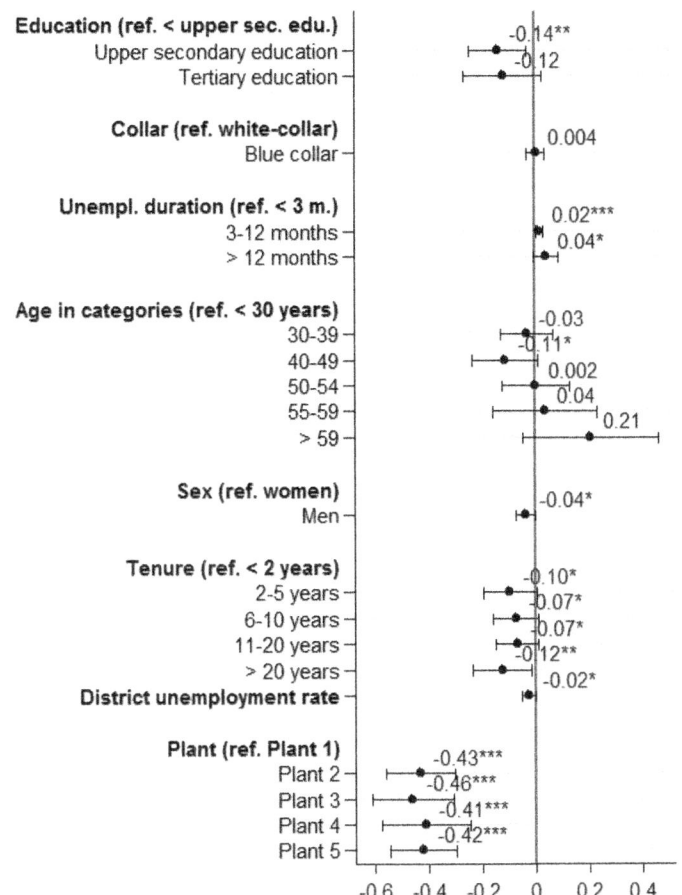

**Fig. 8.2** Average Marginal Effects (AME) for a binomial logistic regression for being reemployed in a non-permanent contract. Note: N=445. Significance levels: * p < 0.1, ** p < 0.05, *** p < 0.01. Standard errors are clustered at the plant level. The dependent variable is binomial and differentiates between two outcomes: (i) reemployed in a non-permanent (fixed-term, temporary, call-off or other) job and (ii) reemployed in a permanent job. Reading example: As compared to workers with less than upper secondary education, workers with upper secondary education are 14 percentage points and workers with tertiary education 12 percentage points less likely to be reemployed in a non-permanent contract

This age-related finding is confirmed by a binomial analysis presented in Fig. 8.2. However, the effects for the older age groups are not statistically significant because of large standard errors. Other covariates, in contrast, have provided us with significant results. In fact, workers with higher levels of education are less likely to be reemployed in non-permanent contracts than workers with less than upper secondary education. In comparison to the other covariates, education has a strong effect on the reemployment contract. It thus seems that education protects workers well from being reemployed in unstable jobs. The longer workers were unemployed, the more likely they were to be reemployed in a non-permanent contract. Workers who were unemployed between 3 and 12 months were 2 percentage points more likely to be reemployed in non-permanent contracts than workers who found their new job within 3 months. Workers who were unemployed for over 12 months had a 4 percentage points higher likelihood. Although the effects are statistically significant, they are small. Men and workers with longer tenure were less likely to be reemployed in a non-permanent contract than women and workers with tenure less than 2 years. It is possible that workers with tenure of less than 2 years were already hired on a temporary or fixed-term contract in their pre-displacement job. If this were the case, it is possible that certain workers have a higher risk of being repeatedly employed in temporary or fixed-term contracts. Finally, workers from Plants 2 to 5 were much less likely to be reemployed in non-permanent jobs than workers from Plant 1. The differences between Plant 1 – the reference category – and the other plants are large and highly statistically significant. This result shows that workers in Plant 1, located in Geneva, had by far the highest risk of being reemployed in temporary or fixed-term contacts. A reason for this result may be the more competitive labor market in Geneva.

## 8.2 Subjective Job Security

An additional approach to examine the workers' job security was made by asking reemployed workers how they estimate the risk of job loss in their new job. Figure 8.3 reveals that 5 % of the workers indicated a very high and 9 % a rather high subjective risk of job loss. 14 % of the reemployed workers thus experienced strong job insecurity in their new job. However, the great majority – altogether 75 % of the workers – reported a medium, rather low or very low risk of job loss. Three out of four reemployed workers thus felt rather safe in their new position. 11 % were not able to assess the risk of job loss.

These descriptive findings correspond approximately to those on contract type. While 4 % of the workers were reemployed in temporary contracts, 5 % feel the risk of job loss to be very high. The 7 % share of workers reemployed in fixed-termed contracts roughly corresponds to the 9 % of workers indicating a rather high risk of

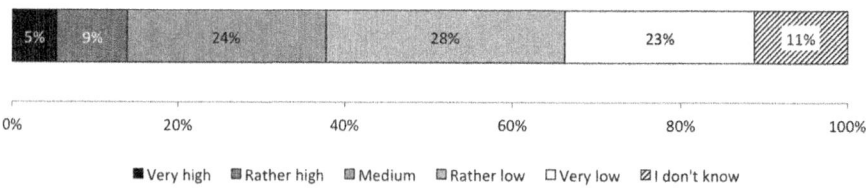

**Fig. 8.3** Subjective risk of job loss in the new job. N=482

job loss. The assumption that probably the same workers indicated working in non-permanent contracts and experiencing low job security is supported by a study based on the European Community Household Panel that shows a clear link between subjective job security and type of contract (Clark and Postel-Vinay 2009). In the 12 European countries under study, they find that subjective job security is highest for workers employed in public service jobs and the lowest for those in temporary jobs. Interestingly, they observe that the more generous the unemployment benefits are in a country, the higher is the subjective job security in all types of jobs, including temporary and private sector jobs.

With respect to the risk of job loss, a descriptive analysis (not shown) reveals a similar pattern for all age groups from 30 to over 60. Here only the youngest cohort differs from the others. Among the under-30s none of the workers experienced a very high risk of job loss, while in all other age cohorts 5–7 % of the workers evaluate their risk of losing their job as very high.

A multinomial logistic regression analysis, presented in Fig. 8.4, shows that only our hypothesis regarding unemployment duration is supported. Workers with unemployment durations of over 1 year are 13 percentage points more likely to be reemployed in a job with very or rather high risk of job loss. Thus, even after controlling for socio-demographic factors, unemployment duration seems to be strongly associated with being reemployed in more insecure jobs. Moreover, unemployment durations over 1 year provide not merely the only statistically significant result of this regression analysis but also display the strongest effect in the entire model. Education provides us neither with statistically significant nor results in the expected direction. With respect to collar, there is a small effect but it is not statistically significant and goes in the opposite direction to what we would have expected.

## 8.3 Skill Match

Skill match refers to the correspondence between workers' skills and the requirements of their jobs. In our survey we asked the workers in a straightforward way whether they thought that the skill requirements of their new job corresponded to their own skills. Possible answers were that the skill match is adequate, that the worker is underqualified, i.e. the skills available are below the requirements, or that the worker is overqualified, i.e. the skills available are over the requirements.

Overall, two out of three reemployed workers (64 %) declared they had found a job with an adequate skill match, 12 % indicated that they were underqualified and 24 % that they were overqualified in their new job (Fig. 8.5). Thus, a majority of the workers found a job that corresponded to their skill level. However, twice as many workers were overqualified as are underqualified and thus more workers encountered a situation where the skill requirements of their new job were below the skill profile they possess. It is possible that workers' self-reported skill match is biased because they rather overestimate than underestimate their skills. Moreover, workers may also have been overqualified in their former job. Still, this result suggests that

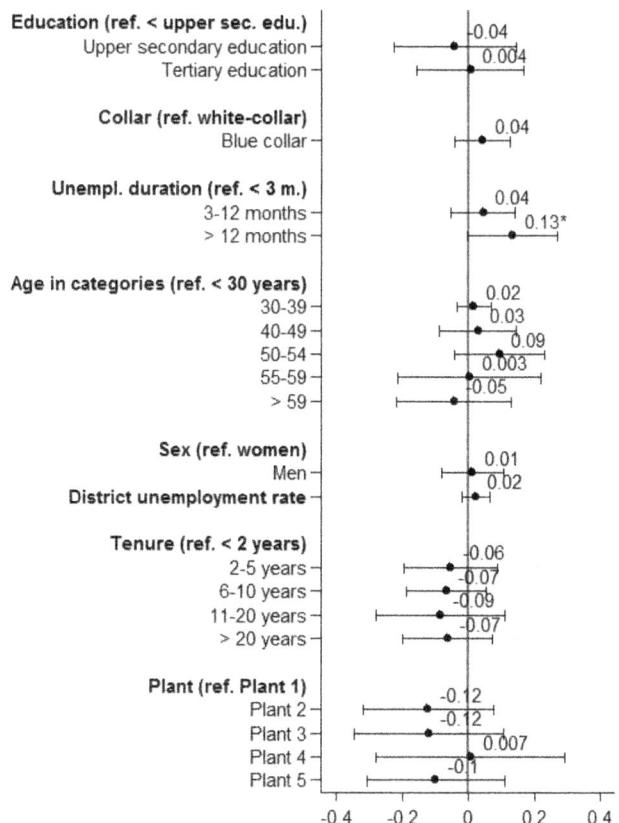

**Fig. 8.4** Average Marginal Effects (AME) for a multinomial logistic regression for being reemployed in a job with higher risk of job loss. N=397. Note: The dependent variable is multinomial and differentiates between three outcomes: reemployed in a job where the worker is at (i) high risk, (ii) intermediate risk and (iii) low risk. Significance levels: * $p < 0.1$, ** $p < 0.05$, *** $p < 0.01$. Standard errors are clustered at the plant level. Reading example: As compared to workers with less than upper secondary education, workers with upper secondary education are 4 percentage points less and workers with tertiary education 0.4 percentage points more likely to be reemployed in a job with high risk of job loss

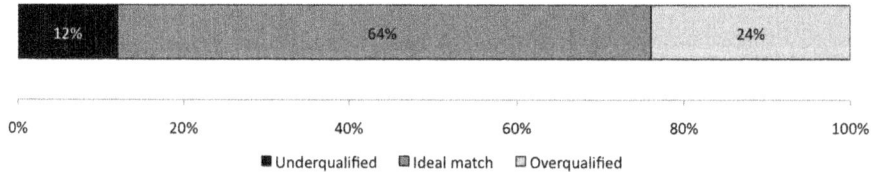

**Fig. 8.5** Skill match in the new job. N=474

workers who found a job in which they cannot tap the full potential of their skills were more numerous than those in the opposite situation.

Overqualification may hinder workers' career advancement and usually goes hand in hand, other things being equal, with lower returns on their skills than for workers in a job with an adequate skill match. Moreover, based on data from the US and Spain it has been shown that overqualifaction is strongly associated with low job satisfaction (Johnson and Johnson 2000: 547; Badillo Amador et al. 2012: 322). In the Spanish study it has been shown, however, that underqualification is even more detrimental to workers' job satisfaction.

Were older workers more often confronted with overqualification in the new job than younger workers? A descriptive analysis (not shown) suggests that this is the case for the oldest category of workers: 36 % of the over 59 year olds indicated that they were overqualified as compared to 27 % for the 50–59 year olds, 22 % for the 40–49 year olds, 29 % for the 30–39 year olds and 20 % for the under 30s. Compared to the extent of the disadvantage that older workers experienced in terms of reemployment chances and wages, their disadvantage in terms of skill match is small.

Nevertheless, using inferential statistics and thus measuring the net effect of the different factors reveals that workers over 59 have a 17 percentage point higher risk of being overqualified in their new job (see Fig. 8.6). For the other age groups however, there is no statistically significant effect. Our multinomial regression analysis on being overqualified in the new job as compared to being adequately qualified or underqualified furthermore shows that workers with tertiary education were 14 percentage points more likely to be overqualified in their new job than workers with the lowest level of education. Workers with upper secondary education were about 6 percentage points more likely to be overqualified than workers with less education, although the effect does not reach statistical significance. This result is not surprising, since low-educated workers are generally unlikely to be overqualified.

Being unemployed for 3–12 months is linked to a 7 percentage points higher risk and being unemployed for more than a year to a 14 percentage points higher risk of being overqualified in the new job as compared to workers who return to a job within 3 months. We find this effect although we control for other socio-demographic characteristics. Accordingly, the duration *per se* seems to have a negative effect on skill match in the new job. This finding may be due to a selection effect, unobservables driving both long-term unemployment and a decrease in job quality, or due to the fact that long unemployment durations are a negative signal to employers. Overall, we can maintain that workers with long spells of unemployment seem to receive the low-end jobs in terms of job quality.

## 8.4 Job Authority

Pre- and post-displacement job authority was measured by asking workers which hierarchical function they had in their former and their new job. We define change in job authority as a situation where workers were in a position of supervision or

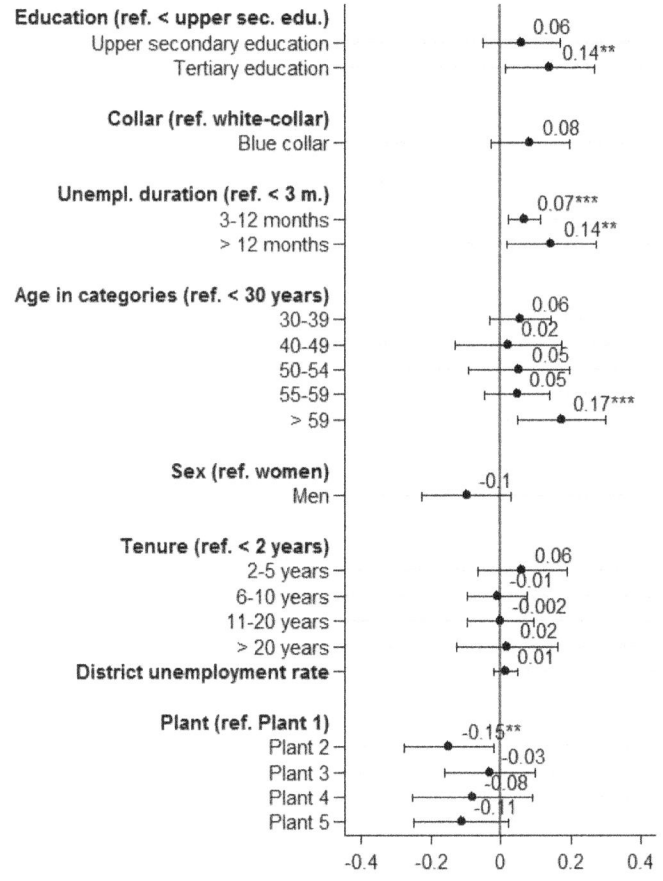

**Fig. 8.6** Average Marginal Effects (AME) for a multinomial logistic regression for being overqualified in the new job. Note: N=440. Significance levels: * p < 0.1, ** p < 0.05, *** p < 0.01. Standard errors are clustered at the plant level. The dependent variable is multinomial and differentiates between three outcomes: reemployed in a job where the worker is (i) overqualified, (ii) adequately qualified and (iii) underqualified. Reading example: As compared to workers with less than upper secondary education, workers with upper secondary education are 6 percentage points and workers with tertiary education 14 percentage points more likely to be overqualified in their new job

management before displacement but without such a position after displacement or the other way around. 77% of the reemployed respondents indicated having the same level of job authority in the new job as in the old job. 16% experienced a downgrading and 7% an upgrading (see Fig. 8.7). Although the majority of the workers indicated that they are reemployed in a job with the same level of job authority and some workers experienced an increase in job authority, still a considerable proportion of workers experienced a downgrading (16% on average).

## 8.5 Job Satisfaction

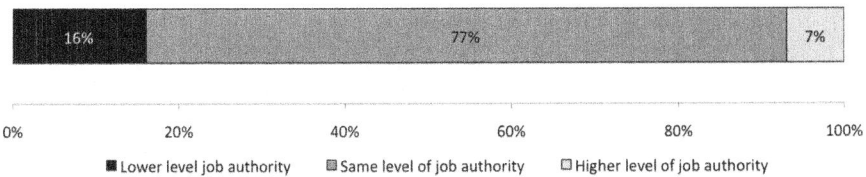

**Fig. 8.7** Level of job authority in the new job as compared to the former job. N=456

These findings confirm earlier research showing that workers who experienced a spell of unemployment were more likely to experience a loss of job authority than workers who had not been unemployed. A study based on European data measuring the impact of job loss on job authority about 2 years after job loss indicates a negative effect of about 8 percentage points for Denmark and the UK (Dieckhoff 2011: 242). Based on data from the US, the negative effect of job displacement on job authority has been estimated to be about 7 percentage points ( Brand 2006: 286).

A descriptive analysis (not shown) of the change in job authority by age reveals that the youngest cohort of the under 30 year old workers had by far the largest proportion (16 %) of workers who experienced an increase in job authority.

This result is confirmed by a multinomial logistic regression analysis, presented in Fig. 8.8, with the usual controls. This finding is not surprising since 94 % of the workers in the youngest cohort did not have a position of supervision before displacement. With respect to education, we find that workers with upper secondary and tertiary education were 8–13 percentage points more likely to experience a decrease in job authority than workers with less than upper secondary education. Again this finding is due to the fact that 90 % of the workers with the lowest level of education did not have a supervision function before displacement, as compared to 70 % of the workers with upper secondary education and 46 % for workers with tertiary education.

## 8.5 Job Satisfaction

The experience of the occupational transition after plant closure also depends on whether workers are satisfied with their new job, or more precisely, how job satisfaction changes as a consequence of displacement. Information about workers' job satisfaction provides us with a subjective evaluation of more objective dimensions of job quality. In fact two recent studies suggest that job satisfaction is closely linked to workers' job quality. Dieckhoff (2011: 243) shows for Austria and Spain that decreases in the availability of permanent contracts lead to decreases in satisfaction with job security. Based on the British Workplace Employee Relation Survey, Gazioglu and Tansel (2006: 1167) report a strong association between job security and job satisfaction as well as between income and job satisfaction. Moreover, they find that women are more satisfied with their jobs than men, low-educated workers

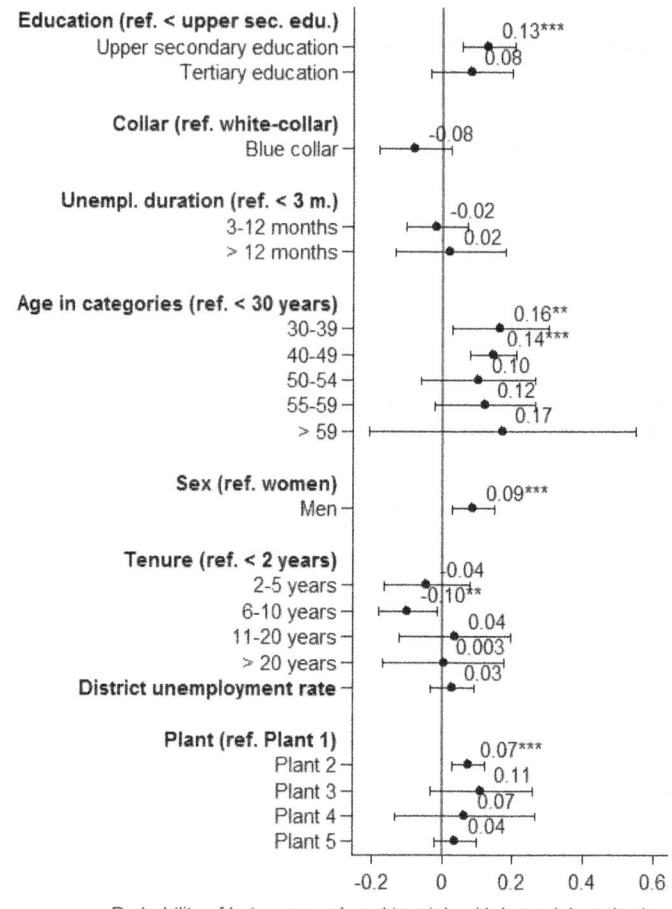

**Fig. 8.8** Average Marginal Effects (AME) for a multinomial logistic regression for being reemployed in a job with lower job authority. Note: N=424. Significance levels: * $p < 0.1$, ** $p < 0.05$, *** $p < 0.01$. Standard errors are clustered at the plant level. The dependent variable is multinomial and differentiates between three outcomes: reemployed in a job where the worker has a (i) lower level of job authority, (ii) the same level of job authority and (iii) a higher level of job authority. Reading example: As compared to workers with less than upper secondary education, workers with upper secondary education are 13 percentage points and workers with tertiary education 8 percentage points more likely to be reemployed in a job with lower job authority

more than highly educated ones, workers who are single more than married ones and that age has a U-shaped relation to job satisfaction.

We first describe workers' pre- and post-displacement job satisfaction, before we try to identify the factors associated with change in workers' job satisfaction. Our analysis takes only reemployed workers into account. Before displacement, workers' job satisfaction was on average 7.7 points while after displacement it was significantly lower at 6.9 points. Figures 8.9a and 8.9b present the distribution of job

8.5 Job Satisfaction

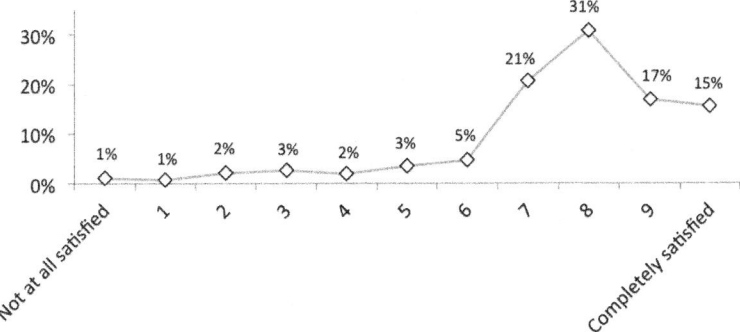

**Fig. 8.9a** Distribution of job satisfaction before displacement. N=474. Reading example: Before displacement, 15% of the workers indicated being completely satisfied with their lives

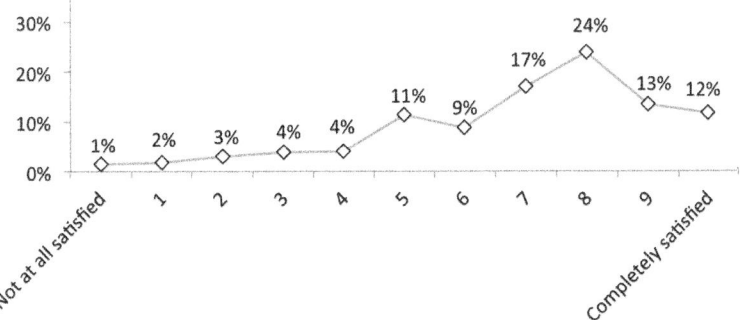

**Fig. 8.9b** Distribution of job satisfaction after displacement. N=474. Reading example: After displacement, 12% of the workers indicated being completely satisfied with their lives

satisfaction before and after displacement on a scale from 0 to 10 points where 0 represents "Not at all satisfied" and 10 represents "Completely satisfied with the job". Figure 8.9a shows that 31% of the workers indicated a job satisfaction of 8 points and 84% between 7 and 10. After displacement, 24% of the workers reported a job satisfaction of 8 points and 64% indicated a level of satisfaction between 7 and 10. At the same time, 20% of the workers reported a job satisfaction of 5 or 6 – a substantially larger proportion than before displacement (8%). The displacement has thus flattened the distribution of job satisfaction and shifted it to the left.

To determine which factors are linked to workers' changes in job satisfaction, we run an OLS regression (see Fig. 8.10). We use within-individual *change* rather than *level* of job satisfaction as a dependent variable since satisfaction measures are typically subject to selection bias. It has been argued that most individuals have a baseline level of satisfaction that remains relatively stable across the life course, although major life events may lead to oscillations around this baseline level (Clark et al.

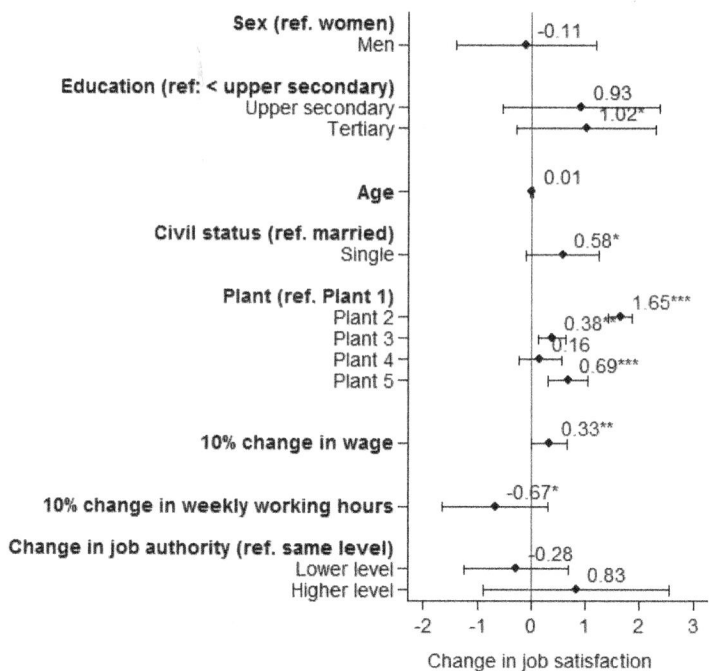

**Fig. 8.10** Coefficients for an OLS-regression analysis for change in job satisfaction for the reemployed. Note: N=332. Significance levels: * p < 0.1, ** p < 0.05, *** p < 0.01. Standard errors are clustered at the plant level. Reading example: As compared to women, men experienced a decrease in job satisfaction by 0.11 points

2008). Our model contains the covariates sex, education, age, civil status, plant, and measures which assess the change between before and after displacement in terms of wages, weekly working hours and job authority.

We find a strong positive effect of tertiary education: reemployed workers with tertiary education experienced on average an increase of over 1 point in life satisfaction as compared to workers with less than upper secondary education. In addition, workers who were single experienced a more positive change in job satisfaction than workers who were married. Workers in Plant 2 experienced a much more positive development of job satisfaction than the workers in other plants. This may be due to the fact that they had known for some time that the plant was in a difficult economic situation – so difficult that they even accepted wage cuts the year before the plant closed – and thus suffered from job insecurity. A 10 % increase in wages was associated with an increase in job satisfaction of 0.3 points. Moreover, longer working hours have a negative effect on job satisfaction: an increase of 10 % in working hours was associated with a decrease in job satisfaction of about 0.7 points. In contrast, changes in job authority do not provide significant effects. In sum, this analysis shows that tertiary education and, curiously, being single cushioned workers against a decrease in job satisfaction. Changes in wages also mattered for workers' job satisfaction, but less than changes in working hours.

## 8.6 Conclusion

The analysis of the quality of the workers' new jobs has provided us with a more in-depth picture about the adjustment process that workers undergo after plant closure. However, we do not find as bleak a picture as might have been expected. Interestingly, 86% of the workers were reemployed in a permanent contract. However, because of the weak employment protection in Switzerland a permanent contract does not automatically imply high job security – but does give higher security than temporary or fixed-term jobs. An analysis of the subjective risk of job loss suggests that while half of the workers think they have a low risk of losing their job, about 40% of the workers indicate a high or a medium risk.

We are not able to identify one single factor that best explains the decreases in all dimensions of job quality. However, what we find is that long unemployment duration is associated with reemployment in non-permanent contracts, a high risk of job loss and overqualification – but is not correlated with changes in job authority. More precisely, our analysis has shown that an unemployment duration of over 1 year goes along with a substantially higher risk of experiencing a decrease in job quality. Higher levels of education are linked to two dimensions of low job quality, overqualification and lower job authority. Finally, an older age seems to be the driver of overqualification, lower job authority and a lower social status.

In a nutshell, unemployment duration seems to be particularly relevant with respect to the quality of displaced workers' new jobs. This finding corroborates our hypothesis H7. However, it needs to be recalled that unemployment duration is not exogenous and is thus likely to be determined by unobservable variables.

This chapter shows that losing one's job goes along with a decline in job quality. From our descriptive analysis we can conclude that in terms of all job quality dimensions some workers are disadvantaged in their new job. Some were reemployed in better jobs – for instance with higher job authority – but those who experienced an improvement are clearly fewer than those who experienced a deterioration. We therefore can maintain that plant closure has a negative impact on workers' careers in terms of job quality. Nevertheless, the outcome is not the same for everyone and a more precise look at the data shows that some workers were reemployed in jobs of about the same and some in jobs of better quality.

**Open Access** This chapter is distributed under the terms of the Creative Commons Attribution 4.0 International License (http://creativecommons.org/licenses/by/4.0/), which permits use, duplication, adaptation, distribution and reproduction in any medium or format, as long as you give appropriate credit to the original author(s) and the source, a link is provided to the Creative Commons license and any changes made are indicated.

The images or other third party material in this chapter are included in the work's Creative Commons license, unless indicated otherwise in the credit line; if such material is not included in the work's Creative Commons license and the respective action is not permitted by statutory regulation, users will need to obtain permission from the license holder to duplicate, adapt or reproduce the material.

# References

Arulampalam, W. (2001). Is unemployment really scarring? Effects of unemployment experiences on wages. *The Economic Journal, 111*(475), F585–F606.

Badillo Amador, L., López Nicolás, Á., & Vila, L. E. (2012). The consequences on job satisfaction of job–worker educational and skill mismatches in the Spanish labour market: A panel analysis. *Applied Economics Letters, 19*(4), 319–324.

Becker, G. S. (1962). Investment in human capital: A theoretical analysis. *Journal of Political Economy, 70*(5), 9–49.

Brand, J. E. (2006). The effects of job displacement on job quality: Findings from the Wisconsin Longitudinal Study. *Research in Social Stratification and Mobility, 24*(3), 275–298.

Clark, A. E., & Postel-Vinay, F. (2009). Job security and job protection. *Oxford Economic Papers, 62*(2), 207–239.

Clark, A. E., Diener, E., Georgellis, Y., & Lucas, R. E. (2008). Lags and leads in life satisfaction: A test of the baseline hypothesis. *The Economic Journal, 118*(529), F222–F243.

De Witte, H. (1999). Job insecurity and psychological well- being: Review of the literature and exploration of some unresolved issues. *European Journal of Work and Organizational Psychology, 8*(2), 155–177.

Dieckhoff, M. (2011). The effect of unemployment on subsequent job quality in Europe: A comparative study of four countries. *Acta Sociologica, 54*(3), 233–249.

Esping-Andersen, G. (2008). *Trois leçons sur l'Etat-providence*. Paris: Editions du Seuil.

Gazioglu, S., & Tansel, A. (2006). Job satisfaction in Britain: Individual and job related factors. *Applied Economics, 38*, 1163–1171.

Gerfin, M., Lechner, M., & Steiger, H. (2005). Does subsidised temporary employment get the unemployed back to work? An econometric analysis of two different schemes. *Labour Economics, 12*(6), 807–835.

Green, F. (2008). Temporary work and insecurity in Britain: A problem solved? *Social Indicators Research, 88*(1), 147–160.

Hipp, L., Bernhardt, J., & Allmendinger, J. (2015). Institutions and the prevalence of nonstandard employment. *Socio-Economic Review, 13*(2), 351–377.

Johnson, G. J., & Johnson, W. R. (2000). Perceived overqualification and dimensions of job satisfaction: A longitudinal analysis. *The Journal of Psychology, 134*(5), 537–555.

Kalleberg, A. L. (2009). Precarious work, insecure workers: Employment relations in transition. *American Sociological Review, 74*(1), 1–22.

OECD. (2004). Employment protection regulation and labour market performance. In *OECD employment outlook* (pp. 61–125). Paris: OECD Publishing.

Pissarides, C. A. (1992). Loss of skill during unemployment and the persistence of employment shocks. *The Quarterly Journal of Economics, 107*(4), 1371–1391.

Wyss, S. (2009). *Stellenverlust und Lohneinbusse durch die Globalisierung ?* University of Basel, Wirtschaftswissenschaftliches Zentrum der Universität Basel Working Paper No. 05/09

# Chapter 9
# Linked Lives and Well-Being

Glen Elder (1994: 6) pointed out that individuals' lives are highly interdependent – or in other words *linked* – and that social regulation and support come about through these relationships. Consequently, the analysis of economic and social processes needs to account for the social relationships in which individuals are embedded. In this light, we argue that plant closure usually does not affect only the displaced workers but also their spouses, families, friends and perhaps even the larger community in which they live. The mechanisms behind this phenomenon are on the one hand that the job loss of a relevant breadwinner affects the financial situation of a household. On the other hand, reduced well-being is likely to harm the quality of social relationships within and outside the household. Moreover, how the displaced workers cope with job loss critically depends on how their significant others respond to this critical event.

Job displacement is known to affect workers' well-being. A large body of scholarship has documented on the basis of longitudinal data that becoming unemployed is associated with a substantial decrease in general life satisfaction (e.g. Winkelmann and Winkelmann 1998; Clark et al. 2008). The previous literature has also shown that job loss is likely to lead to persistent tensions in social relationships and in particular between spouses. We therefore expect that changes in workers' marital relationships crucially determine changes in their well-being, more strongly than changes in their financial situation (hypothesis H8, see Sect. 1.4).

In this chapter we examine how plant closure affects the relationship between the displaced workers and their significant others. We first focus on coping strategies developed on a household level and second analyze how the quality of the workers' relationships has changed. Third, we describe the impact of plant closure on their subjective well-being and discuss how changes in well-being are linked to changes in their social and occupational situation.

© The Author(s) 2016
I. Baumann, *The Plight of Older Workers*, Life Course Research and Social Policies 5, DOI 10.1007/978-3-319-39754-2_9

## 9.1 Coping Strategies

If job loss is followed by an episode of unemployment, it goes along with financial insecurity. Although in Switzerland most workers are entitled to unemployment insurance benefits, the replacement rate is only 70–80 % of the pre-displacement earnings. Moreover, the uncertainty about the duration of job search and about the chance of finding a job may lead workers to deal more cautiously with their expenditures. As we have seen in Chap. 7, even if the workers find a job, they may experience income losses and subsequently an impairment of their quality of life. However, Kalleberg (2009: 14) highlights that workers are not passive victims of their situation but active agents who can develop strategies to cope with their hardship.

The analysis of our data reveals that a substantial proportion of workers adapted their spending and saving behavior. To begin with, 61 % of the workers indicated that in the aftermath of their displacement they had become more cautious in their handling of expenditures. When we asked workers about the domains where they cut their spending, it turned out that vacations were the budget item where the largest proportion of workers (77 %) reduced their expenditure as compared to transportation (51 %), food and drinks (49 %) or housing (21 %). With respect to the workers' post-displacement labor market status there are pronounced differences between the unemployed and reemployed workers in being more cautious in their handling of expenditures (84 % vs. 56 %).

A key factor that influences which strategies workers use is whether they experience a substantial change in their wage. Our data suggests that workers' wage change is linearly associated with measures taken to save money. Not surprisingly, 80 % of the workers who experience a *strong wage loss* of over 20 % were more cautious with their expenditures (e.g. spending less on holidays) while among workers who experienced a *wage increase* of over 20 % only 33 % were more cautious with their expenditures. The saving behavoir slighty differs by gender: Women seem to save less on food and housing but more on transportation than men. Moreover, the women in our sample borrowed money significantly more often than the men.

An alternative strategy on the household level for workers with a spouse may be that the spouse increases her/his employment activity. To expect spouses to adopt this strategy seems plausible since a large share of our sample is male and in Switzerland the majority of women work part-time.[1] Spouses – in most cases wives – thus potentially enter the labor force or increase their activity level in order to improve the household income (Engen and Gruber 2001: 571).

It has been pointed out that the household type is an important determinant of the risk of entering poverty (Vandecasteele 2011: 253). Although the household type is evidently not a strategy, it affects the way in which the household members can cope

---

[1] In 2011, the year when our survey was conducted, 58 % of the women employed in Switzerland worked part-time, part-time being defined as the respondents' perception of their main job (OECD Statistics).

9.1 Coping Strategies

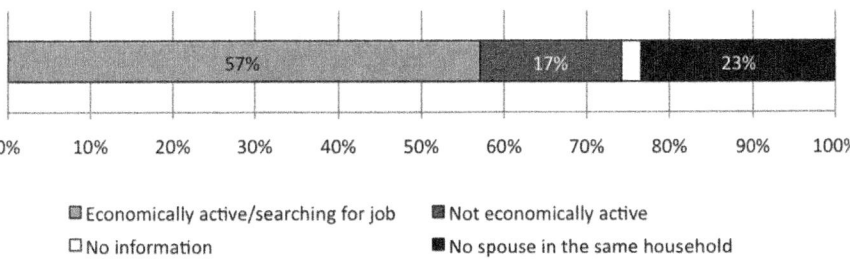

**Fig. 9.1a** Economic activity of the spouse living in the same household. N = 718. Reading example: 57 % of the spouses of displaced workers were economically active or searching for a job

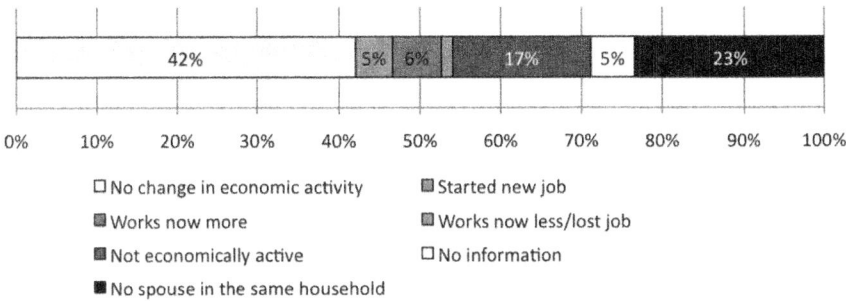

**Fig. 9.1b** Changes in economic activity of the spouse living in the same household. N = 718. Reading example: 5 % of the spouses started a new job after the displaced workers lost their job

with a particular situation. Accordingly, whether workers live with a spouse or alone and whether they have a partner who has a job probably affects how they cope with a drop in income. In our sample, 77 % of the workers live with a spouse and, as Fig. 9.1a shows, 57 % of all workers indicated that their spouse was economically active. For 17 % of all workers the partner was not active, for 2 % there is no information available and 23 % had no spouse in the same household. With respect to changes in spouses' economic activity (see Fig. 9.1b), 42 % of the workers had an economically active spouse who did not change their level of activity subsequent to the worker's job loss. In contrast, the spouses of 5 % of the workers started a new job and the spouses of 6 % increased their level of economic activity.

Which factors favor workers' spouses adapting to the job loss by starting a new job or increasing their working hours? In a descriptive analysis we find that among the reemployed workers there is a link between the magnitude of changes in wages and the likelihood of the partner adapting their hours of employment. Figure 9.2 shows that the spouses of reemployed workers who experienced wage losses are more likely to increase their economic activity relative to the spouses of the workers who experienced wage increases: Among displaced workers who experienced a wage *decrease* of more than 20 %, 31 % of the spouses increased their economic activity as compared to 12 % of the spouses of displaced workers who experienced a wage *increase* of more than 20 %.

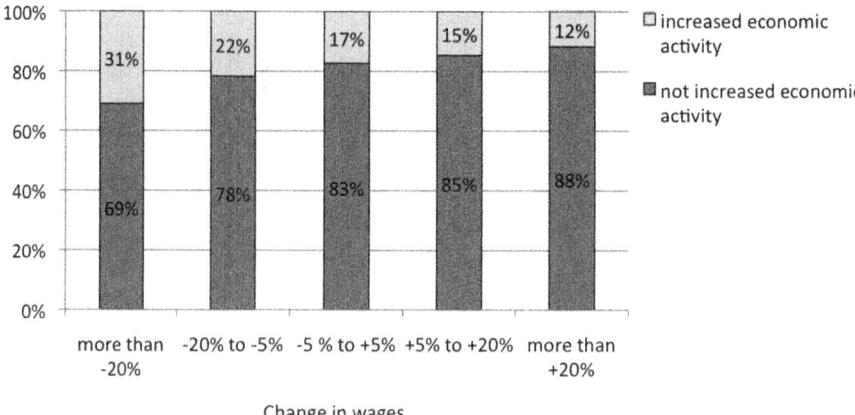

**Fig. 9.2** Reemployed workers' change in wage and change in economic activity by the spouse. N=227. Reading example: Among displaced workers who experienced a wage decrease of more than 20%, 31% of the spouses increased their economic activity

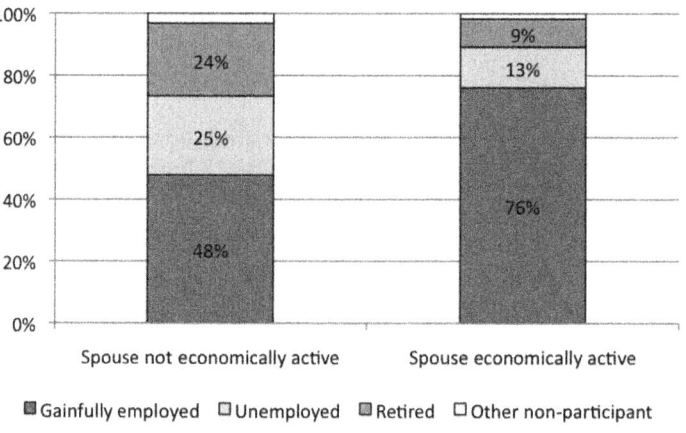

**Fig. 9.3** Labor market status of the displaced workers by economic activity of spouse. N=541 (N spouse not economically active=153, N spouse economically active=388). Reading example: Among workers whose spouse is economically active, 76% were gainfully reemployed after job displacement

If we test this association in a bivariate logistic regression analysis, using a continuous variable of wage difference as independent variable but no other control variables, we find a significant effect. However, if we then add unemployment duration and gender of the spouse to the model, we find that neither of these variables is associated with increased economic activity.

If we take into account all workers – not only the reemployed – there seems to be an association between the labor market statuses of the displaced worker and the labor market status of their spouse. Figure 9.3 highlights that the workers who have an economically active spouse were much more likely to be reemployed at the moment of our survey (76%) as compared to the workers who have an economically inactive spouse (48%). This difference may be due to the fact that the workers with an economically inactive spouse were more likely to go into retirement (24%) than the workers with a working partner (9%). However, the difference was also substantial with respect to unemployment. In fact, 25% of the workers with non-working spouses were unemployed when we surveyed them versus 13% of the workers with working spouses. This result goes in the same direction as findings from earlier studies that point to a polarization between dual-earner and no-earner couples (Gallie et al. 2001: 46). Two studies from Sweden and the UK even show that wives decreased their employment level as their husbands became involuntarily unemployed (Eliason 2011: 609; Davies et al. 1994). This pattern may be due to voluntary reduction of employment or due to involuntary job loss by the spouses. The latter seems to be more plausible since from a financial point of view one would not expect spouses to welcome reductions in income during phases of unemployment of their spouse. If individuals lose their jobs while their spouses are unemployed this may indicate that they are employed in the same economic sector or in sectors that are similarly prone to job contractions. This in turn would be an indicator for homophily, a concept designating the fact that individuals with a similar socio-economic background are more likely to mate.

## 9.2 Sociability

Workers losing their job may experience substantial changes in their sociability. One strand of the literature highlights that workers undergoing a critical event may receive emotional and practical support from spouses, family or friends (Sweet and Moen 2011: 181; Gallie et al. 2001: 47). Another strand of the literature contends that unemployed workers may experience tensions within their couple or become socially isolated as they lose contact with their former co-workers (Atkinson et al. 1986: 320; Larsen 2008: 11).

Empirical evidence suggests that there is no general positive or negative effect of job loss on sociability but instead that the outcome depends on the workers' social roles. It has been shown for Sweden and Norway that the effect of job loss on social relations tends to be more detrimental for male workers (Eliason 2012: 1392; Rege et al. 2007: 18). Men may experience tensions in their social relationships since job loss prevents them from fulfilling their traditional main-breadwinner role. Having children also seems to trigger more pressure on displaced workers to find a new job (Leana and Feldman 1995: 1383).

We start with a descriptive analysis of how workers experienced the change in their relationships with their spouse, family and friends for all workers together and then proceed with a regression to identify potential determinants. Figs. 9.4a, 9.4b and 9.4c show that 3% of the workers suffered a very negative effect of the displacement on their relationship with their *spouse* and 12% a rather negative effect. 56%

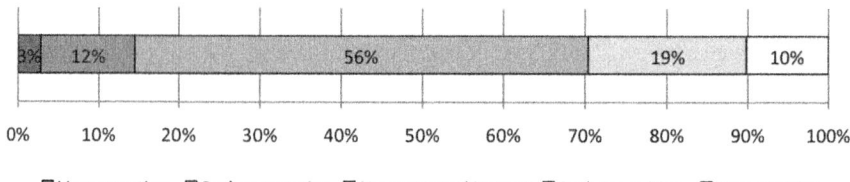

■ Very negative  ■ Rather negative  □ No or neutral impact  □ Rather positive  □ Very positive

**Fig. 9.4a** Impact of displacement on relationship with the spouse. N=659. Note: the sample size of the workers who responded to the question about the relationship with the spouse is larger than the number of workers who indicated that they have a partner living in the same household (as presented in Figs. 9.1a and 9.1b) since partners living outside the household are also considered

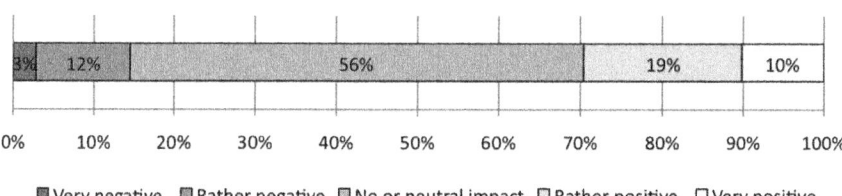

■ Very negative  ■ Rather negative  □ No or neutral impact  □ Rather positive  □ Very positive

**Fig. 9.4b** Impact of displacement on relationship with the family. N=671

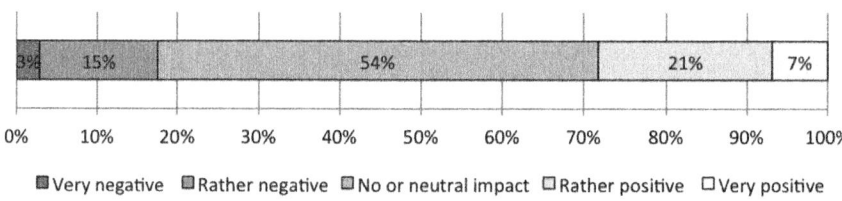

■ Very negative  ■ Rather negative  □ No or neutral impact  □ Rather positive  □ Very positive

**Fig. 9.4c** Impact of displacement on relationship with friends. N=683

of the workers experienced no or a neutral impact. 19% indicate that the job loss had a rather positive impact and 10% a very positive impact on their relationship with their *spouse*. The outcomes are very similar with respect to the workers' relationships with their *family* and their *friends*. This result suggests that rather more than half of the workers were not affected in their sociability by the plant closure. Among the 45% of workers reporting changes in their social relationships, those

## 9.2 Sociability

who experience positive changes are twice as numerous as those who experience negative changes. Our results thus suggest that the experience of plant closure leads to the consolidation of social ties.[2] A possible explanation for this finding may be found in the results from the study by Charles and Stephens (2004: 516–9). The authors show that spouses did not blame their displaced partners if they lost their job because of plant closure (as compared to individual layoff). Accordingly, if spouses know that their partner did not lose their job because of their own fault they rather seem to provide them with support and solidarity.

The similarity of the patterns of Figs. 9.4a, 9.4b, and 9.4c is striking. This outcome may be biased: the survey respondents were possibly primed by the answer they gave to the question about the impact of plant closure on their marital relationship and then checked the same answers for the subsequent questions on family and friends. This would imply that workers accurately answered the first question about the impact of displacement on the relationship with their spouse but inaccurately gave the same answer to the following questions. However, an analysis of the correlation in the three answers reveals that only the answers on relationship with the spouse and relationship with the family are highly correlated (0.81). The correlations between the relationship with spouse and friends (0.51) as well as that with family and friends (0.55) are intermediate. These correlations seem plausible as the strong link between relationship with spouse and family is not surprising, given that the spouse is a central part of the family.

The literature suggests that displaced workers who assume the main-breadwinner role are more likely to experience hardship in their social relationships with their spouses (Eliason 2012; Rege et al. 2007). As men still tend to be the main breadwinner in Switzerland, we tested this argument by examining whether the workers' sex determines how their marital relationship is affected (Joye and Bergman 2004: 88; Bernardi et al. 2013). With respect to relationships with friends, a study based on the European Community Household Panel has shown that unemployed workers tend to see their friends more frequently than employed workers (Gallie et al. 2003). It is however unclear whether there exists a causal effect or whether this finding is due to selection bias.

We compute three models – one for each type of sociability – using the independent variables sex and labor market status, and additionally control for age, education and plant. The results are presented in Table 9.1. We observe strongly negative effects on social relationships for the age group of the 50–54 year olds. The effects are significant for relationships with the family and relationships with friends. With respect to education, our results show that higher levels of education are associated with positive changes in workers' social relationships even though the effects are not statistically significant with the exception of relationship with the family. Contrary to our expectation, we find that men are not significantly more likely than women to experience negative changes in any type of social relationship.

---

[2] However, it is possible that our results are biased as a consequence of non-response in the survey. Workers who were more negatively affected in their relationships may have been less likely to respond to our survey and thus be underrepresented among the respondents.

**Table 9.1** Coefficients for an OLS regression for changes in social relationships

| | Changes in relationship with *spouse* | Changes in relationship with *family* | Changes in relationship with *friends* |
|---|---|---|---|
| | Coef. (SE) | Coef. (SE) | Coef. (SE) |
| Age (ref. < 30) | | | |
| 30–39 | −0.05 (0.14) | −0.06 (0.14) | −0.15 (0.14) |
| 40–49 | −0.14 (0.13) | −0.13 (0.12) | −0.17 (0.12) |
| 50–54 | −0.19 (0.14) | −0.28** (0.14) | −0.36***(0.13) |
| 55–59 | 0.04 (0.15) | 0.03 (0.14) | −0.19 (0.14) |
| >59 | 0.14 (0.17) | −0.02 (0.17) | −0.13 (0.16) |
| Education (ref. less than upper secondary) | | | |
| Upper secondary | 0.12 (0.11) | 0.16 (0.11) | 0.05 (0.10) |
| Tertiary | 0.17 (0.12) | 0.20* (0.12) | 0.02 (0.11) |
| Plant (ref. Plant 1) | | | |
| Plant 2 | 0.19 (0.13) | 0.23* (0.13) | 0.04 (0.12) |
| Plant 3 | 0.05 (0.12) | 0.03 (0.12) | 0.07 (0.12) |
| Plant 4 | −0.001 (0.13) | −0.0004 (0.12) | −0.03 (0.12) |
| Plant 5 | 0.07 (0.14) | 0.15 (0.14) | 0.02 (0.14) |
| Sex (ref. women) | | | |
| Men | −0.005 (0.10) | 0.04 (0.09) | 0.04 (0.09) |
| Labor market status (ref. reemployed) | | | |
| Unemployed | −0.23** (0.11) | −0.09 (0.11) | −0.25** (0.11) |
| Retired | 0.14 (0.16) | 0.42*** (0.16) | 0.15 (0.15) |
| Out of the labor force | −0.19 (0.22) | −0.05 (0.21) | −0.03 (0.21) |
| Constant | 3.11 (0.20) | 3.05 (0.19) | 3.25 (0.19) |
| $R^2$ | 0.04 | 0.06 | 0.04 |
| N | 645 | 658 | 668 |

Note: The dependent variables are the impacts of displacement on relationship with (a) spouse, (b) family and (c) friends with the outcome options (i) very negative, (ii) rather negative, (iii) no or neutral impact, (iv) rather positive, (v) very positive. Significance levels: * $p<0.1$, ** $p<0.05$, *** $p<0.01$. Reading example: As compared to women, men experienced a decrease in quality of family relationship of 4 percentage points

The workers' labor market status turns out to be highly relevant with respect to changes in their social relationships. In fact, being unemployed is associated with substantially higher chances of experiencing deterioration in the *marital* relationship as compared to being reemployed. This may indicate that unemployed workers are particularly prone to tensions within the *couple*. In contrast to earlier findings in the literature we also find that unemployed workers are more likely to suffer negatives changes in their friendships than the reemployed, possibly because long-term unemployment acts as a stigma.

Finally, being retired seems to positively influence changes in *family* relationships. This result is possibly due to the time additional that the retirees have for social activities, in particular with their family. Indeed, retirees are more likely to enjoy their leisure time than the unemployed workers since they do not suffer from the stigma that goes with being out of work and do not have to search for jobs, and possibly also because the value of time available depends on whether significant others have a similar schedule of available time (Young and Lim 2014).

## 9.3 Subjective Well-Being

Studies based on longitudinal data show that those workers who become unemployed experience a short-term decrease in their subjective well-being (Winkelmann and Winkelmann 1998; Lucas 2007; Clark et al. 2008; Oesch and Lipps 2013). A Swedish study comparing the different labor market outcomes after job loss shows that the workers' long-term life satisfaction depends on how they overcome this critical situation (Strandh 2000). Workers who remain unemployed are more likely to suffer lasting harm. Conversely, those who return to the active labor force are expected to regain their pre-displacement level of subjective well-being.

However, recent evidence contradicts the view that reemployment alone allows unemployed workers to regain their former level of life satisfaction. In fact, a study on unemployed workers who find a job shows that on average they have a lower level of well-being after reemployment than before they lost their job (Young 2012: 14). This leads to the question whether factors such as the characteristics of the new job or a lasting depression triggered by the job loss explain the decline in well-being (Brand 2006: 287; Burgard et al. 2009: 376).

Another explanation may be that job displacement affects other domains of workers' lives besides their occupational situation and leaves long-lasting scars. Even if workers are reemployed, job loss may involve status loss (Kalleberg 2009: 9; West et al. 1990: 127). Moreover, as we have seen, their social relationships may be affected.

Based on previous findings, we expect that changes in workers' financial situation affect their well-being. In particular, workers' life satisfaction decreases if they experience wage losses or have to be more cautious with their daily expenditures. The literature about underemployment and commuting gives rise to the prediction that changes in time budget are crucial for workers' well-being. If workers have to work at activity levels below their preferences or are compelled to commute longer distances, their life satisfaction is impaired. We furthermore expect that the achievement of social recognition is associated with life satisfaction. We predict that lower levels of social recognition – for example in the case of reemployment in a job of lower job authority – lead to lower scores of life satisfaction. Finally, we hypothesize that changes in social relationships – in particular marital relationships – following job loss and job change are the most important predictor for changes in well-being.

The concept of subjective well-being as a dimension of individuals' lives has some disadvantages such as the possibility that survey respondents adjust their reported well-being, either because in the context of the study an event is mentally particularly present – a bias that is called substitution – or in order to appear consistent (Lucas 2007: 76; Kahneman and Frederick 2002). Substitution is likely to be an issue in our survey since the question about overall life satisfaction was placed *after* the questions about the characteristics of the reemployed workers' new job. Accordingly, substitution probably leads to an overestimation of the correlation between workers' well-being and their new position. In contrast, the association between the workers' life satisfaction on the one hand and their social relationships or dealing with expenditures on the other hand are likely to be correctly assessed since the life satisfaction question was asked *before* the questions about changes in social relationships or dealing with expenditures.

Despite its flaws, we consider the concept of life satisfaction to be a meaningful indicator that complements objective measures such as wage or contract type. The combined assessment of subjective and objective measures seems crucial in order to shed light on the individuals' experience of critical life-course events (Dieckhoff 2011: 237).

Our data is cross-sectional and we rely on retrospective information about workers' *pre*-displacement well-being. Even though longitudinal studies are always to be preferred, cross-sectional studies using retrospective recall constitute a second-best as this method allows for measurement of within-individual changes (Hardt and Rutter 2004: 261). In addition, the use of data from plant closures addresses the problem of reverse causality that is often present in studies on well-being (Eliason and Storrie 2006: 1402; Brand 2015: 15). Consequently, if we find that job loss goes along with a decrease in workers' well-being, it is legitimate to assume that plant closure caused the drop in well-being and not the other way round (i.e. that the decrease in well-being caused the job loss).

As with wages, a problem that is likely to arise in our data is that we assess the workers' pre-displacement well-being directly before their displacement. As scholars have pointed out with respect to workers' pre-displacement wages, this way of calculating probably underestimates the workers' wage losses as many companies reduced their workers' wages when they first encountered having economic difficulties (Jacobson et al. 1993: 691; Arulampalam 2001: F587; Carneiro and Portugal 2006: 13). Likewise, we can assume that workers' subjective well-being was already starting to decrease in the months before they lost their job (Oesch and Lipps 2013: 959). Accordingly, if the pre-displacement level of well-being is lower than the workers' baseline level, we are likely to underestimate the drop in well-being that they experienced as a consequence of job loss.

Table 9.2 presents a descriptive analysis of the workers' life satisfaction by labor market status before and after displacement. The table reveals that displaced workers who were *reemployed* at the moment of our survey indicate an average life satisfaction of 7.7 points before displacement and 7.5 after displacement. Accordingly, this worker subgroup experienced a slight but statistically significant decrease in well-being. At both time points their well-being is lower than the average of the employed individuals in Switzerland which was – according to calculations based on the Swiss Household Panel – 8.0 points in both 2009 and 2011.

9.3 Subjective Well-Being

**Table 9.2** Average life satisfaction by labor market status before and after displacement

|  | Before displacement | After displacement | N |
|---|---|---|---|
| Reemployed | 7.7 | 7.5 | 480 |
| Retired | 8.3 | 8.4 | 89 |
| Unemployed | 8.2 | 5.4 | 115 |
| Out of the labor force | 8.4 | 5.7 | 20 |

Note: A Student's t-test was run to assess the significance of the change in life satisfaction between before and after displacement. The difference is significant for the reemployed ($p<0.05$), the unemployed ($p<0.001$) and the labor force dropouts ($p<0.01$).

With respect to the *retired* workers we find that they experienced a slight but not significant increase in well-being from 8.3 points to 8.4.[3] For displaced workers who were *unemployed* in 2011 we find an average life satisfaction of 8.2 before displacement and 5.4 after displacement. These workers thus experienced a strong and highly significant decrease in life satisfaction. It has been argued that there exists a mechanism of self-selection of less happy workers into unemployment. However, our analysis shows that even if this phenomenon exists there is an additional drop in well-being at the moment when workers become unemployed. Comparing this result to the average unemployed individual in the Swiss Household Panel in 2011 with a life satisfaction of 6.8 points, workers in our sample indicate a lower well-being. A possible reason for this finding is that while the data from the SHP includes data from individuals with a large variety of unemployment durations – most of them probably of only some months –, our data includes unemployed workers who have been unemployed for more than 1 year. Intriguingly, the unemployed displaced workers indicate a pre-displacement life satisfaction that is higher than that of the average Swiss employed worker in the Swiss Household Panel (which was 8.0 in 2009). This finding probably points to an overestimation of the life satisfaction before displacement if the workers' post-displacement situation is difficult. Since the pre-displacement life satisfaction is a retrospective measure, it is likely to be subject to recall bias. In order to rule out a possible recall bias, we proceed with multivariate analyses that are run separately for the reemployed and the unemployed workers.[4]

---

[3] If we further distinguish between workers who retired regularly and those who retired early (not shown in the figure), we find that the regularly retired experienced a strong increase in well-being from 7.8 to 8.6 points and the early retired a slight decrease from 8.4 to 8.3 points. Whereas the strong increase in well-being for the regularly retired supports earlier findings (Calvo et al. 2007), the stability in well-being of the early retirees reflects an apparently voluntary rather than forced exit from the labor force (as discussed in Chap. 4).

[4] Our analyses were not run for the retirees and the labor force dropouts, the sample sizes being too small.

The labor force dropouts exhibit a similar pattern to the unemployed, expressing a significant decrease in life satisfaction from 8.4 to 5.7 points. However, the confidence intervals are very large for the labor force dropouts and the unemployed and the results thus need to be interpreted with caution.

Within each worker subgroup there is substantial variance in change in life satisfaction. For the reemployed and the retired the pattern of the distribution takes a form that is close to a normal distribution; for the unemployed and labor force dropouts the distribution in contrast is clearly not normal but skewed to the negative values. For instance, among the unemployed about 7 % of them have experienced the maximum decrease of −9 or −10 points. A minority of 10 % experienced an increase between 2 and 7 points, which may reflect the fact that some workers were relieved to lose their former job, which was marked by instability (Sweet und Moen 2011: 24–5).[5]

## 9.4 Unemployed Workers' Changes in Life Satisfaction

We try to explain displaced workers' changes in well-being by resorting to a multivariate analysis. More precisely, we analyze the effect of changes in dealing with money and changes in social relationships on unemployed workers' changes in subjective well-being. The results are presented in Fig. 9.5. Our model includes the variables changes in dealing with expenditures, changes in social relationships sex, education, civil status, age, language, duration since displacement, and plant.[6]

We find that the experience of financial restrictions has a very strong negative impact on workers' well-being. As we will see later, the effect of changes in expenditures is much larger for the unemployed workers than for the reemployed, which is little surprising. We also find a strong negative effect for being less cautious with spending, which is counterintuitive. However, the effects of this variables are not statistically significant. Regarding changes in workers' social relationships we find that marital relationships and relationships with friends affect workers' subjective well-being in an intuitive way, i.e., positive changes lead to positive effects, while negative changes lead to negative effects.[7] Interestingly, workers seem to be particularly sensitive to positive changes. This finding may indicate that workers who received ample empathy and support from their friends were spared the negative effect that unemployment usually has on workers' well-being. With respect to edu-

---

[5] Figures presenting the distribution can be found in a paper related to this analysis (Baumann 2015).

[6] We also tested whether receiving unemployment benefits or not affected the outcomes. However, since this was not the case and the inclusion of this variable considerably reduced the size of our sample, we dropped it.

[7] If we test the same model only on workers who have a spouse, the effects for marital and family relationships are not significant. In contrast, for workers with a spouse, changes in relationships with *friends* are even more important than for all workers together.

## 9.4 Unemployed Workers' Changes in Life Satisfaction

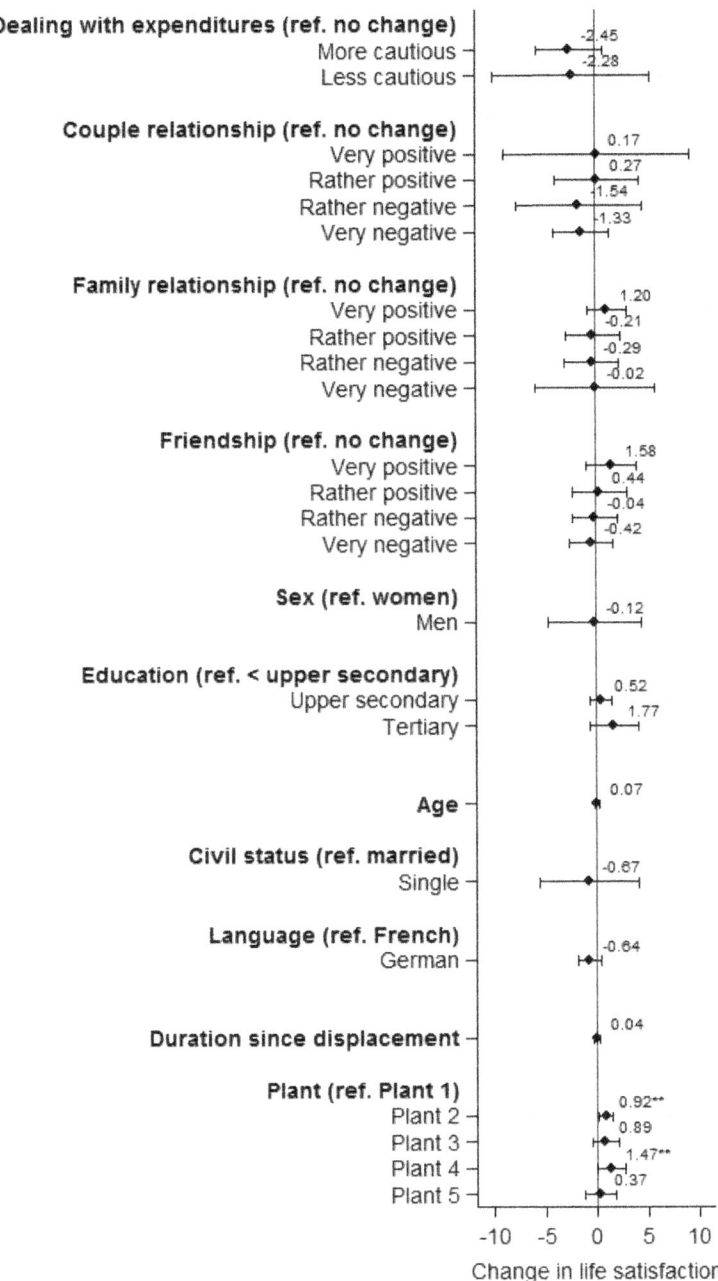

**Fig. 9.5** Coefficients for an OLS regression analysis for the change in life satisfaction for the unemployed workers. Note: N=100. Significance levels: * p < 0.1, ** p < 0.05, *** p < 0.01. Standard errors are clustered at the plant level. Reading example: As compared to unemployed women, unemployed men experienced a decrease in life satisfaction of 0.12 points

cation, workers with tertiary education experienced a much more positive evolution of their subjective well-being than workers with less than upper secondary education, although the effect is not statistically significant. Education thus may have a cushioning effect on workers' well-being. The only statistically significant result in this analysis is revealed for the variable 'plant'. We find that unemployed workers in all companies experienced a more positive development in their well-being than workers in Plant 1 in Geneva. This is possibly due to the more competitive labor market of Geneva with much higher rates of unemployment than in the other regions examined. The workers from the plant in Geneva experienced the longest durations of unemployment (see Figs. 5.6 and 5.7 in Chap. 5) which probably had detrimental effects on workers' well-being.

## 9.5 Reemployed Workers' Change in Life Satisfaction

We proceed with a multivariate analysis to estimate the impact of changes in economic and social factors on changes in *reemployed* workers' well-being. We run an OLS-regression model with the covariates change in wages, dealing with expenditures, change in weekly working hours, change in time spent commuting, change in job authority, change in relationships with spouse, family and friends, sex, education, civil status, age, survey language and duration since displacement. The coefficients are presented in Fig. 9.6.

We begin with the discussion of our expectation that an increase in workers' wages and being less cautious in dealing with expenditures is positively linked to changes in workers' life satisfaction. Although the effects go in the expected direction, the coefficients for both variables are not statistically significant.

We predicted that workers who work fewer hours per week and workers who have to commute longer distances than before displacement tend to experience a decrease in well-being. The analysis of the effect of changes in weekly working hours does not reveal statistically significant results. Nor are the results with respect to commuting time in line with our expectations. Although we find a negative effect of longer commuting distances on workers' well-being and a positive effect of *slightly* shorter commuting distances, we also find the counterintuitive result that *much* shorter distances are associated with a strong and significant *decrease* in life satisfaction. A possible explanation for this result may be that a much shorter commuting time is a proxy for an unobservable variable. For instance, workers who have to commute much shorter distances may be unhappy about being obliged to work in a different city than before displacement and need time to get used to their new environment.

Based on the previous literature we predicted that changes in social recognition are important for workers' well-being. With respect to job authority however, we do not find significant results and both being reemployed in a higher and a lower hierarchical position go along with an increase in life satisfaction. In contrast, workers'

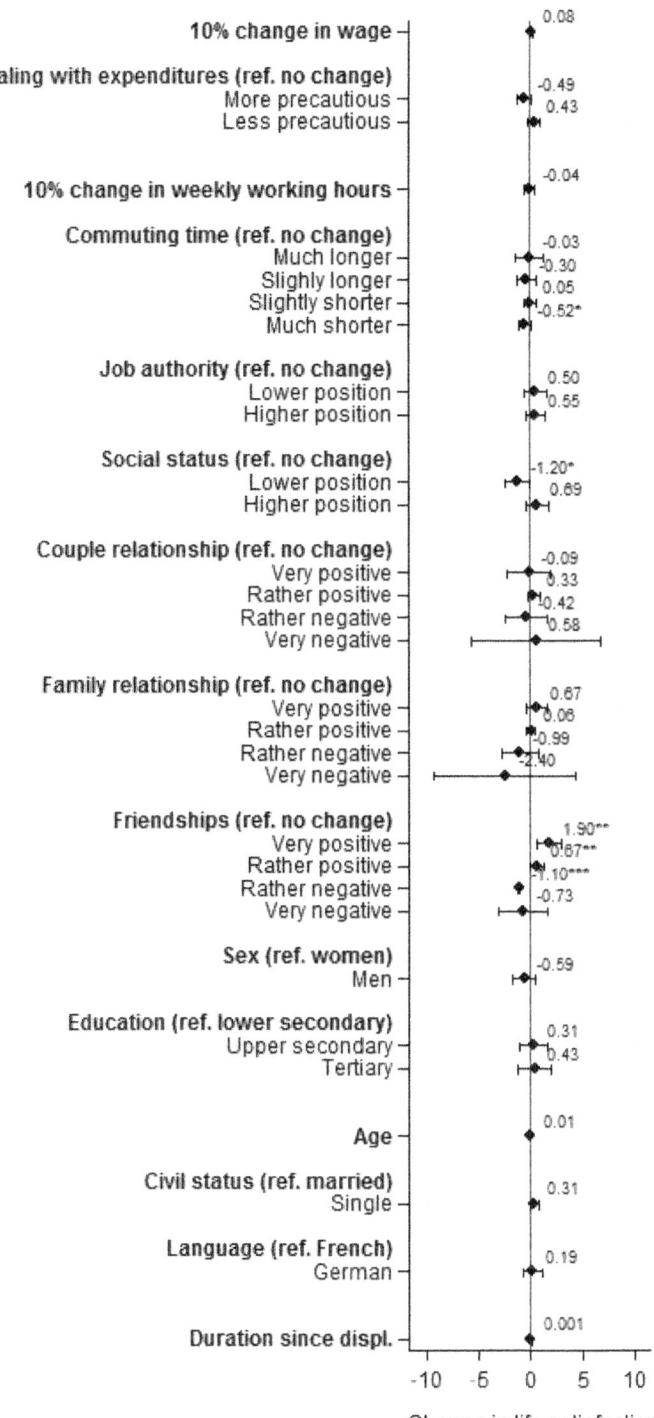

**Fig. 9.6** OLS-regression analysis for change in life satisfaction for the reemployed workers N=307. Note: * p < 0.1, ** p < 0.05, *** p < 0.01. 95% confidence intervals shown. Standard errors are clustered at the plant level. Each dependent variable represents a change. Reading example: Workers who were reemployed in a job with a lower social position experienced a decrease in life satisfaction of 1.2 points

job-related social status seems to be relevant. We find that being reemployed in a job with a lower social status is associated with a strong and significant decrease in life satisfaction by 1.20 points.

We hypothesized that deterioration in couple, family and friendship relationships as a consequence of plant closure has a harmful effect on workers' well-being. While the effect of changes in the workers' marital relationship neither goes in the expected direction nor is linear, the effect of changes in family relationships is more intuitive. As expected, positive changes go along with an increase in well-being and negative changes with a decrease. Very negative changes in family relationships are even associated with a 2.40 points decrease in life satisfaction. However, the standard errors for effects of couple and family relationships are too large to enable the coefficients to be statistically significant.[8] In contrast, changes in friendships are significantly linked to workers' satisfaction with their life. Both deterioration and improvement of these relationships coincide with substantial changes in workers' well-being, the positive effect being even stronger than the negative effect. With respect to the control variables sex, education, age, civil status, survey language and duration since displacement, we do not find statistically significant results.

How do these results compare to earlier studies? The finding that changes in wages are only weakly associated with changes in workers' life satisfaction coincides more strongly with evidence from Germany as compared to evidence from the UK (Ferrer-i-Carbonell and Frijters 2004: 656; Winkelmann and Winkelmann 1998: 12; Gardner and Oswald 2007). This is not surprising since the unemployment insurance in Germany – as in Switzerland – represents a stronger buffer against financial strains than in the UK. As a consequence, changes in the workers' financial situation probably affect workers in Switzerland less than workers in other countries.

Regarding changes in social status a British study on a large sample of managers shows that downward occupational mobility had even more detrimental effects on their life satisfaction than unemployment (West et al. 1990: 132). The authors explain this finding by contending that the expected direction of mobility of managers is upward and a failure strongly affects their well-being. This argument can be extended to workers in general, at least for those who are not close to the end of their career. Brand (2015: 17–18) claims that if hardship caused by job loss was mainly financial, reemployment would have the potential to re-establish workers' well-being. In contrast, if displacement alters workers' place in society more profoundly, regaining the former level of life satisfaction may be difficult.

We find that changes in couple relationships matter little for workers' changes in well-being contradicts earlier research. A recent literature review has shown that deteriorations in marital relationships affect individuals' well-being particularly negatively (Dolan et al. 2008). It is thus surprising that the effects in our analysis are not significant and rather small. A potential explanation may be that changes in

---

[8] If we calculate the effect of changes in relationships with family and spouse only for those workers who have a spouse (there is no information available about workers' children), the results are basically the same but have the downside that the number of observation is smaller.

couple relationships tend to be gradual rather than sudden and that individuals thus have time to adapt to the changes (VanLaningham et al. 2001: 1316–8).

Our finding that relationships with friends are more strongly associated with subjective well-being than relationships with spouses and the family is in line with the meta-analysis by Pinquart and Sörensen (2000: 194) and with a study by Helliwell and Putnam (2004: 1439) on the US and Canada.

How can we interpret this finding? Although we know that reverse causality between job loss and change in well-being is unlikely (i.e. that a decrease in well-being has caused workers to lose their job), it is possible that we are confronted with reverse causality between our dependent and independent variables. Although this interpretation is possible, it seems more likely that the correlation that we found expresses an effect of changes in social relationships on changes in workers' well-being because the wording of our question was causal ("How did plant closure affect your relationship with your spouse/family/friends?").

A more plausible interpretation is that our measure of relationships with friends actually assesses workers' relationships with their former co-workers. If this is the case, positive changes in these relationships may have positive effects on workers' well-being as a consequence of solidarity expressed among former colleagues. As the workers' occupational career is falling apart, they may find and provide important mutual support from and to their former colleagues. The negative effect of deterioration in friendship relationships on workers' well-being may be an expression of suffering over the loss of appreciated former co-workers.

In sum, our analysis provides us with the insight that finding a job after displacement does not guarantee that workers overcome the shock of displacement and restore their pre-displacement level of life satisfaction – even though being unemployed is even a much stronger burden. This suggests that hitherto theories for loss in well-being after job loss do not fully explain the mechanism behind this phenomenon. Our results in fact indicate that additional processes are at stake. Indeed, it seems that workers' lives are enduringly affected by job loss and that these effects persist even after reemployment. This is particularly true for social relationships, which are likely to be affected by job loss and which in turn have paramount consequences for workers' subjective well-being.

## 9.6 Changes in Workers' Health

A substantial body of evidence from the US suggests that job displacement goes along with decreased health conditions, even after controlling for selection effects. Burgard et al. (2007: 379) show, based on longitudinal data, that workers losing their job are more likely to be affected by depression. In line with these findings are the results of Gallo et al. (2006: S225), who report for older workers who experience involuntary job loss that they have an increased likelihood of exhibiting depressive symptoms. However, these effects were usually present only in the mid-term after job loss and disappeared in the long term. Sullivan and von Wachter (2009:

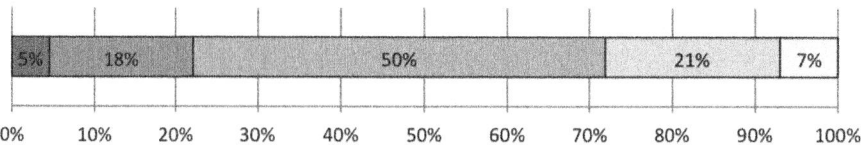

**Fig. 9.7a** Impact of displacement on physical health. N=687

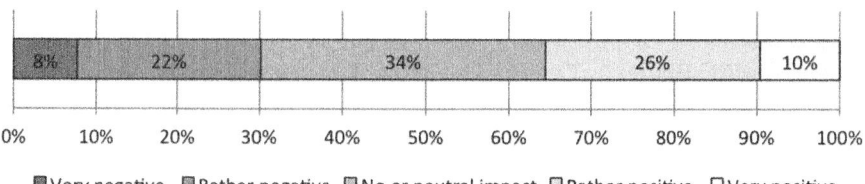

■ Very negative  ■ Rather negative  ■ No or neutral impact  ■ Rather positive  □ Very positive

**Fig. 9.7b** Impact of displacement on psychological health. N=686

1278–9) find that displaced workers have a substantially higher risk of mortality than non-displaced workers.

Although in our study we did not assess extensive health indicators, we surveyed the self-reported impact of job displacement on workers' physical and psychological health. As we can see from Figs 9.7a and 9.7b, half of all workers indicated that job loss had no effect on their *physical* health. However, 23 % of the workers indicated that they experienced negative effects and 28 % report positive effects.

With respect to *psychological* health, only about a third indicated that there was no or a neutral effect. Slightly less than a third experienced a negative impact and slightly more than a third a positive impact. Overall, the two figures point to a stronger impact of plant closure on workers' mental health than on their physical health and, surprisingly, workers reporting a positive health impact outnumber those indicating a negative impact. This finding probably needs to be interpreted in the context of having worked in plants troubled by instability and tensions – hence a particularly stressful context – which ultimately led to plant closure.

## 9.7 Conclusion

Although workers implemented several coping strategies such as reducing expenditures, the strategy that we had assumed to be largely used did not prove to be particularly important, namely the spouses increasing their economic activity. Indeed,

## 9.7 Conclusion

a substantial proportion of workers' spouses were not employed and did not change their occupational situation in order to cope with the job loss of their partner. Moreover, workers who were unemployed at the moment of our survey were more likely than the reemployed workers to have spouses who were not working. This points to a pattern of polarization between dual-earner and no-earner families.

With respect to sociability we find the interesting result that plant closure rather strengthens than weakens the workers' social relationships. This suggests that a critical event that disrupts workers' careers need not similarly disrupt their social lives. However, a small proportion of workers still experienced very negative effects on their relationships and thus have experienced hardship not only in their occupational, but also their private life.

The workers' general life satisfaction strongly depends on their labor market status, reemployed and retired workers having much higher levels of life satisfaction than unemployed workers and labor force dropouts, who experienced strong decreases in well-being. With respect to the determinants of the change in well-being, financial issues seem for the unemployed workers to be more consequential for their well-being than their social relations. This finding may be explained by the unemployed workers' financial vulnerability. Although Switzerland's unemployment benefits system offers comparatively high financial security with a benefit replacement rate of 70–80 % for 18 months, workers are likely to be impaired in their life style and may experience uncertainty about whether they will find a job.

Our hypothesis H8 that changes in social relationships following job loss decisively predict changes in workers' well-being does seem to be more pronounced among the reemployed workers than among the unemployed. In general, contrasting with earlier findings in the literature we do not find clear evidence for the link between change in *marital* relationships and well-being. But we observe that changes in relationships with *friends* are strongly linked to changes in well-being. This finding has been corroborated for both reemployed and unemployed workers. For unemployed workers, a possible explanation for this finding may be that workers have had more time for their friends while they were unemployed and accordingly were happier in this period. An explanation for this result for reemployed workers may be that relationships with friends actually represent workers' relationships with their co-workers. Positive changes in these relationships may either be a sign that they appreciated solidarity and mutual support among former colleagues or that they are happy with their new colleagues. The negative effect of a deterioration in friendship relationships may be an expression of disappointment in the case of loss of appreciated former co-workers.

In sum, our analysis confirms that unemployment is a highly unpleasant experience. We show that finding a job after displacement does not guarantee that workers will immediately overcome the shock of the displacement and regain their pre-displacement level of life satisfaction. It seems that individuals experiencing an occupational transition from one job to another need time to adjust to their new workplace. It is thus not unemployment alone that is arduous but also the period coming after the spell of unemployment. Factors that seem to mitigate potential hardship are social relationships. We show that relationships with friends and colleagues have the most important consequences for workers' subjective well-being – apparently often in a positive way.

The contribution of this chapter is to illustrate how other domains of workers' lives are affected through job displacement. Our analysis adds to the scholarly literature by highlighting the dimensions of unemployment that are beyond the economic sphere. In addition, in this chapter we focus on non-objective indicators such as satisfaction with life. The use of the life satisfaction measure in the analysis of objective outcomes such as the post-displacement labor force status emphasizes that complementing objective indicators with subjective ones provides us with a more comprehensive understanding of the phenomenon of job displacement.

**Open Access** This chapter is distributed under the terms of the Creative Commons Attribution 4.0 International License (http://creativecommons.org/licenses/by/4.0/), which permits use, duplication, adaptation, distribution and reproduction in any medium or format, as long as you give appropriate credit to the original author(s) and the source, a link is provided to the Creative Commons license and any changes made are indicated.

The images or other third party material in this chapter are included in the work's Creative Commons license, unless indicated otherwise in the credit line; if such material is not included in the work's Creative Commons license and the respective action is not permitted by statutory regulation, users will need to obtain permission from the license holder to duplicate, adapt or reproduce the material.

# References

Arulampalam, W. (2001). Is unemployment really scarring? Effects of unemployment experiences on wages. *The Economic Journal, 111*(475), F585–F606.
Atkinson, T., Liem, R., & Liem, J. H. (1986). The social costs of unemployment: Implications for social support. *Journal of Health and Social Behavior, 27*(4), 317–331.
Baumann, I. (2015). *Decreased well-being after job loss: Testing omitted causes* (LIVES Working Paper No. 36).
Bernardi, L., Ryser, V.-A., & Le Goff, J.-M. (2013). Gender role-set, family orientations, and women's fertility intentions in Switzerland. *Swiss Journal of Sociology, 39*(1), 9–32.
Brand, J. E. (2006). The effects of job displacement on job quality: Findings from the Wisconsin Longitudinal Study. *Research in Social Stratification and Mobility, 24*(3), 275–298.
Brand, J. E. (2015). The far-reaching impact of job loss and unemployment. *Annual Review of Sociology, 41,* 359–375.
Burgard, S. A., Brand, J. E., & House, J. S. (2007). Toward a better estimation of the effect of job loss on health. *Journal of Health and Social Behavior, 48*(4), 369–384.
Burgard, S. A., Brand, J. E., & House, J. S. (2009). Perceived job insecurity and worker health in the United States. *Social Science & Medicine, 69*(5), 777–785.
Calvo, E., Haverstick, K., & Sass, S. (2007). *What makes retirees happier: A gradual or "Cold Turkey" retirement?* (Munich personal RePEc archive paper no. 5607). Chestnut Hill: Center for Retirement Research at Boston College.
Carneiro, A., & Portugal, P. (2006). *Earnings losses of displaced workers: Evidence from a matched employer-employee data set* (Estudos e Doumentos de Trabalho working papers No. 14).
Charles, K. K., & Stephens, M. J. (2004). Job displacement, disability, and divorce. *Journal of Labor Economics, 22*(2), 489–522.

# References

Clark, A. E., Diener, E., Georgellis, Y., & Lucas, R. E. (2008). Lags and leads in life satisfaction: A test of the baseline hypothesis. *The Economic Journal, 118*(529), F222–F243.

Davies, R. B., Elias, P., & Pen, R. (1994). The relationship between a husband's unemployment and his wife's participation in the labour force. In D. Gallie, C. Marsh, & C. Vogler (Eds.), *Social change and the experience of unemployment* (pp. 154–187). Oxford: Oxford University Press.

Dieckhoff, M. (2011). The effect of unemployment on subsequent job quality in Europe: A comparative study of four countries. *Acta Sociologica, 54*(3), 233–249.

Dolan, P., Peasgood, T., & White, M. (2008). Do we really know what makes us happy? A review of the economic literature on the factors associated with subjective well-being. *Journal of Economic Psychology, 29*(1), 94–122.

Dolan, P., Layard, R., & Metcalfe, R. (2011). *Measuring subjective well-being for public policy.* Richmond: Office for National Statistics. Crown copyright.

Elder, G. H. (1994). Time, human agency, and social change: Perspectives on the life course. *Social Psychology Quarterly, 57*(1), 4–15.

Eliason, M. (2011). Income after job loss: The role of the family and the welfare state. *Applied Economics, 43*(5), 603–618.

Eliason, M. (2012). Lost jobs, broken marriages. *Journal of Population Economics, 25*, 1365–1397.

Eliason, M., & Storrie, D. (2006). Lasting or latent scars? Swedish evidence on the long term effects of job displacement. *Journal of Labor Economics, 24*(4), 831–856.

Engen, E. M., & Gruber, J. (2001). Unemployment insurance and precautionary saving. *Journal of Monetary Economics, 47*, 545–579.

Ferrer-i-Carbonell, A., & Frijters, P. (2004). How important is methodology for the estimates of the determinants of happiness? *The Economic Journal, 114*(497), 641–659.

Gallie, D., Kostova, D., & Kuchar, P. (2001). Social consequences of unemployment: An east–west comparison. *Journal of European Social Policy, 11*(1), 39–54.

Gallie, D., Paugam, S., & Jacobs, S. (2003). Unemployment, poverty and social isolation: Is there a vicious circle of social exclusion? *European Societies, 5*(1), 1–32.

Gallo, W. T., Bradley, E. H., Dubin, J. A., Jones, R. N., Falba, T. A., Teng, H.-M., & Kasl, S. V. (2006). The persistence of depressive symptoms in older workers who experience involuntary job loss: Results from the health and retirement survey. *Journal of Gerontology: Social Sciences, 61*(4), S221–S228.

Gardner, J., & Oswald, A. J. (2007). Money and mental wellbeing: A longitudinal study of medium-sized lottery wins. *Journal of Health Economics, 26*(1), 49–60.

Hansen, H.-T. (2005). Unemployment and marital dissolution: A panel data study of Norway. *European Sociological Review, 21*(2), 135–148.

Hardt, J., & Rutter, M. (2004). Validity of adult retrospective reports of adverse childhood experiences: Review of the evidence. *Journal of Child Psychology and Psychiatry, and Allied Disciplines, 45*(2), 260–273.

Helliwell, J. F., & Putnam, R. D. (2004). The social context of well-being. *Philosophical Transactions of the Royal Society of London. Series B, Biological Sciences, 359*, 1435–1446.

Jacobson, L. S., LaLonde, R. J., & Sullivan, D. G. (1993). Earning losses of displaced workers. *The American Economic Review, 83*(4), 685–709.

Joye, D., & Bergman, M. M. (2004). Carrières professionnelles: Une analyse biographique. In E. Zimmerman & R. Tillmann (Eds.), *Vivre en Suisse 1999–2000: Une année dans la vie des ménages et familles en Suisse* (pp. 77–92). Bern: Peter Lang.

Kahneman, D., & Frederick, S. (2002). Heuristics of intuitive judgment: Extensions and applications. In T. Gilovich, D. Griffin, & D. Kahneman (Eds.), *Heuristics of intuitive judgment: Extensions and applications* (pp. 49–81). New York: Cambridge University Press.

Kalleberg, A. L. (2009). Precarious work, insecure workers: Employment relations in transition. *American Sociological Review, 74*(1), 1–22.

Larsen, C. A. (2008). *Networks versus economic incentives* (Center for comparative welfare studies working paper no 59). Aalborg: Department of Economics, Politics and Public Administration, Aalborg University.

Leana, C. R., & Feldman, D. C. (1995). Finding new jobs after a plant closing: Antecedents and outcomes of the occurrence and quality of reemployment. *Human Relations, 48*(12), 1381–1401.

Lipps, O., Laganà, F., Pollien, A., & Gianettoni, L. (2013). Under-representation of foreign minorities in cross-sectional and longitudinal surveys in Switzerland. In J. Font & M. Méndez (Eds.), *Surveying ethnic minorities and immigrant populations: Methodological challenges and research strategies* (pp. 241–267). Amsterdam: University Press.

Lucas, R. E. (2007). Adaptation and the set-point model of subjective well-being: Does happiness change after major life events? *Current Directions in Psychological Science, 16*(2), 75–79.

Pinquart, M., & Sörensen, S. (2000). Influences of socioeconomic status, social network, and competence on subjective well-being in later life: A meta-analysis. *Psychology and Aging, 15*(2), 187–224.

Rege, M., Telle, K., & Votruba, M. (2007). *Plant closure and marital dissolution* (Statistics Norway, Research Department, Discussion Papers No. 514). Kongsvinger: Statistics Norway

Strandh, M. (2000). Different exit routes from unemployment and their impact on mental well-being: The role of the economic situation and the predictability of the life course. *Work, Employment & Society, 14*(3), 459–479.

Sullivan, D., & von Wachter, T. (2009). Job displacement and mortality: An analysis using administrative data. *Quarterly Journal of Economics, 124*(3), 1265–1306.

Sweet, S., & Moen, P. (2011). Dual earners preparing for job loss: Agency, linked lives, and resilience. *Work and Occupations, 39*(1), 35–70.

Vandecasteele, L. (2011). Life course risks or cumulative disadvantage? The structuring effect of social stratification determinants and life course events on poverty transitions in Europe. *European Sociological Review, 27*(2), 246–263.

VanLaningham, J., Johnson, D. R., & Amato, P. (2001). Marital happiness, marital duration, and the U-shaped curve: Evidence from a five-wave panel study. *Social Forces, 79*(4), 1313–1341.

West, M., Nicholson, N., & Rees, A. (1990). The outcomes of downward managerial mobility. *Journal of Organizational Behavior, 11*(2), 119–134.

Winkelmann, R., & Winkelmann, L. (1998). Why are the unemployed so unhappy? Evidence from panel data. *Economica, 65*(257), 1–15.

Young, C. (2012). Losing a job: The nonpecuniary cost of unemployment in the United States. *Social Forces, 91*(2), 609–633.

Young, C., & Lim, C. (2014). Time as a network good: Evidence from unemployment and the standard workweek. *Sociological Science, 1*, 10–27.

# Conclusion

This study contributes to the literature by providing an in-depth analysis of the impact of plant closure on workers' careers and lives. Looking at the economic, social and psychological consequences of job loss, it provides a comprehensive understanding of how individuals who were well integrated into the labor market are affected in their career prospects through an exogenous – non-self-inflicted – shock. In addition to our contribution to the scholarly debate, we offer insights on how effective policies may be shaped that assist workers in adjusting to adverse conditions.

We draw on a unique dataset on workers displaced because their plant closed down. Analyzing occupational transitions after plant closure allows us to address the problem of endogeneity inherent in the study of unemployment. If a plant closes down completely, it is unlikely that workers lose their job because they worked poorly. We can thus infer that the reason for job loss is exogenous and that changes in workers' lives in the aftermath of displacement are caused by the plant closure. An additional advantage of plant closure studies is that reverse causality can be excluded. If we find that job loss is accompanied by a strong decrease in workers' well-being we can assume that the drop in well-being is a result of plant closure and not the other way round.

The dataset includes 1203 manufacturing workers who lost their job in 2009 or 2010 and who were surveyed about 2 years later, in 2011. The survey data was complemented with register data from the public unemployment insurance and the plants, a strategy that allows us to control for a number of issues typically occurring in surveys such as nonresponse bias and measurement error. A control group of non-displaced workers, based on data from the Swiss Household Panel, provides us with a counterfactual outcome. This approach enables us to carry out a difference-in-difference analysis, comparing the labor market experiences of displaced workers with those of non-displaced workers. These features of our rich dataset provide us with an exceptional opportunity to understand potential causal mechanisms behind labor reallocation.

## Robust Job Prospects in Manufacturing

Two years after plant closure, more than two-thirds of the workers had returned to a job. Among them, more than two-thirds were reemployed in manufacturing. In addition, more than half of the machine operators and craft workers were able to find a new job in the same occupation as before displacement. Accordingly, the service sector does not constitute a collecting vessel of displaced manufacturing workers. This finding is probably due to the slow pace of deindustrialization in Switzerland: although the crisis of 2008 was accompanied by labor churning in the secondary sector, employment recovered soon afterwards.

However, the Swiss labor market and economy are not as particular as is often assumed. Switzerland shares some common features with Austria and Southern Germany, such as low levels of unemployment, a high importance of vocational education and a flexible manufacturing sector. It is thus legitimate to expect that a survey on plant closure in the adjacent regions of Austria and Germany – Salzburg, Stuttgart or Munich – would produce comparable results to those presented here. Although we cannot assess whether our sample is representative for all displaced workers in Switzerland, it seems to be representative for workers in the manufacturing sector.

In a nutshell, a large share of workers returned to jobs that were similar, in terms of occupation and sector, to their pre-displacement employment. This outcome has the positive implication that workers were able to continue using the skills and knowledge they had acquired through education, on-the-job training and work experience. In addition, a close skill match in the new job is likely to be valorizing for the workers since they were able to retain their social status and identity.

Research on labor market churning and worker turnover (Stevens 1997: 172; Pries 2004: 214; OECD 2009; Autor et al. 2013) as well as quantitative and anecdotic evidence from our study suggests that manufacturing workers have to put up with multiple job loss during their career. Although it seems that they usually manage to return quickly to the labor force after a job loss, the requirement to adapt repeatedly to new jobs is likely to be stressful and represents a great demand in social and psychological skills. In light of accelerating technological advance we may expect that in the future more workers will need to change job several times over their career and adapt to new environments.

## Polarization in Labor Market Experiences

Although a large share of the workers experienced a smooth transition after plant closure, job loss had harmful effects on a small group of workers. The labor market experiences of the workers in our study thus are strongly divergent. Referring to a concept from life-course sociology, plant closure constitutes a "transition" for the majority of the workers – describing an adjustment to their new occupational situation without major frictions. Within this group are the more than two-thirds of workers who returned to employment. Among them, almost half found their new job very quickly. More than four-fifths of them were reemployed on permanent contracts and about a third experienced an increase in their wages. In their relationships with their spouse, family and friends they experienced more frequently positive than negative changes.

The worker subgroups for whom plant closure constitutes a "transition" within their life course, are characterized by a young age – or, if they are older, having retired early –, high levels of education and having been employed in Plant 5 (NWS 2). More precisely, workers under 30 found new jobs most quickly and workers in their 30s had the highest reemployment rates. With respect to wage changes they were the most likely to see their wages increase. Highly qualified workers returned more quickly to a job and were more likely to be reemployed. In addition, high levels of education provided workers with a much higher chance of being reemployed in their pre-displacement occupation. Workers from Plant 5 had the highest reemployment rate and were the most likely to continue working in the manufacturing sector. With respect to workers' life satisfaction, the reemployed and retired workers experienced stability and were thus cushioned from negative effects on their well-being.

However, a small proportion of workers suffered substantial hardship in the aftermath of job loss. For these workers, plant closure constitutes a "turning point", an event that crucially affects their ensuing lives by shifting the direction of their occupational and life trajectory. They were often long-term unemployed and subsequently reemployed in jobs of lower quality. More specifically, they were hired in insecure jobs and jobs which match only little with their skills. Others were unable to return to a job and were still, or again, searching for a job when we surveyed them. Unemployed workers and workers who dropped out of the labor force were particularly prone to find their subjective well-being decreasing. Moreover, they were likely to experience a negative impact of job loss on their social relationships. Overall, plant closure had a clearly detrimental effect for their careers and lives.

This group mainly consists of low-qualified workers, workers who were employed in Plant 1 (Geneva) and older workers. Workers with only compulsory education took longer to find a new job, had lower reemployment rates and were the most likely to be pushed out of their pre-displacement occupations. Workers from Plant 1 had labor market experiences which are in many ways different from workers in other plants, which is possibly due to the particular labor market context of Geneva and the high proportion of workers who live in France and thus were assisted by a different unemployment insurance system. Workers from Plant 1 took by far the most time to find a new job and had the lowest reemployment rate. If they found a job, they were by far the most likely to be reemployed in non-permanent jobs and saw their wages decrease the most strongly. They were also the most likely to be reemployed in the service sector, particularly in often low-paid distributive consumer service jobs.

## Old Age as the Main Disadvantage

Our most noteworthy finding is that whether workers experienced job displacement as a "transition" or as a "turning point" was most strongly determined by their age. Being aged over 55 led to disadvantages in almost every respect. More precisely, older workers not only took longer to find a job but were in the end also less likely to return to employment. If they managed to find a job, they experienced the severest cuts in wages and job quality of all age cohorts.

This finding is in line with a recent report by the OECD (2014: 118) and another study based on survey and register data (Egger et al. 2008: 61) about the employment situation of older workers in Switzerland. The report shows that although Switzerland is among the five countries with the highest employment rates of workers between 55 and 64, older job seekers face high hurdles in the hiring process. This result is striking in the context of the current demographic development. With the baby boomer generation being in this age group during the next 15 years, this phenomenon may concern large shares of displaced workers in the years to come.

This result is surprising and seems difficult to explain from a theoretical point of view. With respect to *reemployment*, human capital theory suggests that employers may try avoid hiring older workers because they have to train them for several years, the investment until the workers' retirement for the company being higher than the returns. Consequently, we would expect employers to be particularly reluctant to hire older workers formerly employed in another occupation. This expectation is however not confirmed by our results which show that older workers experience difficulties independent of whether they change occupation between their pre- and post-displacement job. Our result however contradicts the descriptive analysis by Egger et al. (2008: 63) who find differences in reemployment prospects of older workers by occupation – workers in service occupations having better reemployment prospects than manufacturing workers. However, the authors did not test these findings with regression analyses and thus did not examine whether the results may be confounded by other explanatory factors such as workers' tenure or education. With respect to *wage losses*, human capital theory would predict that older workers experience wage decreases because they had high tenure in the pre-displacement plant and thus acquired a large amount of firm-specific skills on which the returns in the new company are low. However, our models control for tenure but a considerable age effect persists.

Alternatively, unobserved factors may explain the finding of older workers' difficulties in finding a job. For instance, older workers may be more likely to be in poor health conditions than younger workers and thus be less productive. However, this view does not seem to hold, as age *per se* does not provide reliable information about workers' productivity. Indeed, a study from Austria that measures productivity at the firm level finds no link between age and productivity (Mahlberg et al. 2013: 11). A Dutch study shows that although *physical* productivity decreases after the age of 40, *cognitive* productivity is not affected by age (van Ours 2010: 457). Accordingly, if we control for occupation and education, the age effect would be

# Conclusion

picked up. However, in our data we find no evidence that older workers' encounter less difficulties in finding a new job if they have an occupation that demands foremost cognitive skills.

Although the literature suggests that cognitive productivity of the working-aged population is little affected by their aging, it has been argued that younger cohorts are more productive than older ones as they are more adept in using new technologies and keeping up with technological change (Meyer 2011). However, if this argument is valid, we would expect the age disadvantage in our study to increase stepwise by age group. But in contrast there is a threshold at the age of 55 with similar results for all age groups below the threshold. Accordingly, our findings do not seem to comply with this argument. In addition, a study based on German data shows that older workers who remained working during their entire life adapted well to technological changes (Romeu Gordo and Skirbekk 2013: 65). Nevertheless, the Swiss study based on a survey among employees indicates that with increasing age a larger share of workers believe that they are less capable of adapting to new work environments and technologies (Egger et al. 2008: 55).

From the perspective of the human capital theory, older workers may cope with a potential loss of productivity by accepting a lower wage. Since older workers tend to earn more than younger worker in the exact same job, and the employers' old-age pension contributions are higher for older workers, reducing their reservation wage may be a strategy for older workers to enhance their reemployment chances. An experimental study from Switzerland has examined the effect of reducing the reservation wage on reemployment prospects (Arni 2010). The author found that a decline in the reservation wage reduced workers' job search durations but their reemployment rate was not significantly enhanced. Another explanation that has been brought forward to explain older workers' barriers to reemployment is that companies do not want to hire older workers because they will profit for less long from their investment in continuous and on-the-job training. Yet with young workers employers do not have a guarantee that they will stay longer in their company than older workers.

Finally, there is the possibility that our results can be explained by discrimination based on age-related stereotypes. The older age of a job candidate may act as a signal for particular characteristics – positive or negative – such as being difficult to train or high reliability (Brooke and Taylor 2005: 416). Studies by the Eurofound (2013: 42) and the OECD (2014: 119, 150) come to the conclusions for Europe in general and Switzerland in particular that such mechanisms may be at work. In contrast, the Swiss study based on a survey among employees and employers does not find evidence for a negative image of older workers held by employers or younger employees (Egger et al. 2008: 53–4). However, from vignette and correspondence studies we know that employers are reluctant to admit or are unconscious of discriminatory behavior (Jackson and Cox 2013: 40). Nevertheless, discrimination is very difficult to assess and these assumptions thus have to be carefully tested. More research into this question is therefore needed.

## Tackling the Plight of Older Workers

In order to address the hurdles older workers face when searching for a job, knowledge of the mechanisms behind this phenomenon is of central importance. However, as long as there is only little evidence of the triggering factors, policy makers may take measures that seem to improve the workers' situation in any case.

A first measure may be to promote lifelong learning. Our survey included a question on continuous training, but the question referred specifically to training attended during the job search phase after their plant closed down and not to training attended during their entire working life. In Switzerland, workers over 55 are less likely to have undertaken continuous training during their career than younger age cohorts (Bundesamt für Statistik 2007: 14). Accordingly, encouraging workers to engage in continuous training throughout their entire working life may enhance older workers' reemployment prospects (Dieckhoff 2007: 302; Gallie 2003: 69). Particularly in sectors where automation is advancing rapidly, consecutive training on new machines and devices may help workers to keep up with technological change. To enhance older workers' reemployment prospects in the event of job loss, human capital theory suggests that the focus of continuous education should be placed on transferable skills that are valuable in other companies.

Second, employers' awareness of the weak relationship between workers' productivity and their age may be raised. Employers may be sensitized to the importance of the integration of older job seekers into the labor market from the perspective of society as a whole. A study conducted by the European Foundation for the Improvement of Living and Working Conditions recommends initiatives to enhance awareness of the effects of exclusion of older job seekers in the light of current demographic change (Eurofound 2013: 13). The OECD (2014: 124) recommends that employers be better informed about the possibilities of the management of aging and the advantage of mixed-age teams within companies.

Third, investments in age-based workplaces have been shown to be an effective means to keep older workers in the labor force. The adoption of certain features of the workplace – such as the provision of equipment that reduces hearing or vision problems – help to maintain older workers' productivity (Göbel and Zwick 2013: 87). The authors of an experimental study find that cooperation is highest in mixed-age teams and that such teams are consequently more productive as they capitalize synergies between younger and older workers (Charness and Villeval 2007: 21).

Finally, a policy framework that enables a transition into early retirement in the event of job loss is a helpful means to attenuate the negative effects of job displacement for older workers. This may be implemented within the legislation on mass displacements or the unemployment insurance. While such a measure would clearly provide workers with financial security, their social integration may be impaired by early withdrawal from the labor market. A possible policy would therefore ideally provide older workers with financial security in the event of continuous unemployment and simultaneously foster their efforts to return to the labor force.

# Conclusion

In sum, our study provides insights into how plant closure affects workers' careers, social lives and well-being. By considering a large array of outcomes, it contributes to a more comprehensive understanding of the impact of this critical event on the workers concerned. We shed light on the question of which worker subgroups are particularly vulnerable in the face of plant closure by taking into account how their socio-demographic characteristics, the coping strategies and the labor market situation mediate their career outcomes after job loss.

# References

Arni, P. (2010). *How to improve labor market programs for older job-seekers? A field experiment* (pp. 1–49).
Autor, D. H., Dorn, D., Hanson, G. H., & Song, J. (2013). *Trade adjustment: Worker level evidence* (NBER working paper no. 19226). Cambridge, MA: National Bureau of Economic Research (NBER working paper no.
Brooke, L., & Taylor, P. (2005). Older workers and employment: Managing age relations. *Ageing and Society, 25*(3), 415–429.
Bundesamt für Statistik. (2007). *Participation à la formation continue en Suisse*. Swiss Federal Statistical Office.
Charness, G., & Marie-Claire, V. (2007). *Cooperation, competition, and risk attitudes: An intergenerational field and laboratory experiment*. Institute for the Study of Labor (IZA) Discussion Paper Series, No. 2674. Bonn: IZA.
Dieckhoff, M. (2007). Does it work? The effect of continuing training on labour market outcomes: A comparative study of Germany, Denmark and the United Kingdom. *European Sociological Review, 23*(3), 295–308.
Egger, M., Moser, R., & Thom, N. (2008). *Arbeitsfähigkeit und Integration der älteren Arbeitskräfte in der Schweiz – Studie I* (SECO Publikation Arbeitsmarktpolitik, No. 24). Bern: SECO
Eurofound. (2013). *Role of governments and social partners in keeping older workers in the labour market*. Dublin: Eurofound.
Gallie, D. (2003). The quality of working life: Is Scandinavia different? *European Sociological Review, 19*(1), 61–79.
Göbel, C., & Zwick, T. (2013). Are personnel measures effective in increasing productivity of old workers? *Labour Economics, 22*, 80–93.
Mahlberg, B., Freund, I., Crespo Cuaresma, J., & Prskawetz, A. (2013). Ageing, productivity and wages in Austria. *Labour Economics, 22*(100), 5–15.
Meyer, J. (2011). Workforce age and technology adoption in small and medium-sized service firms. *Small Business Economics, 37*(3), 305–324.
OECD. (2009). Employment outlook: How do industry, firm and worker characteristics shape job and worker flows? In *OECD employment outlook* (pp. 117–163). Paris: OECD.
OECD. (2014). *Schweiz. Bessere Arbeit im Alter*. Paris: OECD Publishing.
Pries, M. J. (2004). Persistence of employment fluctuations: A model of recurring job loss. *Review of Economic Studies, 71*(1), 193–215.
Romeu Gordo, L., & Skirbekk, V. (2013). Skill demand and the comparative advantage of age: Jobs tasks and earnings from the 1980s to the 2000s in Germany. *Labour Economics, 22*, 61–69.

Stevens, A. H. (1997). Persistent effects of job displacement: The importance of multiple job losses. *Journal of Labor Economics, 15*(1), 165–188.
Van Ours, J. C. (2010). Will you still need me: When I'm 64? *De Economist, 157*(4), 441–460.

# Annex

## Tables

**Table A.1** OLS-regression analysis of the determinants of the pre-displacement wages on the basis of the survey and register data

|  | Dependent variable: pre-displacement wage (in CHF) | |
|---|---|---|
|  | Survey data | Register data |
| Age (ref. < 30) | | |
| 30–34 | 1119 (898) | 1108 (639)* |
| 35–39 | 1180 (929) | 1141 (662)* |
| 40–44 | 1395 (824)* | 1563 (587)*** |
| 45–49 | 2121 (739)*** | 1957 (526)*** |
| 50–54 | 1578 (734)** | 1475 (523)*** |
| 55–59 | 1857 (746)** | 2180 (531)*** |
| >59 | 1956 (754)** | 1751 (537)*** |
| Sex (ref. women) | | |
| Men | 1562 (376)*** | 1645 (268)*** |
| Nationality (ref. Swiss) | | |
| France, Germany, Italy and Austria | 697 (715) | 734 (509) |
| Spain and Portugal | −560 (727) | −64 (517) |
| Non-EU countries | −683 (716) | −445 (509) |
| Education (ref. less than upper secondary education) | | |
| Upper secondary education | 450 (622) | 428 (442) |
| Tertiary education | 2532 (675)*** | 2073 (480)*** |
| Constant | 1301 (1081) | 1145 (770) |
| Adjusted R2 | 0.26 | 0.38 |
| N | 157 | 157 |

Note: * $p<0.1$, ** $p<0.05$, *** $p<0.01$

**Table A.2** Coefficients for a bivariate probit model with Heckman selection correction on the probability of being employed in the service sector as compared to manufacturing, conditional on being reemployed

| | Outcome equation on being reemployed in services (as compared to being reemployed in manufacturing) | | Selection equation on being reemployed (as compared to being unemployed or out of the labor force) | |
|---|---|---|---|---|
| | Coef. | (SE) | Coef. | (SE) |
| Sex (ref. woman) | −0.37** | (0.17) | | |
| Men | | | | |
| Education (ref. less than upper secondary) | | | | |
| Upper secondary | 0.09 | (0.15) | 0.59*** | (0.14) |
| Tertiary | 0.07 | (0.20) | 0.85*** | (0.16) |
| Tenure (ref. < 2 years) | | | | |
| 2–5 years | 0.10 | (0.12) | 0.66*** | (0.22) |
| 6–10 years | 0.16 | (0.13) | 0.32*** | (0.12) |
| 11–20 years | 0.28 | (0.27) | 0.08 | (0.23) |
| >20 years | −0.16 | (0.15) | −0.06 | (0.28) |
| Occupation (ref. white-collar) | | | | |
| Blue-collar | −0.04 | (0.08) | | |
| Unemployment duration (ref. < 3 months) | | | | |
| 3–6 months | 0.26 | (0.20) | | |
| 7–12 months | 0.22 | (0.16) | | |
| 13–24 months | 0.31** | (0.14) | | |
| Age in years (ref. < 30) | | | | |
| 30–39 | | | 0.32 | (0.22) |
| 40–49 | | | 0.25 | (0.20) |
| 50–54 | | | 0.01 | (0.41) |
| 55–59 | | | −0.86*** | (0.27) |
| >59 | | | −2.26*** | (0.23) |
| Plant (ref. Plant 1 (Geneva)) | | | | |
| Plant 2 (Biel) | −0.58*** | (0.31) | 1.12*** | (0.07) |
| Plant 3 (NWS 1) | −0.89*** | (0.44) | 1.00*** | (0.11) |
| Plant 4 (Bern) | −0.83*** | (0.59) | 0.62*** | (0.04) |
| Plant 5 (NWS 2) | −1.12*** | (0.31) | 1.26*** | (0.11) |
| Civil status (ref. married) | | | | |
| Single | | | −0.24** | (0.09) |
| District unemployment rate | −0.03 | | | |
| Constant | −0.06 | (0.14) | −0.54 | (0.41) |
| Rho | | | 0.26 | (0.16) |

Note: The outcome equation contains the same variables as Fig. 6.2
N observations: 658; censored observations: 220
Standard errors are clustered at the plant level. Significance levels: * $p<0.1$, ** $p<0.05$, *** $p<0.01$
The Wald test is not significant ($p=0.12$)

# Figures

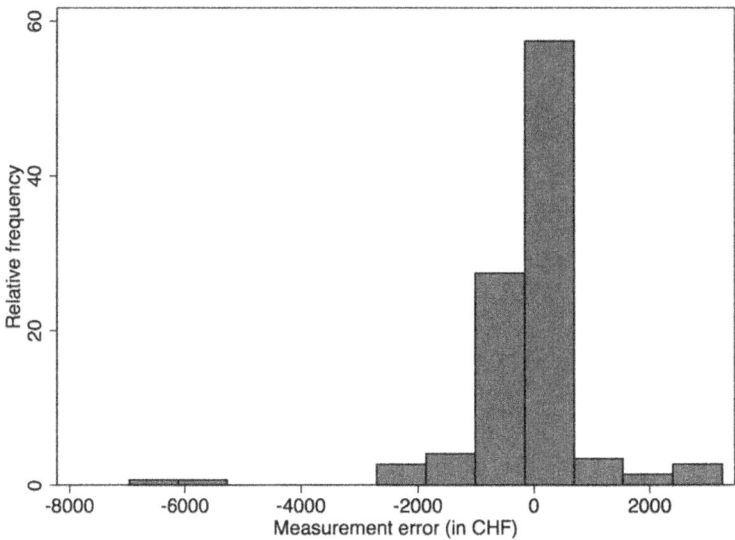

**Fig. A.1** Relative frequency of the measurement error for pre-displacement wages. N=150

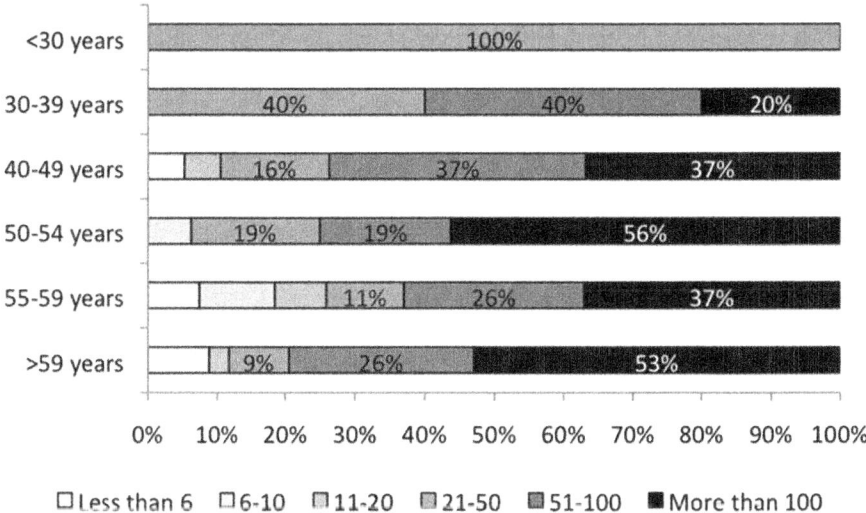

**Fig. A.2** Number of job applications for the still or again unemployed workers by age category. N=102

# Index

**A**
Antonakis, J., 41
Apprenticeship, 26, 54, 66, 70, 72
Autor, D., 4

**B**
Becker, G.S., 14, 127, 143
Bias
  nonresponse bias, 40, 43, 47, 48
  selection bias, 35–36, 137, 153, 163
  survey bias, 35, 40–42, 58
Blue-collar worker, 70, 76, 104, 112, 114, 116, 137
Bonoli, G., 7, 8, 10, 93, 109
Brand, J.E., 1, 3, 17, 20–22, 35, 53, 54, 143, 151, 165, 166, 172
Breen, R., 77
Burda, M.C., 2, 54, 131
Burgard, S.A., 165, 173

**C**
Career, 1–11, 13, 15, 16, 23, 72, 76, 78, 89, 91, 97, 127, 140, 143, 144, 149, 155, 172, 173, 175
Clark, A.E., 21–23, 147, 153, 157, 165
Clerks, 4, 13, 46, 47, 70, 104, 110, 114, 119–121, 124
Commuting, 9, 22, 95–97, 104, 165, 170
Constraints, 8, 18, 83
Contract
  fixed-term contract, 144, 146
  permanent contract, 16, 144, 151, 155
  temporary contract, 16, 97, 144, 146

Control group, 2, 35, 44, 52–53, 63, 67, 78, 128, 130, 131, 140
Coping, 18–19, 24, 157–161, 174
Couch, K.A., 2, 6, 14, 15, 77
Craft workers, 46–48, 70, 88, 114, 118–121, 124
Critical event, 18, 157, 161, 175

**D**
Deferred compensation, 6, 15
Deindustrialization, 57, 109
Dieckhoff, M., 16, 17, 22, 56, 101, 143, 151, 166
Discrimination, 7
Displacement, 26, 36, 39, 44–47, 50–53, 55, 64–69, 71, 76–78, 81, 83, 87–89, 91, 95, 98, 99, 110, 117, 118
Dorn, D., 4, 10, 89
Downgrading
  occupation downgrading, 25, 109, 114, 119, 121, 125
  social downgrading, 26, 91
Downturn, 132, 134
Duration dependence, 3, 99

**E**
Economic boom, 2
Elder, G., 18, 157
Eliason, M., 2, 7, 18, 20, 36, 77, 161, 163, 166
Employability, 3, 9, 97
Employer, 2–5, 7, 8, 11, 12, 14, 24, 26, 36, 38, 42, 45, 56, 63, 65, 76, 85, 96, 99, 105, 110, 112, 117, 125, 127, 134, 141, 149

## F

Fallick, B.C., 2–4, 12, 52, 78
Farber, H.S., 5, 11, 44, 76, 78, 97, 132
Financial crisis, 57
Flückiger, Y., 3, 5, 22, 57

## G

Gallie, D., 16, 18–20, 91, 161, 163
Gebel, M., 3, 96, 99
Geneva, 37, 40, 47, 57, 69, 71, 74, 82, 85, 101, 105, 114, 117, 123, 146, 170

## H

Hamermesh, D.S., 1, 3, 78
Hiring, 7, 8, 15, 65, 76, 141
Household, 18, 20–24, 42, 53, 157–159, 162
Human capital theory, 3, 12, 14, 127, 139, 143

## I

Inequality, 129
Institution, 10, 24, 43, 55, 56, 75, 76, 86

## J

Jacobsen, L.S., 2
Jahoda, M., 21
Job, 91, 92
    authority, 16, 17, 143, 149–152, 154, 155, 165, 170
    quality, 16–17, 22, 25, 26, 91, 104, 121, 125, 143–155
    satisfaction, 22, 125, 143, 149, 151–154
    search
        formal job search, 92
        information job search, 92
        job search intensity, 91
    security, 16, 23, 143, 146–148, 151, 155
Jolkkonen, A., 5, 6, 44, 54, 65, 76, 78, 98, 134
Joye, D., 41, 48, 163

## K

Kahneman, D., 9, 22, 95, 135, 166
Kalleberg, A., 16, 23, 91, 143, 158, 165
Kletzer, L., 2, 7, 15, 44, 64, 65, 76, 78, 132
Kuhn, P.J., 3, 65

## L

Laganà, F., 41
Lalive, R., 10
Life course, 68, 153

Life satisfaction, 21–23, 25, 54, 77, 87, 154, 157, 165, 166, 168–173, 175
Linked lives, 157–176
Lipps, O., 21, 41, 165, 166
Longitudinal data, 2, 3, 8, 9, 11, 17, 18, 21, 22, 42, 54, 77, 115, 157, 165, 173
Low-skilled workers, 4

## M

Machine operators, 4, 46, 47, 70, 88, 101, 114, 118–121, 124
Macroeconomic, 8, 101
Managers, 16, 23, 45, 46, 48, 70, 93, 110, 114, 119–121, 124, 172
Measurement error, 40–42, 50, 51, 58, 119, 128
Mertens, A., 2, 54, 132
Motivation, 3, 4, 8, 35, 44, 99, 143

## N

North-Western Switzerland, 38, 39, 86, 101, 123

## O

Occupations/occupational
    change, 5, 13, 110, 118, 119, 122–125
    elementary, 46, 47, 70, 88, 101, 114, 119–121
    manufacturing, 119
    mobility, 118
    trajectory, 1
    transition, 1, 24–26, 55, 56, 90, 109, 119, 127, 140, 151, 175
    upgrading, 5
    service, 13
OECD, 3, 4, 10, 12, 13, 16, 55, 68, 76, 97, 109, 115, 130, 132, 144, 158
Oesch, D., 5, 8, 13, 15, 21, 36, 65, 119, 165, 166
Older workers, 5, 6, 10, 12, 13, 15, 17, 25, 26, 38, 57, 63, 70, 75–78, 81–83, 86, 88, 89, 97, 99, 101, 127, 140, 149, 173

## P

Polarization, 4, 5, 18, 161, 175
Policy
    active labor market policy (ALMP), 105
    policy decision, 89
Productivity, 3, 4, 15, 65, 77, 127, 134, 136
Professionals, 13, 16, 46–48, 56, 70, 93, 104, 114, 119–121, 124
Propensity score matching, 53, 54, 67, 129

# Index

**R**
Recession, 7, 132
Redundancy plan, 38, 39, 47, 55, 74, 77, 83–86, 89
Reemployment, 1, 2, 4–10, 12, 14, 16, 23, 25, 26, 35, 38, 44, 47, 52, 63–68, 70–72, 74–78, 81, 83, 86, 88, 90, 91, 96, 99, 101, 105, 109–112, 114, 116–119, 121, 124, 127, 134, 135, 139, 140, 143, 144, 149, 155, 165, 172, 173
Relationship
 couple, 172
 family, 164, 168, 172
 social, 19, 23, 25, 26, 157, 162–164, 168, 173, 175
Resources, 14, 47, 86
Retirement
 early, 10, 25, 38, 39, 52, 55, 64, 68, 70, 71, 77, 81–90
 regular, 38, 39, 77, 83, 86
Ruhm, C.J., 2, 15

**S**
Sampling, 35, 37, 53, 54
Scarring, 26, 165
Sectors, 111, 116, 117
 industrial, 109
 manufacturing, 4, 12, 37, 54, 58, 66, 68, 78, 98, 109, 110, 113, 116, 117, 124, 137, 139
 secondary, 111
 service
  business services, 111, 116, 117
  distributive and consumer services, 116, 117
  social and public services, 116, 117
 tertiary, 111, 114, 117, 139
Signaling theory, 3, 4, 127, 139
Skills
 firm-specific, 15, 56, 63, 65, 136, 137
 industry-specific, 56, 66
 sector-specific, 110, 137
 skill biased technological change (SBTC), 4
 skill mismatch, 14, 17, 93, 104
 skill regime, 24, 55, 56, 137
 social, 8, 35, 110
 transferable, 109, 125
Sociability, 1, 19, 25, 161–163, 175
Spence, M., 3
Spitz-Oener, A., 13
Storrie, D., 2, 7, 36, 77, 166

Swiss State Secretariat of Economic Affairs (SECO), 43, 97

**T**
Technicians, 46, 47, 70, 93, 114, 118, 120, 121, 124
Tenure, 6, 12–15, 24, 25, 38, 39, 63, 65, 71, 72, 85, 86, 101, 110, 112, 116, 117, 122, 129–132, 136, 139, 143, 146
Termination pay, 38, 39, 55, 74
Trade union, 38, 39, 56, 93
Training
 continuous, 76
 vocational, 14, 26, 56, 66, 77, 101, 109, 112, 137
Transferability, 12, 25, 127
Transition, 1, 10, 12, 24, 55, 56, 78, 81, 86, 90, 91, 96, 101, 109, 119, 127, 140, 151, 175

**U**
Unemployment
 benefits, 18, 37, 38, 45, 55, 57, 64, 66, 74, 77, 83, 85, 91, 95, 97, 129, 132, 147, 168, 175
 long-term, 11, 16, 18, 25, 26, 37, 78, 81, 90, 114, 124, 143, 149, 164

**V**
Vulnerability/vulnerable, 11, 16, 20, 76, 78, 143, 175

**W**
Wages
 wage loss, 2, 12, 14, 16, 22, 26, 52, 93, 96, 110, 127, 130–132, 134, 136, 137, 139, 140, 144, 158, 159, 165, 166
Weder, R., 2, 6, 44, 64, 134
Well-being
 subjective, 1, 21–24, 26, 54, 87, 157, 165–168, 173, 176
White-collar worker, 70, 77, 104, 110, 112–114, 116, 137, 143
Works council, 37, 40, 47
Wyss, S., 2, 5, 6, 44, 64, 76, 98, 101, 134, 144

**Y**
Young, C., 3, 22, 165

CPSIA information can be obtained at www.ICGtesting.com
Printed in the USA
BVOW06*0219200916

462691BV00008B/33/P